John William Dawson

Fossil Men and their Modern Representatives

An Attempt to Illustrate the Characters and Condition of Pre-Historic Men in

Europe

John William Dawson

Fossil Men and their Modern Representatives
An Attempt to Illustrate the Characters and Condition of Pre-Historic Men in Europe

ISBN/EAN: 9783337417055

Printed in Europe, USA, Canada, Australia, Japan

Cover: Foto ©ninafisch / pixelio.de

More available books at **www.hansebooks.com**

FOSSIL MEN

AND

THEIR MODERN REPRESENTATIVES.

*AN ATTEMPT TO ILLUSTRATE
THE CHARACTERS AND CONDITION OF PRE-HISTORIC
MEN IN EUROPE, BY THOSE OF THE
AMERICAN RACES.*

BY

J. W. DAWSON, C.M.G., LL.D., F.R.S., F.G.S.,
*Principal of McGill College and University, Montreal;
Author of
"The Story of the Earth and Man," "The
Origin of the World," etc.*

THIRD EDITION.

London:
HODDER AND STOUGHTON,
27, PATERNOSTER ROW.

MDCCCLXXXVIII.

Butler & Tanner,
The Selwood Printing Works,
Frome, and London.

TO HIS FRIEND,

PETER REDPATH, Esq.,

OF MONTREAL,

𝔗his work is Dedicated

BY THE AUTHOR,

IN COMMEMORATION OF PERSONAL KINDNESS,

AND OF

AID LIBERALLY RENDERED

TO

SCIENCE EDUCATION IN CANADA.

PREFACE.

No subject of Geological investigation is perhaps in a more unsatisfactory state than that which relates to the connection of the modern or human period with preceding epochs. Difficult and complex problems, yet unsolved, and even imperfectly understood in their data and conditions, encompass the history of that remarkable Glacial Age which seems to have preceded the advent of man and the modern mammalia in the Northern Hemisphere. Much uncertainty and liability to error attach to the study of the superficial deposits which alone contain the remains of man and his works. Further, the Geologist, the Archæologist, and the Historian, the Philologist and the Anthropologist, approaching this obscure region from different directions, all claim to be heard, and often vie with each other in dogmatic assertions respecting facts and inferences of the most uncertain character.

The present work is intended as a popular exposition of some of the more important topics, from the point of view of the Geologist and Naturalist, and on that principle of referring to modern causes for the explanation of ancient effects, which is the basis of theoretical geology, the principal modern facts relied on being those furnished by the aboriginal tribes of America. It cannot pretend to be exhaustive of a department of inquiry yet in its infancy; but may claim the merit of being suggestive.

The substance of this work appeared in a series of papers in the *Leisure Hour*, entitled "The New World and the Old," but has been considerably extended and in some parts re-written.

J. W. D.

McGill College, Montreal.
Jan. 1880.

CONTENTS.

Chapter I.
Explanatory and Introductory 1

Chapter II.
An Old Story of the New World 18

Chapter III.
Glimpses of Pre-historic Times 45

Chapter IV.
The Remains of Cities of the Stone Age . . . 70

Chapter V.
Implements and Weapons of the Stone Age . . . 111

Chapter VI.
Lost Arts of Primitive Races 146

Chapter VII.
Physical Characteristics of Pre-historic Man . . . 177

Chapter VIII.
Antiquity of Man 205

CHAPTER IX.

Primitive Ideas of Religion, the Idea of God . . . 250

CHAPTER X.

Primitive Ideas of Religion, the Instinct of Immortality . 282

CHAPTER XI.

Unity and Continuity 307

APPENDIX 340

LIST OF ILLUSTRATIONS.

	PAGE
LES ROCHES PERCÉES	*Frontispiece*.
IMPLEMENTS OF CHIPPED STONE, EUROPE	12
IMPLEMENTS OF CHIPPED STONE, NORTH AMERICA	13
IMPLEMENTS OF POLISHED STONE, EUROPE	14
IMPLEMENTS OF POLISHED STONE, NORTH AMERICA	15
ORNAMENTS, ETC., OF A RED INDIAN OF NEWFOUNDLAND	21
SECTION OF THE STOCKADE OR WALL OF HOCHELAGA	38
PLAN OF HOCHELAGA	39
THE TOWN OF HOCHELAGA	41
SKETCH-MAP SHOWING THE PROBABLE LINES OF MIGRATION AND DISTRIBUTION OF THE AMERICAN TRIBES	48
ALLEGHAN, TOLTECAN, PERUVIAN, AND MODERN CROW HEADS	54
MODERN MANDAN, AND ANCIENT AZTEC HEADS	55
COPPER AXES, SPEARS, AND KNIFE OF THE ALLEGHANS	58
COPPER BRACELET, DISC, BEAD, AND BUTTONS OF ALLEGHANS	59
MODE OF SUSPENDING EARTHEN POTS	72, 73
FRAGMENT OF EARTHEN VESSEL, HOCHELAGA	75
EARTHEN POT	77
HEAD FROM AN EARTHEN POT	79
HEAD IN POTTERY	81
PLAN OF HOCHELAGAN HOUSE FOR FIVE FAMILIES	83
EARTHEN POT FOUND ON THE UPPER OTTAWA	87
FRAGMENTS OF POTTERY	91
EARTHEN PIPES, HOCHELAGA	94
RED PIPESTONE PIPE	95
STONE ARROW-HEADS, MODERN	123
BONE NEEDLE AND SPEARS, HOCHELAGA	135

ILLUSTRATIONS.

	PAGE
BONE HARPOONS	137
SHELL AND TERRA COTTA BEADS, HOCHELAGA	141
GROTESQUE FIGURE, QUEEN CHARLOTTE ISLANDS	148
PIPE CARVED OUT OF HARD PORPHYRITIC STONE	150
GROUP OF HURON WOMEN	156
GROOVED HAMMER	171
OUTLINES OF THREE PRE-HISTORIC EUROPEAN SKULLS COMPARED WITH ONE FROM HOCHELAGA	194
OUTLINE OF A CRO-MAGNON SKULL AS SEEN IN FRONT, AND HOCHELAGAN SKULL ON A SMALLER SCALE	195
FRONT VIEW OF ANOTHER HOCHELAGAN SKULL OF A SIMILAR TYPE	196
PROFILE VIEW OF SAME SKULL	197
CHIPPEWA CHIEFS, FROM PHOTOGRAPHS	253
TOTEMS OF CHIEFS OF THE PENOBSCOT INDIANS	265
TOTEMS OF FAMILIES OF THE REINDEER AGE IN FRANCE	267
PICTOGRAPH ON A PIECE OF REINDEER HORN FROM A CAVE IN THE DORDOGNE	269
AMERICAN PICTOGRAPH FROM SCHOOLCRAFT	270
TOTEMS SCULPTURED ON THE ROCHES PERCÉES	272
ADJEDATIG, OR GRAVE-POST OF WABOJEEGSE, THE "WHITE FISHER"	289
CHIPPEWA GRAVES AND MOURNERS	291

CHAPTER I.

EXPLANATORY AND INTRODUCTORY.

SOMEWHERE in the past, the long ages of the prehuman geologic record join and merge into the human period. The day when the first man stood erect upon the earth and gazed upon a world which had been shaped for him by the preceding periods of the creative work, was the definite beginning of the Modern Period in Geology. If that day could be fixed in the world's calendar, on reaching it the geologist might lay down his hammer and yield the field to the antiquarian and the historian. On that day a world, for long ages the abode of brute creatures, became for the first time the habitation of a rational soul. On it the old and unvarying machinery of nature first became amenable to the action of a conscious, independent earthly agent. On it a new and marvellous power—that of human will—was introduced upon our planet. No wonder, then, that in our critical and sceptical time, when men are no longer satisfied with traditions, or even with sacred history, questions as to this mysterious meeting-place of the past and present should be agitated with an engrossing interest, and that all our varied stores of scientific and historical knowledge should be brought to bear on it. Nor need we wonder that obscurity still rests upon the subject when regarded from the standpoint of science and secular history. It is connected, in so far as geology is concerned, with difficult and controverted questions of the Glacial period and its close, and in the domain of archæology with the darkness that antedates the beginning of literature. It thus forms an appropriate battle-ground for active spirits eager to reach new truths. The evolutionist searches in its obscurity for the transition from apes to men. The geologist painfully gathers the faint traces of forgotten tribes preserved in caves and gravels, and the archæologist joins him in his quest.

The result has been the accumulation of a great mass of facts, of which, however, many are doubtful in their import, the initiation of many controversies, and the production of a general vague impression that science has unsettled all our previous views as to the origin and antiquity of man. While popular writers have boldly asserted this last conclusion as established beyond dispute, the more cautious, and those who have the best opportunities of weighing the evidence, are well aware of its doubtful and uncertain character; and the attempt recently made by one of the greatest and most judicial minds among English geologists to sum up the actual results,*

* Lyell, "Antiquity of Man," fourth edition.

while it startles the reader with the magnitude and strangeness of the questions suggested, appals him with their complexity and difficulty.

To those who, like the writer of these pages, have long been familiar with the manners of the American aborigines and with the antiquities of America, the facts detailed in such publications as Lyell's "Antiquity of Man," Christie and Lartet's "Reliquiæ Aquitanicæ," Morlot's Memoirs on the Swiss Lake Habitations, and Dupont's on the Belgian Caves, appear like a new edition of a familiar story; and as Dr. Wilson has well shown in his "Pre-historic Man," existing humanity, as it appears in the native American, is little else than a survival of primeval man in Europe. In short, the early voyagers who first met the American tribes really held conference with their now ancestors, or with men among whom still lived manners and customs extinct in Europe before the dawn of history. Why, then, should not that method of reasoning from existing causes to explain ancient facts, by which geology has achieved its greatest triumphs, be applied to the extinct tribes of the old world? Why should not the enormous mass of existing information as to rude man in America be employed to illustrate and explain conditions long since passed away in the eastern continent?

To attain successfully such a result requires something more than the desultory and imperfect references which have been casually made by writers on European archæology. It requires that large and systematic views of the culture of the American nations should be placed beside the results of European research, and that such comparisons shall not be overloaded with details, but shall be given in a distinct and pictorial form. It has occurred to me that this may best be done by taking up our position on the antiquities of one tribe or locality, connecting the others with this, so as to show the homogeneous nature of the American culture, and then applying the whole to European facts and difficulties.

I shall therefore take as my first starting-point the primitive town of Hochelaga, the predecessor of the fair city of Montreal, and shall present to the reader American and European prehistoric times as they would appear to an inhabitant of that ancient town. We shall thus at least obtain a novel insight, remote from that of the ordinary geologist or archæologist, and which may aid us in interpreting some things which from his point of view are most difficult to understand. We shall, I hope, find that such change of base in our attack on prehistoric times may afford advantages of a peculiar character, and may enable us to correct some of the fanciful and enthusiastic impressions of those who look back on prehistoric times in Europe from the, perhaps, too elevated standpoint of a mature civilization, to which the rude hunter, with his weapons of stone and bone, seems a creature almost too remote to have approached within thousands of years, and rather to be pushed back into the mists of an archaic and forgotten antiquity, to consort with the mythical anthropoid apes from which the evolutionist proposes to derive our species.

Since, however, in the following chapters we shall be occupied almost exclusively with American facts, and must refer from them to the discoveries made in Europe, and as the reader may not be familiar with the aspects of pre-historic time to European geologists and antiquarians, I may here shortly explain the usually received views with reference to those times anterior to history, and the terms by which they are designated.

We have the misfortune, according to archæ-ologists, to live in the " Iron Age," a fact of which we are also reminded by our roads and ships, and by the too great prevalence of a cold, dead materialism, to which all that is not iron and steel, or their equivalent in money, is mere superstition, and which derides the beliefs of the world's earlier times. This Iron Age represents, in Europe at least, the period of written history, for even in Greece the earliest literature goes back merely to the time when the Iron Age of that country was beginning. In the East a far earlier literature exists, but this also does not go beyond the earlier age of iron in that part of the world—the Iron Age of the East having apparently antedated the Iron Age of Europe, much as the latter did that of America. The date of the beginning of the Iron Age is a point altogether indefinite. In Asia Tubal-Cain may have inaugurated it before the Deluge. In

America it is making its way to-day in direct conflict with the age of Stone among the more remote tribes. When we speak, therefore, of the Iron, Bronze, and Stone Ages, it is useless, if we wish to attach any definite meaning to our language, to extend its application beyond the temperate latitudes of Western Europe.

Copper, and bronze, the alloy of copper and tin, were in prevalent use before iron*; and bronze, with its ingredients well proportioned, was no bad substitute for the most useful of metals, having the advantage besides of not perishing by rust, and of being easily molten into any required shape. The Bronze Age precedes the date of written history in Western Europe, though in the East it is cöeval with the early Bible history, and in Greece it reaches to the Trojan war. It attained its acme before the Roman legions had swept over the European plains, when the civilising element was mainly represented by Phœnician traders visiting the coasts, and when the rude primeval tribes were shaping themselves into nations, and acquiring the arts of life from the more cultivated peoples of the south and east. As in the case of the Iron Age, we can attach no definite limits to its

* It would seem that in Africa and elsewhere iron may have been used as early as or earlier than bronze, in consequence of the occurrence of iron ores easily reduced. For this reason, Virchow, quoted with approval by Tylor in an address delivered at the Sheffield meeting of the British Association, has proposed to merge the Bronze and Iron Ages in a " Metal Age."

beginning or to its end. There must have been a time when the Iron Age was fully established on the shores of the Mediterranean, while yet in the inland and northern nations the Age of Bronze coexisted with the earlier Age of Stone, and in some places the Iron Age must have come abruptly into conflict with that of Stone, without the intervention of the Age of Bronze, as it has done in America.

This last Age, that of Stone, in the South of Europe, antedates all written history. In the many-sided East, however, we find cutting instruments of stone in use in Egypt and Syria long after the dawn of literature, and intruding themselves into Europe in some of the detachments which joined the army of Xerxes; while in remote corners of the North of Europe some uses of stone weapons reached almost into the Middle Ages. The earlier Stone folk are known to us only by their graves, and remains of their habitations and implements. The ancient barrows and cromlechs of Britain and France, and the gallery tombs of Scandinavia, contain the bones of the nameless warriors of this Age buried with their flint arrows and stone hatchets. The curious lake habitations of Switzerland, built by unknown tribes on piles over the water, also afford their remains, though some of these strange dwellings reach up to the time of Bronze and Iron. The shell-heaps of the primitive fishermen of the coast of Denmark, and the peat-bogs of various districts of Europe, afford additional remains of the people of this Age.

Wilson may furnish us with a specimen of a monument of this period, which is everywhere in Europe known to us only by monuments, and not by written history. It is the mount called Knock Maraidhe, or Hill of the Sailors or Sea-rovers, standing till 1838 in the Phœnix Park, Dublin, in the midst of modern civilisation. It was of no mean size, being fifteen feet high, and one hundred and twenty in diameter, but no history tells its origin or the cause of its name. It had to be levelled, and then it appeared that it had been built by human hands. Under the centre was a massive stone tomb, or cromlech, holding the remains of two male skeletons in a sitting or crouching posture, and other bones, possibly of a dog. Shells of the common Littorina, perforated for stringing, lay beside the skulls, and a stone arrow-head and a pin or hair-support of bone. Around the margin of the tumulus were stone cists, each containing a small vase and calcined bones, the remains of offerings to the dead. This, as we shall see in the sequel, is an almost precise counterpart of some of the oldest American interments in those remarkable mounds of the river valleys of the West, which, though some of them are of great antiquity, undoubtedly represent a mode of burial pursued up to the time of the European discovery.

Here is another picture. It is a " Gallery grave " in Sweden, as described by Nilsson. The walls consist of flat slabs of granite or gneiss, carefully joined together, forming a chamber from twenty to thirty feet long, and five to six feet high, which is roofed over with flat slabs of gneiss. In the centre of the long side, fronting the south, is a door leading outward through a gallery, also of stone, sixteen to twenty feet long, three feet high, and two to three feet broad. Around the sides of the chamber are stalls or niches, separated by partitions of wood or stone, and in these are the skeletons of the old people, seated with their legs bent under their bodies, or with the bones fallen together in a heap and the skull on top, and beside them their stone weapons and ornaments of shell and amber. The whole structure is buried under a mound or tumulus of earth. This, again, is the style of the family sepulchres of the modern Esquimaux, and is apparently borrowed from the plan of their ordinary dwellings, as the existing plan of a Lapland house is thought to represent that of the ancient gallery graves of Sweden. These instances represent the absolute Stone period of Europe before the use of bronze; but they belong to what has been called the Neolithic or later Stone period, in which stone implements of the most perfect kind existed, and in which the physical features and animal inhabitants of Europe were the same as at present.

In an earlier part of the Stone Age, animals now locally or wholly extinct still survived, and there were climatal and geographical conditions somewhat different from those of the present time. In France and Belgium, for example, there are indications that the reindeer, now confined to Lapland, and not known in Germany since the time of Cæsar, while there is no written record of its former existence in Gaul, afforded a large part of the food of the inhabitants. There is even evidence that these earlier Stone people hunted the now extinct mammoth and its contemporaries. We may take as an example the cave of Bruniquel in the south of France. It has apparently been used both as a house and as a place of sepulture, and since its occupation a layer of hard stalagmite has accumulated over the earth and carbonaceous matter of its floor. Professor Owen, who examined the bones obtained in it, estimated the number of reindeer represented in his collections at 1000.* There were also numerous bones of a species of horse. With these were remains of ten human beings, abundance of flint flakes, and numerous bone implements, including harpoons exactly like those now used by the Esquimaux. On many of the bones were carved figures of animals. Portions of four implements made of mammoth ivory, and needles and pins of bone, were also found, and sea-shells both from the Mediterranean and Atlantic, some at least of which must have been used as ornaments merely. At the time when these and similar earlier Flint folk lived, France would seem to have been in part overgrown with dense forests, and in part connected with great steppes or prairies extending over all central Europe; its climate must have been cool enough for the reindeer, and possibly the

* " Transactions of the Royal Society."

mammoth or extinct European elephant may not have disappeared.

But a still earlier Stone period, that more properly named the Palæolithic, appears to be indicated by quantities of roughly-shaped flint implements found in the valley of the Somme, at Hoxne in Suffolk, and many other places, imbedded in clays and gravels of the river-beds, and in the earth and stalagmite of caverns along with remains of extinct mammals; * but as yet without any human bones. If these remains truly indicate a primitive Stone period of rough implements only, then man must have inhabited Europe before some of the later changes in its physical geography, at a time when the European land was more extensive than now, when many large mammals now extinct still lived, and before the great movements of subsidence which have brought the European continent to its present form.

For reasons to be stated in the sequel, however, it is doubtful if there really was a distinct Palæolithic period, properly so called. Many of the so-called implements are probably natural, and the manner in which they are found renders it possible that those actually fabricated by man belonged merely to special stations of tribes who may have had other and better implements elsewhere. Still there seems to be evidence of the existence of the earlier Flint folk before the disappearance of the great Post-pliocene mammals now extinct, and before the last great subsidence or

* " Story of the Earth and Man," 1873.

diluvian catastrophe of the northern continents. The men of this early age, if not properly "Palæolithic," were at least possibly antediluvian.

Penetrating beyond the so-called Palæolithic period, we find ourselves in the Post-pliocene or Glacial age of geology, in the later part of which it seems evident

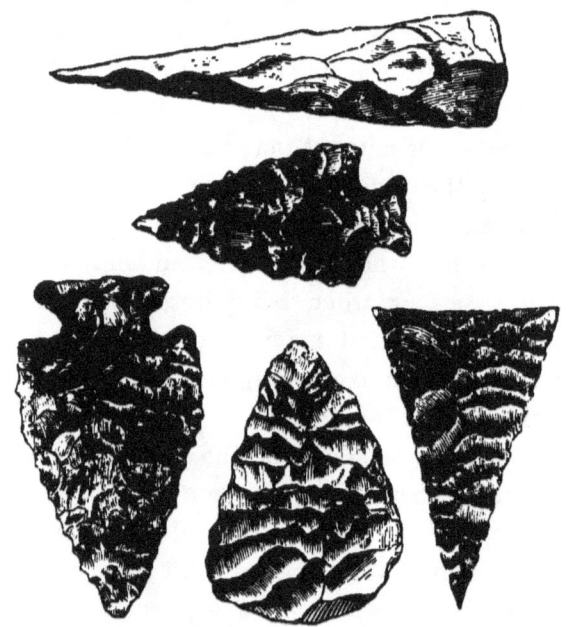

Fig. 1.—Implements of Chipped Stone, Europe.
(*After Nilsson and others.*)

that nearly all the European land was under the sea, and the islands which remained were subject to a climate almost arctic in its character. Here we lose all traces of man; and if he existed in this period, it must have been in some of those portions of the world to which the subsidence and cold climate of the Glacial age did not extend. It is true that the supposed Palæolithic men are often called Post-pliocene, but when this term is used in a strict sense, as it is by Sir C. Lyell, it is with the limitation that human remains occur only at the close of the Post-pliocene; or the beginning of the modern period.

Fig. 2.—IMPLEMENTS OF CHIPPED STONE, NORTH AMERICA.
(*After Squier.*)

Whatever dates we may assign to these several stages of prehistoric man, and whatever value we may attach to such classifications, or whatever new light subsequent research may throw upon them, American facts enable us to attain to absolute certainty on some material points. Of these, one is that the oldest populations known to us in Europe were not inferior

14 FOSSIL MEN.

either in physical character or the arts of life to the aborigines of America at the time of its discovery. Another is, that in their rude manufactures, their habits of life, their social institutions, and their religious beliefs, they must have resembled the Ame-

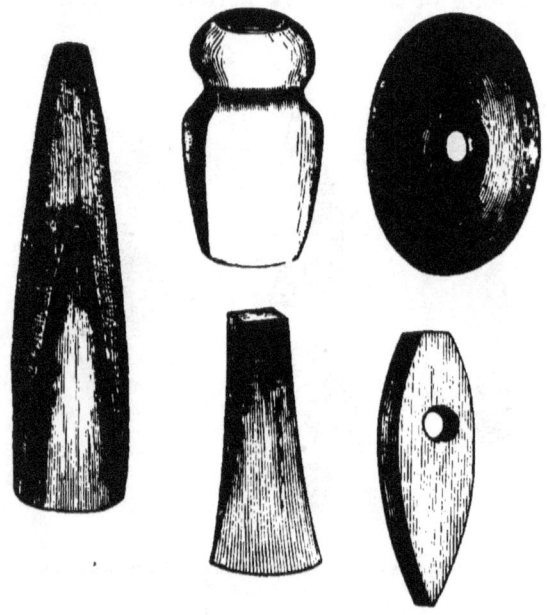

Fig. 3.—Implements of Polished Stone, Europe.
(*After Nilsson.*)

ricans in the closest and most precise manner. These two great leading truths it will be my province to establish and illustrate in the following pages. In the meantime I may appeal to the eye by a few woodcut illustrations of implements and weapons of the Stone

EXPLANATORY AND INTRODUCTORY. 15

Age in Europe and America. In figure 1, are given, from Nilsson and others, tracings of some common forms of arrow and spear heads of the best and

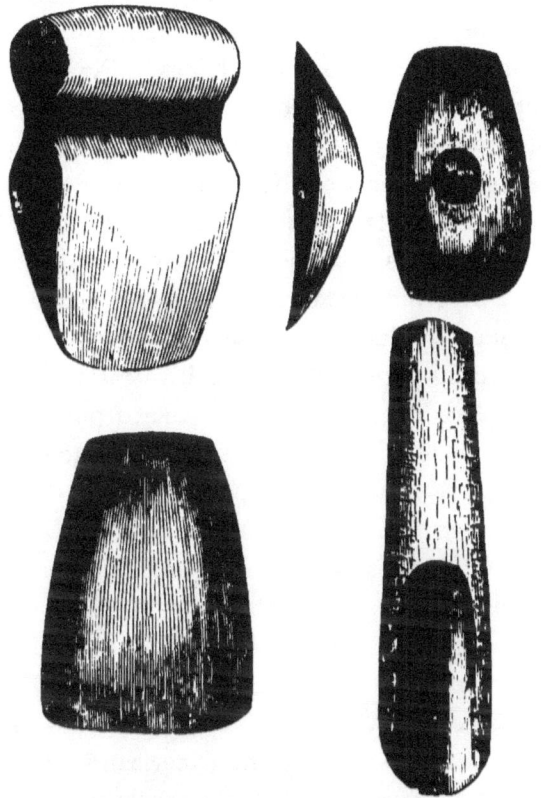

Fig. 4.—IMPLEMENTS OF POLISHED STONE, NORTH AMERICA.
(Partly after Squier.)

the rudest styles of chipped flint, one of them being a weapon of the ancient Amiens type. In figure 2 are some similar tracings from Squier's memoir on the ancient natives of the Mississippi Valley. I have selected these as belonging to one of the most cultivated of the primitive populations of America, who were agriculturists, weavers, and skilful potters and workers in metal, yet used flint implements exactly similar to those of the ruder tribes. Figure 3 shows a group of polished stone implements from Nilsson, all European and of the so-called later Stone Age. In figure 4 are similar stone implements used in America by the same peoples who used those in figure 1, and at the same time. These, let it be observed, are not obtained by arbitrary selection of a few similar things out of many dissimilar. On the contrary, it would be possible to fill pages with such illustrations, showing that the handiwork of the red man, from Terra del Fuego to Baffin's Bay, is of similar character to that of pre-historic man in Europe. I cannot dwell here on all that is implied in such resemblance. To those who know the uses of such implements, every one of them tells, not of a fancied instinct to make things of one form as birds make their nests, but of a wide range of similar wants and habits leading to similar contrivances. Take, for instance, the hollow chisel or gouge in figure 4, used by the American Indian to tap the maple-tree, to extract its saccharine juice in spring, and also to hollow out wooden troughs to hold it; and consider all that is implied in the fact that precisely the same sort of chisel is found abundantly in Scandinavia, as represented in figure 3. Or, take the grooved axes in figures 3 and 4, and consider how much of experience in woodcraft is implied in the construction, handling, and use of such an implement, and with how many possible industries in wood it connects itself. Or take the rudely-chipped flint implements of "Palæolithic" type from the gravels of the Somme, in connection with the fact that an implement of somewhat similar style used by the semi-civilised mound-builders of the Mississippi Valley is held with much probability by some American antiquaries to have been an agricultural hoe, and what strange revelations may we have of the primitive farmers who possibly cultivated the alluvial flats of the Somme Valley with such tools, while they, perhaps, built their towns on hills beyond the reach of inundations. Such comparisons will grow and multiply on us as we proceed, and I must not anticipate them here. In following out these comparisons, moreover, I do not wish to restrict myself to the mere similarity of implements and other remains, but to present such pictures of the actual life of the American Indian as may enable us to place ourselves in his position, and to view things from his standpoint. By thus sitting at the feet of the red man, we may chance to discover some truths which the learned archæologists of the old world have not yet attained; and in any case may hope to present some interesting and instructive pictures of primitive man in the old world and the new.

CHAPTER II.

AN OLD STORY OF THE NEW WORLD.

NOTHING can be more interesting than the narratives which remain to us of the first contact of Europeans with the Indian tribes of the West; and perhaps no such narrative is more touching than the unvarnished yet circumstantial story of the old Breton navigator of St. Malo, who first entered the St. Lawrence and held intercourse with the tribes of Canada.

In the spring and summer of 1534, Jacques Cartier, following on the track of Cabot and of the Breton and Basque fishermen, who even at this early date visited the coast and banks of Newfoundland, the "Island of Baccalaos,"—had entered the Gulf of St. Lawrence by the Strait of Belleisle; and in search of a way to the Indies, coasted along the south side of Labrador, and visited the Magdalen Islands, and the coast of New Brunswick. He then passed up the deep Baie des Chaleurs, so named by him because of the hot summer sun which beat fiercely on its forest-clad shores, and finally took refuge from the fogs and storms of autumn in the lovely Bay of Gaspé.

On the coast of Labrador, which, he quaintly says, from its barren and forbidding aspect, must have been the land that God gave to Cain, he found a tribe of

Americans, the first that he saw. They were large, well-built people, with their skins painted red, clothed in furs, their hair tied up in a knot, secured with a bone pin, and ornamented with feathers. They used canoes of birch bark, and were hunting seals, in search of which they gave the French navigator to understand they had come from a country farther to the south. There can be little doubt that they were the Red Indians or Bœotics of Newfoundland, a race now extinct, mercilessly exterminated by the European settlers of that island, and by the Micmacs of Nova Scotia, but who were of old most extensive hunters of the reindeer, the seal, and the walrus, and skilful carvers of ivory and fabricators of bone implements, and who, in respect to their physical character, food, and mode of life, were very like the men of the so-called Reindeer Age in France itself, subsisting like them very much on the carriboo, or American reindeer, then abundant in the interior of Newfoundland. There is reason to believe that the Red Indians were an eastern extension of the Tinné or Chipewyan race, which once extended across the continent between the Esquimaux on the north and the Algonquins and other Indian tribes on the south. The old Breton here stood in the presence of the precise equivalent of the Flint folk of his own country, just as they would have appeared, if raised from their graves in the French caverns, with their flint arrows, bone spears, harpoons and shell ornaments. But Cartier knew as little of these things as the Red Indians did of the ocean telegraph which now ties their island to Europe. In figure 5 I have given a representation of the ornaments and one of the weapons of a Red Indian warrior, found in a cavern, with the bones of their owner, on an island on the eastern coast of Newfoundland.* The strung shells are those of *Purpura lapillus*. The beads are made from the shell of a large species of Mactra; the pendants are neatly carved in the ivory of the walrus; the arrow-head is quite palæolithic. These objects were taken from a grave which also contained the oxidized remains of an iron hatchet, some red ochre used as paint, and a portion of a walrus tusk, part of which had been cut away for use. The date is probably that of the earliest French visitors of Newfoundland, and presents a curious association of the ages of iron, of bone, and of rudely chipped stone.

Crossing to the opposite side of the gulf, he had some slight intercourse with the Micmacs of the coast of New Brunswick, whom he rightly characterises as a coast tribe, going from place to place in their bark canoes, of which he saw as many as forty or fifty together; living in summer mainly on fish, and forming extensive shell heaps on the coast, though in

* "Transactions of Nova Scotia Institute," vol. i. These remains were found in 1847 by Rev. M. Blackmore. Beside the objects mentioned above, there were glass beads, a bone spear, and the remains of an iron knife. All the objects were near the head of the skeleton. This had been wrapped in birch bark, and near it were fragments of a carved piece of wood.

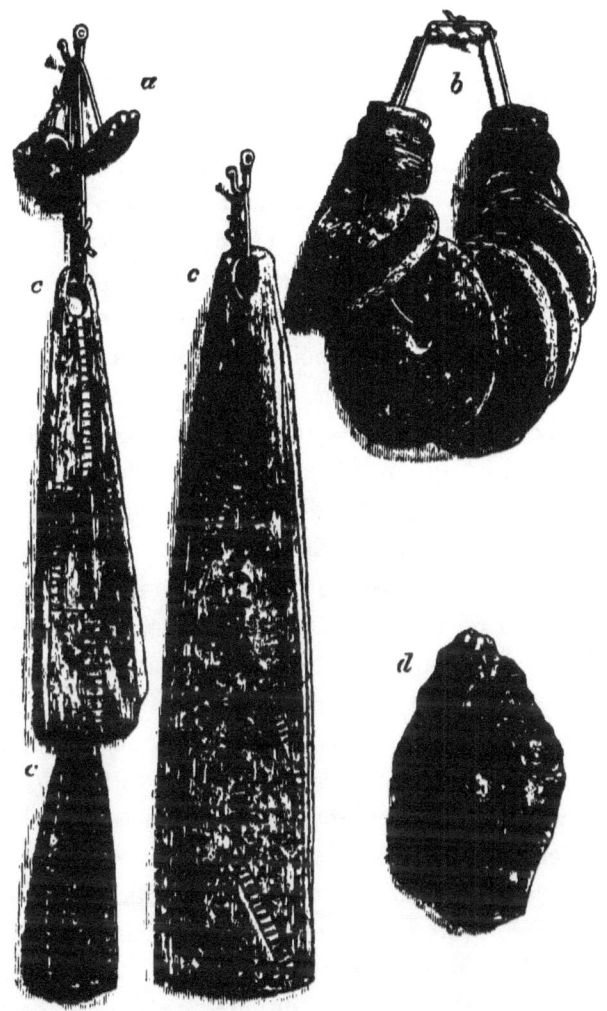

Fig 5.—ORNAMENTS, ETC., OF A RED INDIAN OF NEWFOUNDLAND.
  (a) Pierced Shells of *Purpura lapillus*.
  (b) Wampum of Shell of *Mactra*.
  (c) Pendants of Ivory of *Walrus*.
  (d) Flint Arrow-head.

winter they retired into the interior and hunted the elk and reindeer. They still exist in a semi-civilized state, and we shall have more to say of them in the sequel. In the time of Cartier they were a nation of hunters and fishermen, destitute of agriculture, fabricating very rude pottery, making their wigwams and canoes of birch bark, and their weapons and implements of chipped and polished stone, knowing no metal but native copper, and employing this apparently merely for ornamental purposes, but having for their chief ornament and currency the strings of wampum made from the shell of the quahog (*Venus mercenaria*). These people were shy and threatening in their first approaches to the French, but soon opened an exchange of skins for knives, hatchets, and trinkets, and manifested great eagerness to become possessed of these new and precious treasures. Perhaps these were the least advanced in the arts of life of any of the peoples that Cartier met with, yet it is interesting to observe that with these, as all others, the idea of bartering property already existed, and that they at once understood the importance to them of the improved implements of the strangers, whom they evidently recognised as men like themselves, to be treated with on terms of equality, and to be received in a hostile or friendly manner as their intentions might seem to warrant.

The ancient traditions of the Micmacs, as collected by Mr. Rand, an able missionary worker among them, show that they recognised the Baie des Chaleurs, Moweboktăbāāk, "the Biggest of Bays," as the northern boundary of the Micmac country, and Gaspé, the Great Cape, or cape *par excellence*, which forms the south portal of the St. Lawrence, as the beginning of Canada, a land inhabited by the hostile tribes of the Kwedeches, with whom they waged long and bloody wars, and whom in the struggles that succeeded the French occupation they replaced in Gaspé. Here accordingly Cartier found a different nation. They were engaged in fishing mackerel with nets of their own manufacture. The voyager here notes for the first time the shaven head and scalp-lock so characteristic of many of the American tribes. Here also he notes in their possession Indian corn or maize, the aboriginal bread-corn of America, with grains "as large as peas," and also beans and dried plums. They rejoiced with great joy when Cartier gave them knives and trinkets, and showed their delight by dancing and songs, the universal language of gladness. The erection of a cross by the French led to an official visit from the chief, and a long speech in which this aboriginal sovereign, clad in a bearskin, was understood to assert his right to the country, and the impropriety of setting up any such sign or token of the white man without his permission. Neither party in the scene understood the other's words, yet the significant act was the same to both. To the Frenchman it was the symbol of taking possession of the new country for his sovereign. To the American it was the setting up of the totem or national mark of a strange tribe, and the meaning was identical. We may imagine, therefore, the Canadian potentate as saying, "If you strangers understand this erection as we do, namely, as the sign or totem of your tribe, then we object to it, as indicating a claim on your part to a territory which is ours of right." Whatever the words of the chief, the end was that he and his retinue were induced to go on board the ships, where they were loaded with presents, and the chief's two sons were retained as hostages, and finally taken with Cartier to France. There can be little doubt that these people were not the Micmac or Malicete tribe afterwards known to the French as Gaspesiens, but that they were an outlying branch, or wandering party of the Algonquin or Huron tribes of Canada. This was the ultimatum of Cartier's first voyage; for after beating for some days against the west winds in the strait between Gaspé and Anticosti, he was obliged to bear away for Belle Isle and to return to France.

Next year he returned, and with little difficulty reached the entrance of the St. Lawrence, which his Indian captives had already taught him to call the Great River of Hochelaga, and the highway of Canada. He found at the mouth of the Saguenay certain Canadian fishermen in the pursuit of seals; and farther up, at Isle aux Coudres, so named by him from the abundance of hazel-nuts, was another party engaged in the more formidable sport of hunting the white whale or Beluga of the St. Lawrence, the Adhotuis of the natives, a strange and beautiful creature, which excited the astonishment of the French seaman, and which he correctly characterises as living between the sea and the fresh water of the St. Lawrence, and as peculiar to the estuary of that river. He does not mention how the natives captured this formidable creature, often twenty feet in length; but the modern Indians, like the Esquimaux, use a harpoon with a cord and float. We may imagine that the means in Cartier's time were the same, only that the iron of the modern harpoon would be represented by a triangular stone point, or a many-barbed head of bone.*

The Canada of Cartier's time began at the bottom of the Isle of Orleans, not far below Quebec, and extended thence half-way to Montreal. It was the native name of a district bounded by Saguenay on the east and Hochelaga on the west, and of which Stadacona, on the site of the present Quebec, was the capital. The name Quebec, meaning a strait, was then applied to the narrow part of the river, at the foot of Cape Diamond. Opposite the Island of Orleans,

---

* The *Beluga catodon*, white whale or white porpoise of the St. Lawrence, still exists, though less abundant than formerly. It is strictly an estuarine animal, found only in the St. Lawrence and in parts of Davis' Straits. Its bones, found in the post-pliocene Leda clay of the St. Lawrence, show that it existed in the glacial period, when it must have had a far wider range than at present, over portions of North America now land, but then submerged. Its bones have been found in the vicinity of Lake Champlain and near Brockville on the St. Lawrence. Though the species found in the post-pliocene has been named *Beluga Vermontana*, a comparison with the recent animal shows that it is the same species.

Donnacanna, the reigning Agouhanna, or chief of
Canada, met the voyagers in state with twelve canoes,
and made a long speech, with much gesticulation,
which was interpreted by the two Canadians, who had
returned with Cartier, as expressing welcome and
goodwill. At Stadacona, accordingly, Cartier laid up
his ships, preparatory to his further intended explora-
tion of the River Hochelaga, and had many feasts and
quarrels with his friend Donnacanna, whom at length
he treacherously seized and carried off to France.

Here, first at Stadacona, and afterwards at Hochelaga, Cartier found himself at the head-quarters of
the primitive men of the more advanced Stone Age.
We shall first accompany him to the latter place,
and then inquire in detail as to the actual character
of the Flint folk, and the remains which they have
left.

Donnacanna and his advisers were, when their education and opportunities are considered, little inferior
to their successors in American public life in devising
political expedients. They seem at a very early
period of their intercourse with the French to have
discovered that it was not for the public good to
allow their visitors to proceed any farther up the St.
Lawrence. It was clearly the interest of Stadacona
that foreign trade should be limited to it, and that the
precious commodities of the strangers should be distributed inland only at the price set upon them by the
Quebec dealers. The commercial jealousy of the cities
on the St. Lawrence was already in full force. The

first device was to represent that the river was dangerous or not navigable. Finding this not sufficient, Donnacanna, after a present of fish and a solemn dance and song, drew a circle in the sand (an action for which had he known it, there are classical precedents) around Cartier and his companions, in token that they were to remain where they were, and then formally presented him with a girl and two boys, children of the best families in the town, as pledges of alliance and friendship. Even this, however, proved of no avail, and then the sanctions of religion were invoked. Three medicine-men with blackened faces, dog-skin or skunk-skin dresses, and huge horns on their heads, appeared suddenly in a canoe, as messengers from the Great Spirit, Coudragny, to reveal the news that at Hochelaga the ice and snow would be so formidable that the French would all be destroyed. This, however, the captain refused to believe, alleging that the Indian god had no power over the followers of Christ: and the expedients of Donnacanna were exhausted, so that the adventurous Breton was allowed to proceed on his way.

On the 17th day of September Cartier began his long and toilsome ascent of the great river, arriving at Hochelaga on the 2nd of October, thus occupying thirteen days in a voyage which the magnificent river-boats of the St. Lawrence now perform in as many hours. He was struck with the grandeur of the great stream, the fertile lands on its banks, and the magnificent forests, now beginning to assume their splendid autumnal hues. He saw many huts on the banks, occupied by fishermen, who came to his boats with as great confidence and nonchalance as if the French had been well-known friends and neighbours, and at the mouth of the Richelieu he was visited by a great chief, apparently tributary to him of Stadacona, with many professions of friendship. There seems little doubt that the news of the arrival of the French had preceded them far up the river, and that as allies of Donnacanna they were everywhere received as friends.

At length, on the evening of the 2nd of October, amid all the autumnal glories of the Canadian forest, Cartier moored his boats at the foot of the current of St. Mary, opposite what is now a suburb of Montreal, and in sight of the wooded trappean hill which overlooked the town of Hochelaga as it now overlooks the chief city of Canada.

The arrival of the voyagers was speedily made known in the town, for before night more than a thousand persons had assembled on the bank, and signified their joy and welcome by dances, in which the men, women, and children performed separately, and by throwing fish and corn-bread into the boats. Not content with this, they lighted fires on the shore, and kept up their dances all night, with cries of *Aguiazé*, which Cartier interpreted as a word of welcome.

The place where the boats halted, and to which the Europeans have now restricted the once more extensive name of Hochelaga, was about three miles from the actual town, on going to which the traveller would first pass over the low alluvial bank of the river for some distance, and then ascend to a sandy terrace on which the town was built, as Cartier describes it, at the base of the mountain, on a level sandy plain, intersected by a few small brooklets. This being premised, we may give the account of the visit in the words of the old voyager, as translated by Hakluyt, with a few verbal emendations :—

"The captaine the next day very earely in the morning, having attired himselfe, caused all his company to be set in order to go to see the towne and habitation of those people, and a certaine mountaine that is neere the citie; with whom went also five gentlemen, and twenty mariners, leaving the rest to keepe and looke to our boates : we tooke with us three men of Hochelaga to bring us to the place. All along as we went we found the way as well beaten and frequented as can be, the fairest and best country that possibly can be seene, full of as goodly great okes as are in any wood in France, under which the ground was all covered over with faire akornes. After we had gone about foure or five miles, we met by the way one of the chiefest lords of the citie, accompanied with many moe, who so soone as he sawe us beckned and made signes upon us, that we must rest in that place where they had a great fire, and so we did. Then the said lord began to make a long discourse, even as we have saide above, they are accustomed to doe in signe of mirth and friendship, shewing

our captaine and all his company a joyfull countenance,
and good will; who gave him two hatchets, a paire of
knives and a crucifix which he made him to kisse, and
then put it about his necke, for which he gave our
captaine heartie thankes. This done, we went along,
and about a mile and a halfe farther, we began to
finde goodly and large cultivated fieldes, full of such
corn as the countrie yeeldeth. It is even as the Millet
of Bresil, as great and some what bigger than small
peason, wherewith they live even as we doe with our
wheat. In the midst of those fields is the citie of
Hochelaga, placed neere, and as it were joyned to a
great mountaine,* that is tilled round about, very
fertill, on the top of which you may see very farre, we
named it Mount Roiall. The citie of Hochelaga is
round, compassed about with timber, with three course
of Rampires, one within another framed like a sharp
spire, or pyramid, but laid acrosse above. The middlemost of them is perpendicular. The Rampires are
framed and fashioned with pieces of timber, layd along
very well and cunningly joyned togither after their
fashion. This inclosure is in height about two rods.†
It hath but one gate or entrie thereat, which is shut
with piles, stakes, and barres. Over it, and also in
many places of the wall, there is a kind of gallery to
runne along, and ladders to get up, all full of stones

* Literally—" which surrounds it, well cultivated and very
fertile."
† French—"deux lances." The drawing in Ramusio's
translation would give a height of about sixteen feet.

and pebbles for the defence of it. There are in the towne about fiftie houses, at the utmost about fiftie paces long, and twelve or fifteen broad, built all of wood, covered over with the barke of the wood, as broad as any boord, very finely and cunningly joyned togither according to there fashion. Within the said houses, there are many roomes. In the midest of every one there is a great hall, in the middle whereof they make their fire. They live in common togither: then doe the husbands, wives and children each one retire themselves to their chambers. They have also on the top of their houses certaine granaries,* wherein they keepe their corne to make their bread withall; they call it Caracony, which they make as hereafter shall follow. They have certaine peeces of wood, like those whereon we beat our hempe, and with certain beetles of wood they beat their corne to powder; then they make paste of it, and of the paste, cakes or wreathes, then they lay them on a broad and hote stone, and then cover it with hote pebbles and so they bake their bread instead of ovens. They make also sundry sorts of pottage with the said corne and also of peas and beanes, whereof they have great store, as also with other fruits, great cowcumbers and other fruits. They have also in their houses certaine vessels as bigge as any But or Tun, wherein they keepe their fish, causing the same in sommer to be dried in the smoke, and live therewith in winter, whereof they make great provision, as we by expe-

* Corn-cribs.

rience have seene. All their viands and meats are without any taste or savour of salt at all. They sleepe upon barkes of trees laide all along upon the ground being over-spread with the skinnes of certaine wilde Beastes, wherewith they also clothe and cover themselves, namely of the Dormouse,* Beaver, Martin, Fox, Wild Cat, Deer, Stag, and other wild beasts, but the greater part of them go almost naked (during the summer). The thing most precious that they have in all the world they call Esurgny; which is white and which they take in the said river in Cornibots,† in the manner following. When any one hath deserved death, or that they take any of their enemies in warres, first they kill him, then with certain knives they give great slashes and strokes upon their buttocks, flankes, thighs and shoulders; then they cast the same bodie so mangled downe to the bottome of the river, in a place where the said Esurgny is, and

* Query, musk-rat.
† This word seems to have puzzled the translators. It is probably a vulgar local name for some shell supposed to resemble that of which these Indians made their wampum. I would suggest that it may be derived from *cornet*, which is used by old French writers as a name for the shells of the genus *Voluta*, and is also a technical term in conchology. In this case it is likely that the Esurgny was made of the shells of some of our species of *Melania* or *Paludina*, just as the Indians on the coast used for beads and ornaments the shells of *Purpura lapillus* and of *Dentalium*, etc. It is just possible that Cartier may have misunderstood the mode of procuring these shells, and that the statement may refer to some practice of making criminals and prisoners *dive* for them in the deeper parts of the river.

there leave it ten or twelve houres, then they take it up againe, and in the cuts find the said esurgny or cornibots. Of them they make beads, and use them even as we doe gold and silver, accounting it the preciousest thing in the world. They have this vertue in them, they will stop or stanch bleeding at the nose, for we proved it. These people are given to no other exercise, but onely to husbandrie and fishing for their sustenance: they have no care of any other wealth or commoditie in this world, for they have no knowledge of it, and never travell and go out of their country, as those of Canada and Saguenay doe, albeit the Canadians with eight or nine villages more alongst that river be subject unto them.

"So soone as we were come neare the towne, a great number of the inhabitants thereof came to present themselves before us, after their fashion, making very much of us: we were by our guides brought into the middest of the towne. They have in the middlemost part of their towne a large square place, being from side to side a good stone cast, whither we were brought, and there with signes were commanded to stay, and so we did: then suddenly all the women and maidens of the towne gathered themselves together, part of which had their armes full of young children, and as many as could came to kiss our faces, our armes, and what part of the bodie soever they could touch, weeping for very joy that they saw us, shewing us the best countenance that possibly they could, desiring us with their signes, that it would please us to

D

touch their children. That done, the men caused the women to withdraw themselves backe, then they every one sate down on the ground round about us, as if we would have shewen and rehearsed some comedie or other shew: then presently came the women againe, every one bringing a fouresquare matte in manner of carpets, and spreading them abroad on the ground in that place, they caused us to sit upon them. That done, the Lord and King of the country was brought upon nine or ten men's shoulders (whom in their tongue they call Agouhanna, sitting upon a great stagges skinne, and they laide him downe upon the foresaid mats neere to the capitaine, every one beckning unto us that hee was their lord. This Agouhanna was a man about fiftie yeeres old: he was no whit better apparelled then any of the rest, onely excepted that he had a certain thing around his head made of the skinnes of hedgehogs * like a red wreath. He was full of the palsie and his members shronke together. After he had with certain signes saluted our captaine and all his companie, and by manifest tokens bid all welcome, he shewed his legges and armes to our capitaine, and with signes desired him to touch them, and so he did, rubbing them with his own hands: then did Agouhanna take the wreath or crowne he had about his head, and gave it unto our capitaine, that done they brought before him diverse diseased men, some blinde, some criple, some lame and impotent, and some so old that the haire of their

* Porcupines.

eyelids came downe and covered their cheekes, and layd them all along before our capitaine, to the end they might of him be touched; for it seemed unto them that God was descended and come down from heaven to heale them. Our capitaine seeing the misery and devotion of this poore people, recited the Gospel of St. John, that is to say, 'In the beginning was the Word,' making the sign of the cross upon the poor sick ones, praying to God that it would please him to open the hearts of this poore people, and to make them know our holy faith, and that they might receive baptisme and christendome, that done, he took a service-booke in his hand, and with a loud voice read all the passion of Christ, word by word, and all the standers by might heare him, all which while this poore people kept silence, and were marvellously attentive, looking up to heaven, and imitating us in gestures. Then he caused the men all orderly to be set on one side, the women on another, and likewise the children on another, and to the chiefest of them he gave hatchets, to the other knives, and to the women beads and such other small trifles. Then where y children were, he cast rings, counters and broaches made of tin, whereat they seemed to be very glad. That done, our capitaine commanded trumpets and other musicall instruments to be sounded, which when they heard, they were very merie. Then we took our leave and went away; the women seeing that, put themselves before to stay us, and brought us out of their meates that they had made readie for us, as fish,

pottage, beanes, and such other things, thinking to
make us eate, and dine in that place; but because
the meats were not to our taste we liked them not,
but thanked them, and with signes gave to understand
that we had no neede to eate. When we were out of
the towne, diverse of the men and women followed us,
and brought us to the toppe of the foresaid mountaine, which wee named Mount Roial, it is about a
quarter of a league from the towne. When as we were
on the toppe of it, we might discerne and plainly see
thirtie leagues about. On the north side of it there
are many hilles to be seene running west and east, and
as many more on the south, amongst and betweene the
which the countrey is as faire and as pleasant as possible can be seene, being levell, smooth, and very
plaine, fit to be husbanded and tilled, and in the middest of those fieldes we saw the river further up a
great way than where we had left our boates, where
was the greatest and the swiftest fall of water that
any where hath beene seene which we could not pass,
and the said river as great wide and large as our sight
might discerne, going southwest along three fair and
round mountaines that we sawe, as we judged about
fifteen leagues from us. Those which brought us
thither tolde and shewed us, that in the sayd river
there were three such falles of water more, as that
was where we had left our boates; but we could not
understand how farre they were one from another.
Moreover they showe us with signes, that the said
three fals being past, a man might sayle the space of

three months more alongst that river, and that along the hills that are on the north side there is a great river, which (even as the other) cometh from the west, we thought it to be the river that runneth through the countrey of Saguenay, and without any signe or question mooved or asked of them, they tooke the chayne of our capitaines whistle, which was of silver, and the dagger-haft of one of our fellow mariners, hanging on his side being of yellow copper guilt, and shewed us that such stuffe came from the said river, and that there be Agojudas, that is as much to say, an evill people, who goe all armed even to their fingers' ends. Also they shewed us the manner of their armour, they are made of cordes and wood, finely and cunningly wrought together. They gave us also to understande that those Agojudas doe continually warre one against another, but because we did not understand them well, we could not perceive how farre it was to that country. Our capitaine shewed them redde copper, which in their language they call Caquedaze, and looking towarde that countrey, with signes asked them if any came from thence, they shaking their heads answered no; but they shewed us that it came from Saguenay, and that lyeth cleane contrary to the other. After we had heard and seene these things of them we drewe to our boates accompanied with a great multitude of those people; some of them when as they sawe any of our fellowes weary, would take them up on their shoulders, and carry them us on horseback."

This, let it be observed, is the picture of an absolutely primitive people, previously unvisited by Europeans—" flint-folk " in so far as weapons and implements are concerned. They may serve to us as a type of those still older aborigines of Europe whose remains are now exciting so much attention, and we may consider in the following pages their history and probable origin, the remains which they have left, their arts and manufactures, their knowledge, culture, and religion, their physical characteristics, and other

Fig. 6.—Section of the Stockade or Wall of Hochelaga. (*After Cartier.*)

American nations their contemporaries, and may as we proceed apply the result to the explanation of prehistoric man elsewhere.

The plan and section of the city and its defences, given in figures 6 and 7, are reduced from those in Ramusio's edition of Cartier's Voyages, and are apparently sketches from memory. The stockade was probably of round trunks of trees rather than of planks, but the town was, no doubt, a regular circle, with the houses on one plan. This plan and the social relations connected with it we shall have to notice in the sequel. Our sketch, fig 8, may be taken as pretty nearly representing the actual appearance of Hochelaga. The features of the country are accurately given, and the oak-tree in the foreground is a sketch

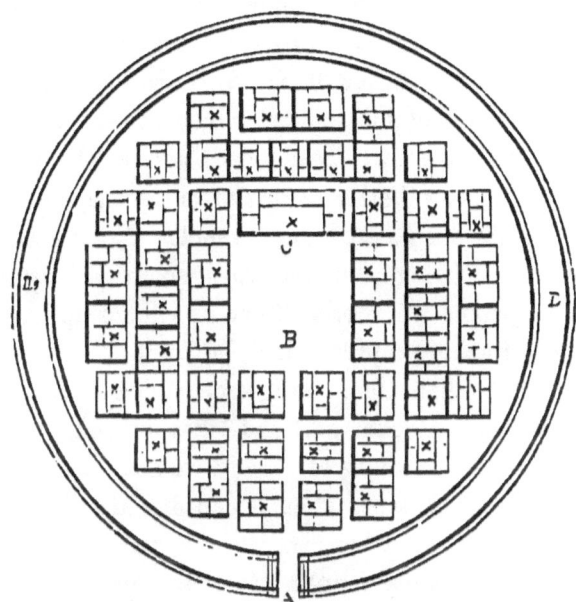

Fig. 7—PLAN OF HOCHELAGA (*after Cartier*).
(A) Gate.
(B) Square.
(C) Chief's House.
(D) Wall or Stockade.

of one now standing on McGill College grounds, Montreal, near the ancient site.

What was the fate of Hochelaga? The question may be prompted by an interest in these primitive people, and the answer has in it much material for thought as to other perished nations. Cartier, finding that the great River Hochelaga was no highway to the Indies, but learning that towards its source was the land of "Saguenay," celebrated for its metallic wealth, made it an object in his third voyage to reach the land of Saguenay,* now known to us as the copper region of Lake Superior. He failed, however, to surmount the rapids of the St. Lawrence, and from the fragments of his journal which remain seems to have found reason to dread hostilities on the part of the natives, now better informed as to the ambitious and selfish designs of the French. No mention is made of Hochelaga, but the voyager was entertained by the people of another town or village apparently near the Lachine rapids, which he names Tutonaguy.

In 1603, when Champlain ascended the St. Lawrence, either Hochelaga had disappeared, or the explorer heard nothing of it, and we hear no more of its site till 1642, more than a century after the voyages of Cartier, when the Sieur de Maisonneuve selected the locality for the site of the future Montreal —an instance of the fact which perpetually recurs in the history both of the old world and the new, that the exigencies of defence or the convenience of subsistence and communication have dictated to the primitive peoples of bygone ages the selection of localities which have approved themselves to their successors up to our own time. An isolated and de-

* This name, like many others, has been restricted in use to a locality scarcely that to which it was originally applied.

Fig. 8.—THE TOWN OF HOCHELAGA, as it appeared to Cartier in 1535; with Corn-fields and a "Gr at Oak," drawn from one now on McGill College Grounds, in the foreground; and Mount Royal in the distance.

fensible position, with fertile soil, and a hill commanding an extensive view of the great Canadian plain, and this at the foot of the rapids which close the free navigation of the St. Lawrence, and at the confluence of the two greatest rivers of Canada, constituted a combination of advantages ·equally appreciable to the aborigines and to the French settlers, and which still give to Montreal the first position as a Canadian city.

Sometime in the interval between 1535 and 1642, Hochelaga had been utterly destroyed, and the encroachments of the warlike Five Nations, or Iroquois, from the south, had even made the island a sort of frontier debatable land in which no man lived, and to which it was dangerous to resort even for hunting. A tradition current long afterwards among the Algonquins, and preserved by Charlevoix, told of a long and bloody war between them and the Hochelagans, terminated by a treacherous surprise at the little River Becancour, between Hochelaga and Stadacona, in which the Hochelagans were defeated with the loss of so many warriors that the stream acquired the name of the putrid river from the number of dead bodies left in it. This was a serious blow to Hochelaga, leading afterwards to its fall by the hands of another enemy. According to certain Indians who represented themselves as the survivors of the nation, and who visited the French colonists in 1642, the town was finally taken and burned by the Hurons, and its few remaining people had taken refuge with the nomadic tribes of the Ottawa. They represented themselves as the last remnant of a great people who had once possessed broad lands and many towns on both sides of the St. Lawrence. Their tribal name had been Onontchataranons, but by the French they were called Iroquet, a name apparently expressing a supposed affinity with their bitter enemies the Iroquois. The French invited them to return to Montreal, and a few families accepted the invitation, but remained only for a short time, being driven away by the dread of the Iroquois, from whom they doubted the ability of the French to protect them. This is the last historical notice of Hochelaga. Its site was overgrown with trees, and subsequently cleared and cultivated. Its name was transferred to Cartier's landing-place, at the foot of the current of St. Mary. In 1860 the excavations for foundations of houses in the western part of Montreal uncovered its old hearths and kitchen-middens and burial-places. In the next and following chapters we shall direct attention to its history and remains, and to the light which these throw on the primitive relations of the American tribes.

In the meantime let us think of the instructive fact that within three hundred years of the time when the French explorer found at the foot of Mount Royal a populous Indian town, strongly fortified and surrounded by cultivated ground, its very site had been forgotten, and was occupied with fields showing no sign above the green sward of the remains beneath.

The mountain remains as of old, but a new city of a strange people has grown up, and but for Cartier's narrative, those who dig up the curiously ornamented earthen vessels, the stone implements, and the bones of the old Hochelagans, might suppose that they were dealing with the relics of a people who may have perished thousands of years ago. The historical facts of the existence of the town in 1535, and of its destruction before the settlement of Montreal, while they take away the romance which might otherwise connect itself with the remains, give to them, as we shall find, a double value as interpreters of the prehistoric antiquities of old America and Europe.

CHAPTER III.

GLIMPSES OF PRE-HISTORIC TIMES.

WHAT were the ethnic relations of the old Hochelagans, whose reception of Cartier was noticed in our last chapter? The answer furnishes a strange illustration of the evanescent nature of the history of tribes without written records; but when pursued to the end casts a flood of light on the pre-Columbian history of North America. Dr. Wilson has shown that notwithstanding a general physical resemblance of the primitive North Americans, they present distinct types of skull corresponding to the long and short-headed forms (Dolichocephalic and Brachycephalic) of European races. Now the skulls obtained from the cemeteries of the ancient Hochelaga are of the long-headed form characteristic of the Iroquois and Huron nations, that is, of the historical enemies, not of the later political allies, of this ancient people. We shall find also that the patterns of their pottery and tobacco-pipes correspond with those prevalent among the other tribes in the neighbourhood of the St. Lawrence, but more especially resemble those of the ancient Eries, a tribe also hostile to the Iroquois, though allied to them by language. The language of Hochelaga, in so far as can be judged from the short vocabulary preserved by Cartier, was not Algonquin, or like that of the tribes north of the St. Lawrence, nor was it precisely like that of the Iroquois or Hurons, but a separate dialect resembling these in many leading words. On the other hand, the early French explorers regarded all the St. Lawrence tribes except the Hurons as of Algonquin race. In Cartier's time and subsequently the Iroquois and Hurons were hostile to Hochelaga, while the Algonquins seem to have been allies, and Hochelaga seems to have enjoyed a political headship over the St. Lawrence tribes to the eastward and northward. Lastly, Hochelaga was finally destroyed by the Hurons, and the survivors, if we are to believe their tale, had identified themselves with Algonquin tribes on the Ottawa.

The solution of the difficulty is that the Hochelagans were not precisely either of the Iroquois, Huron, or Algonquin stock, but a remnant of an ancient and decaying nation to which the Eries and some other tribes also belonged, and which had historical relations originally with the now extinct Alleghans, or mound-builders of the Ohio and Mississippi rivers, and latterly with the Iroquois and Hurons, but which at the epoch of the French discovery was on the point of extinction, hemmed in between the aggressive Iroquois nations in the south, and the barbarous Algonquins in the north, and holding the stronghold of Hochelaga as one of its last fortresses on the St. Lawrence. Before the French colonisation of the St. Lawrence valley these people had disappeared, and the Algonquins had replaced them, and their former residence had become an unpeopled frontier between the Iroquois and Algonquins. Had Cartier visited Hochelaga a few centuries earlier, he would have found it connected with a great and powerful group of similar nations extending to the valley of the Ohio. Had he ascended the St. Lawrence a century later, he would have found no trace of such a city.

The evidence and the historical application of this result will require us to consider the ante-Columbian distribution of the North American nations, and the changes and movements in progress among them; and it will be the most perspicuous mode to adopt the historical style for what is in regard to its evidence a matter of archæology.

It was a tradition of one of the American tribes that in old times the Indians were increasing to such an extent that they were threatened with want, and the Great Spirit then taught them to make war, and thus to thin one another's numbers. The tradition, as we shall find, embodies the historic truth that peaceful primitive nations had been overthrown by warlike invaders. But without absolutely believing in this mythical period of peace, there is good reason at least to show that before the European discovery a series of great movements and conquests had commenced and was in progress. Before these movements, we learn from monumental and linguistic evidence the distribution of races marked on the little sketch-map on the following page.

Across the Arctic regions of the continent lay as now the Innuit, Kalalik, or Greenlanders, better known to us by the Algonquin nickname of Esquimaux (Eskumaget, "he eats raw flesh"). On the eastern side

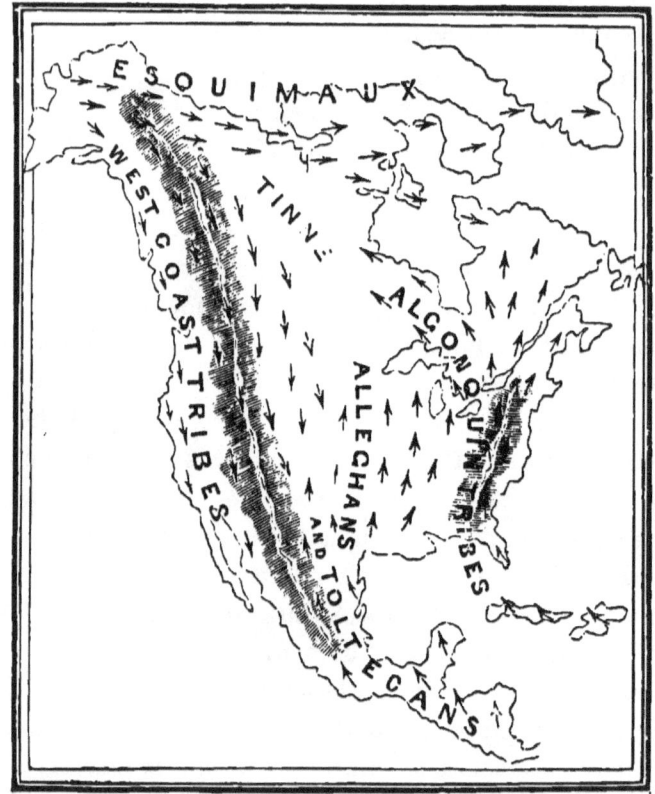

Fig. 9.—SKETCH-MAP SHOWING THE PROBABLE LINES OF MIGRATION AND DISTRIBUTION OF THE AMERICAN TRIBES.

of the continent these poor people have always been separated by a marked line from their Indian neighbours on the south, and have been regarded by them with the most bitter hostility. On the west, however, they pass into the Eastern Siberians on the one hand, and into the West-coast Indians on the other, both by language and physical characters. They and the northern tribes at least of West-coast Indians, belong in all probability to a wave of population spreading from Behring Strait. They were the Skraelings, or dwarfs, of the ancient Icelandic voyagers who early visited and colonised Greenland; and as they represented the inhabitants of Vinland, which seems to have been on the coast of New England, as Skraelings, it has been supposed that the Esquimaux formerly extended farther to the south than at present. It is, however, not unlikely that the Northmen may have regarded the Indians also as Skraelings.

South of the Esquimaux there extends, from near the west coast far into the interior, a series of tribes whose languages and manners are intermediate between those of the last mentioned people and the Indians to the south. These are the Tinné, or Chippewyans. There is reason to believe that at one time they extended quite to the Atlantic coast, and that some of the primitive tribes of Labrador, the Red Indians of Newfoundland, and the pre-historic peoples who are said by tradition to have been displaced by the Algonquin tribes of Nova Scotia and New England, belonged to this stock. The Tinné are either a mixed people, intermediate between the Indians and Esquimaux, or a more ancient people than either, hemmed in between the northern and southern streams of migration.

Between the Esquimaux and Tinné on the north and the St. Lawrence and its lakes on the south, and stretching down the Atlantic coast as far as Florida, lay the numerous tribes of Algonquins and their allies, resembling each other in physical characters and language, and whom tradition and other indications concur in tracing to a migration entering America from the equatorial Atlantic. Many of these tribes were hunters and fishermen, but in the temperate and warmer regions they had acquired the rudiments at least of agriculture. They are the typical American Indians of the early English colonists.

In Central America, Mexico, and the rich alluvial plains of the Mississippi and its tributaries, were the Toltecans, or primitive Mexicans, and the Alleghans, or "mound-builders" of the Mississippi and Ohio—a people now known by little more than their bones and the remains of their works. In physiognomy and bodily frame they seem to have presented some of the softer features of the Polynesians, from whom perhaps they were in whole or in part derived. Simple and primitive tillers of the soil, they possessed a higher degree of the instinct of combination for great public works and of artistic skill than the other North American tribes. Their huge communistic barracks or hotels, the so-called palaces of Central America, Yucatan, and Mexico, the Pueblos of the Colorado, and the mound-villages of the Mississippi, with their sacrificial and burial-mounds, still remain as gigantic monuments of their skill and industry.

In some parts of the western territories the manner in which these are perched on almost inaccessible cliffs affords a testimony to the skill and enterprise of these people, and an affecting evidence of their struggle against the encroachments of the more warlike and barbarous tribes. They were clever weavers, potters, and workers in copper and silver, and had made an amount of progress in the arts of life which in Mexico astonished their Spanish conquerors. They held all the great fertile plains and tablelands between the Rocky Mountains and the Alleghanies, and had extended themselves to the mineral districts of Lake Superior, where they worked extensive mines of copper and silver. They have even left traces of their presence in the valley of the St. Lawrence. But they held their wide possessions by a precarious tenure. Their arms were not superior to those of the ruder races that surrounded them. Tradition and their buried skeletons testify that they were of greater physical strength than the savage tribes, and they excelled in numbers, military skill, and the art of fortification. Still they were subject to continual raids and attacks, and before the discovery of America, the Aztecs, a people of truly American physiognomy and of savage instincts, had conquered Mexico, while the region of the western plains, the meeting-place of the three great waves of immigration, and the Scythia of North America, rearing a numerous and bold population of buffalo-hunters, had overwhelmed with its swarms the northern mound-builders. These, when cut off from the copper mines of the north and the fisheries of the great lakes, probably decayed rapidly, and the old trees growing on their earthworks when the first European explorers visited their country, testify to the lapse of centuries since their destruction or expatriation.

Originally these Alleghans were bounded on the north by the Algonquins, but the earlier waves of conquest from the north and west severed this connection. These earlier migrations, however, in time became partially absorbed and civilized, and formed a belt of semi-Alleghan and semi-Algonquin territory along the great lakes and the St. Lawrence, the people inhabiting which had borrowed some of the arts and modes of life of the Alleghans. To this probably belonged such nations of agricultural and village-dwelling Indians as the Eries, the Neutrals, the Hurons, and the Hochelagans, which eventually cultivated friendly relations with their neighbours on the south, and with the Algonquins on the north, and carried on to some extent the copper-mining and agriculture of their civilized predecessors. But other waves of migration from the west followed, and at the time of the early French discoveries the Iroquois and other fierce and warlike tribes were inserting themselves like a wedge between the remains of the Alleghans on the south, and the Eries, the Hurons, and the Hochelagans on the north.

Such is the history as its general features present themselves to my mind, after long study of the fragmentary evidence which remains. I could not, without several chapters of discussion, give the details of this evidence, but shall devote the remainder of this chapter to some portions of it which especially concern my present purpose.

The features of the old Alleghans, or civilised mound-builders, are preserved to us only by their sculptures and terra-cottas, and principally by the heads represented on the curiously-formed tobacco-pipes, which they devoted in great numbers on their "altar hearths" to their gods or manitous; and the few skulls which have been secured from the grave-mounds correspond with these representations. They were people with rounded, short, and sometimes high heads; and features, which while American, were less marked and softer than those of the more barbarous tribes. The same cast of countenance appears, according to Wilson, on pottery, attributable to the Toltecans or primitive Mexicans and the Central Americans, while the features of the intrusive Aztecs were more of the ordinary Indian type. To illustrate this I give a few profiles—that of a mound-builder from a pipe, those of two ancient Central Americans from Palenque, that of a Peruvian from an earthen vase, and that of a woman of the mound-builders, also from an earthen vessel. To contrast with these are an Aztec chief from a Mexican painting, and a modern Mandan Indian belonging to a nomadic tribe. The Toltecan and Alleghan features obviously show the American type softened and refined either by foreign intermixture or by long ages of civilized culture. A similar but somewhat different style of refinement in the American countenance appears in the Inca race of Peru. It is remarkable in connection

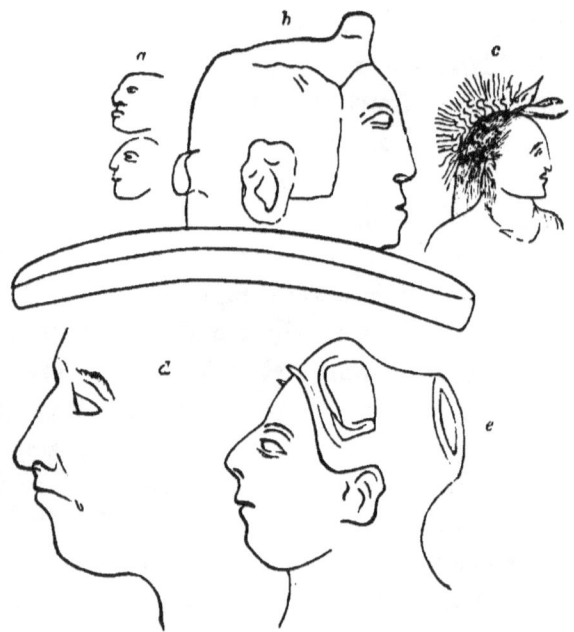

Fig. 10.—ALLEGHAN, TOLTECAN, PERUVIAN, AND MODERN CROW HEADS.
(a) Toltecan from Palenque.
(b) Mound-builder on a pipe.
(c) Crow.
(d) Mound-builder on a vase.
(e) Peruvian on a vase.
(*After Wilson, Foster, and Catlin.*)

with this that the Alleghans and Toltecans are the oldest North American aborigines of whom we have any record. Whatever age may be assigned to the buildings of Central America, Yucatan, and Mexico, there seems the best reason to believe that some of the Mississippi mounds are very ancient. Very old trees were found growing on them, and there were indications of previous generations of trees. The "garden beds" of extinct and forgotten tribes are found to have extended themselves over the earthworks of earlier people. Professor Swallow, of Missouri, informs me that he opened two ancient burial

Fig. 11.—MODERN MANDAN, AND ANCIENT AZTEC HEADS.
(*After Catlin and Wilson.*)

mounds in that State, on which vegetable soil two feet thick had accumulated, and around which six feet of alluvial silt had been deposited, apparently in consequence of a subsidence of the soil on which the mound had been built, in some pre-historic earthquake, similar, perhaps, to those which in modern times produced the sunk country of New Madrid in the same region. In the alluvium which had accumulated was found the tooth of a mastodon. Perhaps no American interment can lay claim to greater antiquity, and the bones of the buried corpses had been resolved almost entirely into dust. Yet earthen vessels found with them showed the high Alleghan type of features, and the only skull secured was of the same type. I have in my own collection a tooth of the mastodon, and a human skull, probably of a woman, which were found, as I am informed, together, in river alluvium, near Kankakee, Illinois, and the statement is corroborated by the state of preservation of the remains. The skull, while of decided American type, is of a short and high form, more allied to the Toltecan head than to that of the more barbarous Indian races. In North America, therefore, a comparatively civilised and well-developed race would seem to have precedence of all others, a statement which we shall find may apply to Europe also, notwithstanding the mythical notions of a palæolithic age of barbarism.

It is remarkable, however, that two types of head are represented in these old monuments, one short and high, with a respectable frontal development; another low-browed, and retreating in the frontal aspect. According to Foster both these types appear in the burial mounds of the Alleghans. This may indicate different castes or tribes, or conquering and subject or servile races. It is certain, however, that similar differences exist among the modern Indians, and that those with low foreheads, even when not artificially compressed, are not deficient in intelligence.

For instance, Catlin has remarked and figured in his sketches the peculiar Toltecan face in the Upsarokas, or Crows, a small tribe inhabiting the Upper Missouri. He notices its resemblance to the Yucatan figures, and particularly refers to the low and retreating forehead, which he, however, affirms is not artificially flattened. He describes the Crows as tall and athletic men, intelligent and cleanly, and remarkable for the superior neatness and ingenuity of their arms, garments, and lodges. They are, however, a migratory people, though the allied Minatarees are more stationary, and are cultivators. He further remarks, however, that the Mandans, who have salient features like those of the Aztecs, represent the Toltecan features on their drawings on buffalo skins. May this not be a conventional style of art handed down from an earlier period?

Another people of the west, who may be regarded as lineal descendants of the Toltecans or Alleghans, are the Moquis, or Village Indians of New Mexico, who still retain the semi-civilized habits and arts of these ancient peoples. From an excellent series of photographs of these people, for which I am indebted to the officers of the United States Geological Survey of the Territories, I infer that they have the semi-Polynesian and refined style of features referred to above. A comparison of these photographs with others in my possession of natives of Easter Island, shows a striking resemblance; and it is interesting that the latter, in their system of totemic carving on wood of family records, and in the character of the megalithic images with which they adorned their burial places, also show affinity with the nations of Western America.

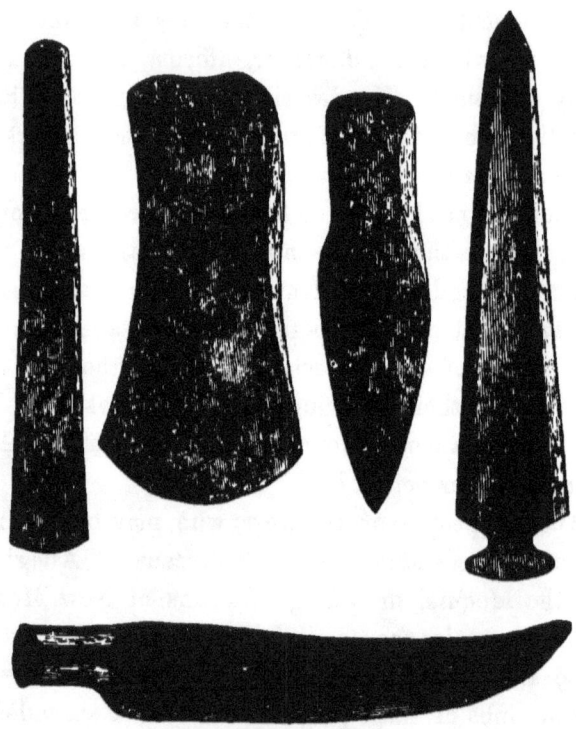

Fig. 12.—COPPER AXES, SPEARS, AND KNIFE OF THE ALLEGHANS.
(*After Squier and Foster.*)

The traditions of the Delawares and Iroquois concur in testifying to their former wars against a great people, the Allegwi or Alleghans, dwelling to the south-west, and who were finally expelled from their territories, and in accordance with this the researches of Squier and Davies have shown that the earthworks of the ancient mound-builders extend up the Ohio valley towards western New York, so that these

Fig. 13.—COPPER BRACELET, DISC, BEAD, AND BUTTONS OF ALLEGHANS.
(*After Squier.*)

people were once conterminous with the Iroquois and allied tribes. Still more remarkable evidences exist that the power of the Alleghans extended as far north as Lake Superior and the St. Lawrence valley. I may take two illustrations from Wilson. One is an ancient burial-place discovered by Dr. Reynolds near Brockville. Here were buried, about fourteen feet below the surface, twenty skeletons, arranged in a circle with their feet towards the centre. Some of the skeletons were of gigantic proportions, but their bones had well-nigh crumbled into dust. With them were found well-made spears and chisels of native copper, stone-chisels, gouges, and arrow-heads, and a curious terra-cotta mask, which Wilson has figured, and which he remarks is Toltecan rather than Indian in its features, and which resembles the heads on earthen vessels of the mound-builders, while he evidently regards the interment as not corresponding with those of the Canadian tribes. It does, however, correspond with old Alleghan interments already mentioned as discovered by Professor Swallow. In one of the mounds explored by him, the bodies, whose bones were in the last stage of decay, lay in the same position as in the Brockville grave, and each had an earthen vessel at its head with a representation of a human face. This mode of burial, the warriors lying in death as they would lie with their feet to the watch-fire, and each with his vessel of water or food at his head, like Saul, King of Israel, of old,* seems to have been peculiar to the Alleghans, and has been recognised in several localities. War parties at least of this people, and possibly also permanent settlements, must have extended themselves to the St. Lawrence river.

* 1 Samuel xxvi. 11.

The evidence of copper mining on Lake Superior in pre-historic times is equally conclusive. In the Ontanogan district, where extensive mines of native copper are now worked, ancient excavations long since deserted and overgrown with the aboriginal forest are found on the outcrops of the veins. Some of these are twenty-five to thirty feet deep, and in the bottom of them are found the stone mauls and picks and decayed wooden shovels of the ancient miners.* In one place a mass of native copper, weighing six tons, had been dislodged from its matrix, and mounted on a wooden frame, but afterwards abandoned, either because of its great weight, or because the miners had been driven away by some hostile invasion. These ancient works are said to be found over an extent of nearly 150 miles on the south side of Lake Superior, and on the north side of the lake they also occur, though on a smaller scale. I have myself explored some of them at Maimanse. Here they are confined to the outcrop of the veins in which the native copper, associated with quartz and other minerals, projects in irregular masses and strings above the enclosing trap. Following these indications, the ancient miners had traced the veins along the hills, and had not only broken off the projecting masses with stone mauls which were found in their trenches, but had, perhaps with the aid of fire, followed the larger masses downward for several feet, throwing out the broken quartz in heaps at the sides. That these mines were not

* Wilson, "Prehistoric Man."

worked by the present Indian tribes of the country is evident, that some of them are of great antiquity is proved by the silt and vegetable soil with which they are filled, the former sometimes containing skeletons of wild animals, which have fallen into these old excavations, and the latter being overgrown with the ancient trees of a primeval forest. Further, deposits of manufactured implements indicate that they were made on the spot, and their style, especially that of some knives inlaid and ornamented with native silver, shows that the artists were the same with those who made the implements of the Mississippi mounds. These people had, in short, explored all the rich localities of native copper only recently re-discovered by Europeans. To some extent, however, the tribes that expelled the primitive miners preserved their arts, for the copper of Lake Superior was known to the Hochelagans and Stadaconians of the time of Cartier, though possessed by these people in much less abundance than by the old Alleghans.

There is also evidence that the original supplanters of the Alleghans were themselves in process of being supplanted at the period of the French discovery. The strange story of the Eries or Neutrals, as it has been preserved by Schoolcraft, belongs to this category. This people, who have given a name to one of the great American lakes, held a political position at the time of the French discovery which entitled them to the name of the neutral nation. Occupying a fertile territory south of Lake Erie, and inhabiting walled villages, they were distinct from the Iroquois on the one hand and the Algonquins on the other, just as the Wyandots or Hurons were on the north of Lake Ontario and the Hochelagans in their island on the St. Lawrence. Further, in language they were allied to the Iroquois and Hurons, being called by them Attiwendaronks, or people differing little in language or speaking a cognate dialect, as distinguished from the Algonquins, who were to them barbarians. This was also the linguistic position of the Hochelagans relatively to the Iroquois. Cartier says that the Hochelagans enjoyed some sort of hegemony over the St. Lawrence tribes. In like manner these people were recognised not only as neutrals, but as pacificators. Their political ruler was a queen, and her council fire was recognised as a sacred place of refuge and of arbitration of differences. This female rule was also, as we shall find, in all probability an institution borrowed from the Alleghans. The more bitter animosities consequent on the European invasion led to events which plunged the Eries into war with the Iroquois, and after a severe struggle they were driven from their homes, and obliged to retreat to the southward, where, according to information collected by Schoolcraft, they became identified with the Katawbas of Virginia and Carolina, one of the noblest and most amenable to culture of the native tribes of the Southern States of the American Union. The Hurons were also in like manner dislodged by the Iroquois, and this extermination of large and populous nations after the discovery of America seems but the completion of a great intrusive movement breaking up the tribes which had previously replaced and mixed with the Alleghans, or which had perhaps been allies of theirs on the north, partially impregnated with their culture and pursuing their industries long after they were cut off. It accords with this that there is a very strong resemblance of detail between the arts and implements of the Eries, Hurons, and Hochelagans, indicating a close connection at that traditional time when their towns and villages occupied the wide regions afterwards seized by their enemies the Iroquois.

"Many hundred years ago," said an aged Iroquois chief, in accounting to an American antiquarian * for the many ancient forts scattered over western New York, "a long war occurred between the Iroquois and other powerful nations, during which many fortifications, often stockaded and enclosing villages, were built throughout all this region, but their enemies were finally repulsed, and passed far to the southwest." Whether this legend refers to the expulsion of the Eries and their allies, which happened as late as 1655, or to the far earlier expulsion of the Alleghans, or whether it includes a mixture of both, it would perhaps be impossible to say. "The traditions of the Delawares," says Dr. Wilson, "hold that the Alleghans were a strong and mighty nation, reaching to the eastern shores of the Mississippi, when in remote

* Cheney, "Report on Monuments of New York."

times they came into the great valley from the west. But the Iroquois, who had established themselves on the head waters of the chief rivers which have their rise to the south of the great lakes, combined with the Delaware or Lenapé nation to crush the power of that ancient people of the valley, and the surviving remnant of the decimated Alleghans were driven down the Mississippi, and their name blotted out from the roll of nations. The very name of the Ohio is of Iroquois origin, and given to the river of the Alleghans by their ruthless conquerors. The Susquehannocks, who are believed to be of the same ancient lineage, excited the ire of the dominant nation, and were in like manner extirpated. At a later date the Delawares fell under their ban, and the remnant of that proud nation, quitting for ever the shores of the noble river which perpetuates their name, retraced their steps into the unknown west." Three hundred years of European colonisation and warfare have brought the same fate on the conquering Iroquois themselves, whose small remnants exist in a few scattered settlements, fading away and mingling with the pale faces, and of no political importance among the strange people who have usurped that heritage which they had wrested from others.

Thus we find in America the Europeans displacing in historic times Indians who had themselves not long before displaced others, and these last retaining the clear tradition of those they had displaced at a still earlier time. The Alleghans are represented only by remains of unknown date, and the Eries, Hurons, and Hochelagans would have been in the same position but for the arrival of the French in time to witness their decadence. Let us observe also that such a history implies primitive civilization fading into barbarism until it shall be replaced by some new culture. The Alleghans of the Ohio and Mississippi had their council fires quenched by barbarians long before Cortez attacked the new Mexican empire of the Aztecs. Our poor Hochelagans, within less than a century of Cartier's time, had been destroyed or reduced to the condition of wandering hunters. The pre-Columbian America seemed hastening to return to barbarism.

Let us observe also that the aboriginal Americans, though probably reaching the continent from the old world by three distinct lines of migration, one from Southern Asia by the Pacific, one from Northern Asia by Behring's straits, and one from Western Europe by the Atlantic and its islands,* had brought with them essentially the same beliefs and customs, and not very dissimilar physical characteristics; so that they naturally and readily blended into a more or less homogeneous American type, with local modifications of physical aspect, customs, and arts. At the time therefore when America was first colonised, there must have been a remarkable uniformity in the populations inhabiting Asia and Europe, similar to that which obtained in prehistoric America. In other

* See the discussion of this subject by Wilson, "Pre-historic Man."

words, the prevalent or universal type of the people of the Eastern or Eurasian continent must have been that which we now call Turanian or American. In America the local varieties and more or less cultured members of this great race had again and again replaced each other over wide regions, so that the same varieties of Dolichocephalic and Brachycephalic races, and the same ages of Stone and Bronze, recognised in Europe, with the addition of an intermediate age of native Copper, could have been made up by the antiquary, did we not know that they were contemporary, and that over wide areas, almost equalling the whole of Europe, the age of Copper and of civilization preceded that of barbarism.

May this not, then, be an American epitome of pre-historic Europe? Simple and industrious colonists spreading themselves over new lands: barbarous and migratory tribes and families wandering from the centres of civilization over the untilled wastes, and then recoiling in successive waves on the more cultivated tribes with rude and desolating violence. So the struggle of opposing races would go on from century to century, strewing the land with strange and unaccountable traces of semi-civilization and barbarism—the forests growing over them and river floods sweeping them away and depositing them in unlikely places, until Rome did for Europe what Europe has been doing for America; and then in both cases the pre-historic ages recede into dim obscurity, and under the manipulation of the archæologist may be stretched indefinitely into the past, and arranged according to his fancy in successive periods of barbarism and semi-civilization.

It is true that this view seems in direct contradiction to the theories promulgated with so much confidence of the primitive barbarism or semi-brutal character of man. Yet there are facts, in the old world as well as in the new, which point in this same direction. For example, it is admitted that the wild Veddahs of Ceylon are proved by their Sanscrit tongue and their physical characters to be a degraded branch of that great Aryan family to which the civilized Hindoo belongs. The Hottentots and even the Bushmen of South Africa can be shown by language and customs to be merely depauperated descendants of that great Ethiopian nation which in Upper Egypt founded one of the oldest known civilized kingdoms. Physiological considerations point in the same direction; for man, unarmed and naked, must originally have been frugivorous, and then to some degree a horticulturist, before he could have developed into a savage hunter and warrior. To suppose that the savage hunters of our day are the primeval type of man, is one of the most unfounded assumptions of that materialistic philosophy which disgraces the intellect as well as the right feeling of our time. At the same time, it has been the policy of this philosophy to gather up and parade all that is discreditable and low in the condition and manners of the modern savage, so as to approximate him as nearly as possible to brutes; and having done this, to exhibit him as the existing representative of our pre-historic ancestors. Thus there is created at once a double prejudice, hostile to true views of human origin and history, and to the brotherhood of humanity, as well as to its spiritual relations and higher aspirations.

CHAPTER IV.

THE REMAINS OF CITIES OF THE STONE AGE.

THE modern Montreal has now overgrown the site of Hochelaga, and it met with no obstacles in doing so save the natural inequalities of the ground. Less than three hundred years have elapsed, and the clearing of the young forest which must have covered the site, and the ploughing of the fields, had sufficed to remove all traces except those which might remain beneath the greensward. Thus, its very place unknown, the old city reposed until the bones of its sleeping inhabitants were disturbed by the excavations of streets and foundations of houses. For some time this work proceeded without any attention being given to the antiquities uncovered. In levelling the ground large quantities of sand were removed to be used in making mortar, and the workmen merely reburied the bones in the underlying clay, where they may some day serve to convince enthusiastic believers in the antiquity of man that our species existed in Canada at the time of the marine Post-pliocene. At length attention was directed to the subject, and a somewhat rich harvest was obtained of relics—which are now preserved in public and private collections.

It will be interesting here to note what actually

remained to indicate the site. The wooden walls described by Cartier, and the bark houses, were no doubt burned at the time of the final capture of the town, which was probably taken by a sudden surprise and assault, and its inhabitants butchered, with the exception of those who could escape by flight, while all portable articles of value would be taken away; and this would especially apply to the implements and trinkets left by the French, the report of whose vast value and rarity may perhaps have stimulated the attack.

In a dry sandy soil and in an extreme climate, wooden structures rapidly decay, and such parts of the buildings as the fire may have spared would soon be mingled with the soil. No trace of them was seen in the modern excavations except a few marks of the spots where posts or stakes may have been sunk in the earth. When the sod was removed, the position of a dwelling was marked merely by its hearth, a shallow excavation filled with ashes and calcined stones, and having the soil for some little distance around reddened by heat. Around and in these hearths might be found fragments of earthenware pots and of tobacco pipes, broken stone implements and chips of flint, bones of wild animals, charred grains of corn, stones of the wild plum, with other remains of vegetable food, and occasional bone bodkins and other implements. In depressed places, and on the borders of the small brooks and creeks which traversed or bounded the town, were accumulations of kitchen-midden stuff, in some places two or three feet in thickness, and of a black colour. This was full of fragments of pottery and bones, and occasionally yielded interesting specimens of stone and bone implements. Around the outskirts of the town, and in some cases within its limits, were skeletons which have been buried in shallow graves in a crouching

Fig 14.—Mode of Suspending Earthen Pots. (*Outside of angle of mouth of vessel.*)

position and lying on their sides, and over each skeleton could usually be detected the ashes and burned soil of the funeral feast. The soil being dry, all vestiges of hair and of the skins in which the bodies had probably been wrapped had perished, and the bones had lost their animal matter, had become porous and brittle, and were stained of a rusty colour like the sand in which they lay.

With regard to the evidence that the site referred to is actually that of the town described by Cartier, I may mention the following additional points. A map or plan of Hochelaga, purporting to have been taken on the spot or from memory, is given in Ramusio's Italian version of Cartier's Voyages (1560). It shows

Fig. 15.—MODE OF SUSPENDING EARTHEN POTS. (*Inside of angle of mouth, with head for suspension.*)

that the village was situated at the base of Mount Royal, on a terrace between two small streams. It enables us to understand the dimensions assigned to the houses in the narrative, which evidently refer not to individual dwellings, but to common edifices inhabited by several families, each having its separate room. It gives as the diameter of the circular enclosure or fort about one hundred and twenty yards, and for each side of the square in the centre about thirty yards. This corresponds with the space occupied by the remains above referred to. It is to be understood, however, that the fort or city, which was quite similar to those occupied by most of the agricultural American tribes, was intended merely to accommodate the whole population in times of danger or in the severity of winter, and to contain their winter supplies of provisions; but that in summer the people would be much scattered in temporary cabins or wigwams in the fields, or along the rivers and streams.

Further, according to the description of the old navigator, the town was four or five miles distant from the place where Cartier landed, and nearer the mountain than the river, and the oak-forest and the cornfields which surrounded it must have been on the terrace of Post-pliocene sand now occupied by the upper streets of the modern city, and about one hundred feet above the river. If the village was destroyed by fire before 1603, the date of Champlain's visit, no trace of it might remain in 1642, when the present city was founded, and the ground it occupied would probably be overgrown with shrubs and young trees. I have seen clearings in the American woods covered with tall young trees in less than thirty years. But the Indian tradition would preserve the memory of the place; and if, as the narrative of the Jesuits informs us, the point of view to which Maisonneuve and his French colonists of 1642 were conducted by the

Fig. 16.—FRAGMENT OF EARTHEN VESSEL, HOCHELAGA (NATURAL SIZE).
(Showing points of the human finger.)

Indians who professed to be survivors of the Hochelagans, was the front of the escarpment of Mount Royal, the same with that occupied by Cartier, their Indian informants would have at their very feet the old residence of their fathers, and their remarks as to its soil and exposure would be naturally called forth by the view before them. The story of the Jesuit fathers is that the two aged Indians who accompanied Maisonneuve to the mountain top after the ceremony of founding the new town, said that they were descendants of the original inhabitants; that their tribe had at one time inhabited all the surrounding country even to the south of the river, possessing many populous villages; that the Hurons, who at that time were hostile to them, had expelled them; that some of them had taken refuge among the Abenaquis, others among the Iroquois, others among the Hurons themselves. They were now associated with a band of Algonquins from the Ottawa. Their grandfathers had cultivated their corn in the very spot at their feet, but they had been driven to become migratory hunters.

The only other probable explanation of the remains would be that they belong to the more recent settlement of the Indians above referred to when invited by the French to return. This, however, was a very temporary occupation, not sufficient to give so large an amount of remains. Further, at a time when the Indians were in constant association with the French, and when missionaries were labouring among them, it is probable that their place of residence would

THE REMAINS OF CITIES OF THE STONE AGE.   77

afford some indication of intercourse with Europeans, and would be nearer to the French fort. With reference to the extent of the remains, I may state that my own private collection contains fragments

Fig. 17.—EARTHEN POT (REDUCED). (*Site of Hochelaga.*)

belonging to from 150 to 200 distinct earthen vessels, and these are of course only a very small fraction of the amount actually present. The interments in a limited space around the supposed town must have amounted to several hundreds, though it is not improbable that the Hochelagans, like some other Canadian tribes, periodically disinterred their dead, and removed their bones to a common tribal ossuary. Lastly, making every allowance for the nature of the soil, the condition of the skeletons would seem to require an interment of at least three centuries. For all these reasons, I can entertain little doubt that the site referred to is actually that of the Hochelaga of Cartier.

The only objects indicating intercourse with Europeans which I have yet found, are an iron nail without the head, and with the point rounded so as to form a sort of bodkin, a piece of iron shaped into a rude knife or chisel, a small piece of sheet brass about half an inch long by a quarter wide, and apparently cut roughly from a larger piece. These were, I think, mixed among the *débris* from one of the kitchens.

I quote here from a notice published in 1861, when the details were fresh in my memory, a few additional facts bearing upon the above points. "In a limited area, not exceeding two imperial acres, twenty skeletons have been disinterred within twelve months, and the workmen state that many parts of the ground excavated in former years were even more rich in such remains. Hundreds of old fireplaces and indications of at least ten or twelve huts or lodges, have also been found, and in a few instances these occur over the burial-places, as if one generation had built its huts over the graves of another. Where habitations have stood, the ground is in some places, to the depth of three feet, a black mass saturated with carbonaceous matter, and full of bones of wild animals, charcoal, pottery, and remains of implements of stone or bone. Further, in such places the black soil is laminated, as if deposited in successive layers on the more depressed parts of the surface. The length of time during which the site was occupied is also indicated by the very different states of preservation of the bones and bone implements; some of those in the deeper parts

Fig. 18.—HEAD FROM AN EARTHEN POT.

of the deposit being apparently much older than those near the surface. Similar testimony is afforded by the great quantity and various patterns of the pottery, as well as by the abundance of the remains of animals used as food throughout the area above mentioned. All these indications point to a long residence of the aborigines on this spot, while the almost entire absence of articles of European manufacture in the undisturbed portions of the ground, implies a date coeval with the discovery of the country. The few objects of this kind found in circumstances which prevented the supposition of mere superficial intermixture, are just sufficient to show that the village existed until the appearance of Europeans on the stage." On the whole, the situation and the remains found not only establish the strongest probability that this is the veritable site, but serve to vindicate Cartier's narration from the doubts cast upon it by subsequent explorers, who visited the country after Hochelaga had disappeared.

Since the days when Cain went forth as the first emigrant and built a city, defence and shelter have ranked among the primary wants of man. The means by which they are secured depend partly on the state of civilization which may have been reached, and partly on the materials at hand; but chiefly on the latter. In rocky regions, caverns and over-hanging ledges afford the most convenient shelter, and stones afford the materials of cyclopean walls for defence. On treeless, alluvial plains the nomad makes his tent of skin, and when he becomes settled has recourse to earthen walls or sun-dried brick. In forest countries wood or bark forms the most convenient material, whether for savage or civilized nations. The American tribe of the Moquis, in the rocky tablelands of New Mexico, build stone structures as massive as any ordinarily constructed by civilized man. The modern inhabitants of the plain of the Euphrates use brick and sun-dried clay exactly as the earliest settlers in the plain of Shinar must have done. The European settlers in Eastern America have adopted houses of wood as their usual habitations.

Neither antiquity, therefore, nor culture are marked by any particular material for building. But the material used will make a vast difference with reference to the remains left. A nation, however rude or ancient, that has been able to use caverns for habitation or to

Fig. 19.—HEAD IN POTTERY.

build of stone, will leave some permanent, nay, indestructible evidences of its presence preserved in cave-earth, or rising from the surface of the ground. A nation that has built of clay will leave merely mounds. The nations that built habitations of clay in the alluvial plain of Mesopotamia, or the valley of the Mississippi, were not necessarily less civilized than those who built with stone in Peru or Egypt. The New England villager who lives in a neat wooden house and worships in a wooden church, is not necessarily less civilized than the people who built magnificent stone edifices in Yucatan, though if the New England village were deserted, no trace of it, except in a little broken pottery, or a few hearth and chimney stones, might remain in a century or two. Nations living by river-sides, and whose only remains are a few indestructible flint implements, may have been, and probably were, more highly civilized than those whose *debris* preserved in caves furnishes far more numerous and curious antiques. Our Hochelagans were woodbuilders. Bark peeled from trees in wide sheets, and supported on poles, forms the cheapest and most comfortable abode for dwellers in the forest, and the people of Hochelaga had houses of this kind with several rooms, and an upper storey to be used as a granary. They were, possibly, more comfortable and suited to the habits of their builders than the huts of mud and rough stone occupied by thousands of the peasants of modern Europe. Their habitations belonged to a type which seems to have been nearly universal among the more settled populations of America, and which Morgan has shown to be connected with peculiar customs of patriarchal communism akin to those of which traces remain in the tribes and *gentes* of early Europe and Asia. Cartier's plan of a Hochelagan house, as given on the following page (Fig. 20), shows a series of rooms surrounding a central hall, in which was a fireplace. Now, we know from the customs of the Iroquois and Hurons, as described by

THE REMAINS OF CITIES OF THE STONE AGE. 83

Champlain and other early French explorers, that each room was occupied by a family, while all the families in the house had the cooking-place in common, and cultivated their cornfields and went on hunting expeditions in common. In such a community, according to the ancient American idea of "women's rights," all the women were related—the husbands might be, probably of necessity were, of different tribes. In some of the Indian nations, indeed, communal houses of even greater size and with several

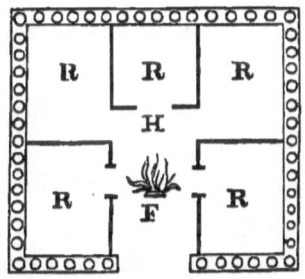

Fig. 20.—PLAN OF HOCHELAGAN HOUSE FOR FIVE FAMILIES. (*After Cartier.*)
R. Rooms, each for one family. H. Common hall. F. Common fire.

fires were used. The stone "pueblos" of the Moquis are of this character. The winter houses of the Greenlanders are on the same plan, which Nilsson has shown is that also of the "gallery graves" and gallery houses of Sweden. Further, as Morgan has proved, the so-called palaces of Mexico, Yucatan, and Peru, were merely large communistic edifices, each occupied by a whole tribe, whose members lived in common, and were related by a bond of consanguinity dependent on descent through the female line.* It seems not impossible that the tradition of the Tower of Babel includes the construction of a huge communistic building on this plan, intended to bind together the early tribes of men in a communistic league, and investigations should be made as to the probability of similar arrangements among the cave-dwellers and other primitive inhabitants of Europe. At this day there remain Pueblos of this kind on the table-lands of New Mexico, where they are inhabited by the Moqui tribes; and ruined edifices of the same type, known to have been occupied by the ancestors of these people at the time of the Spanish conquest, are from 300 to 400 feet in length, with four to seven storeys of stone rooms rising in successive terraces, and one of these is said to have been capable of lodging 600 families. When we come to consider the domestic institutions of these people, and to compare them with those of pre-historic Europe, we shall have occasion to return to this subject.

Instead of a rampart of earth, perhaps with palisades on top like those of the forts of the Iroquois and the mound-builders, the Hochelagans had a wall

* It seems in every way probable that tribes whose families combined to erect such structures as the Swiss lake habitations, retained the primitive tribal communism. Their houses as restored, for example in the papers of Mr. Walker (*Leisure Hour*, Nov. 1873), resemble the "long houses" of the Iroquois, and Sir John Lubbock has figured in his "Pre-historic Times" what he regards as a clay model of a lake hamlet, which in the essential features of its plan is similar to the houses of Hochelaga.

framed of wood, a gigantic public work to be executed by a tribe destitute of metallic tools. If we understand rightly Cartier's description, the rampart of the town consisted of a central support of vertical palisades, with an outer row inclined inwards and resting on this, and a similar inclined row supporting it within. It must have been made, not of planks or boards, but of unhewed logs, each about twenty feet in length, cut with stone hatchets and carried on men's shoulders. By the plan of construction adopted, the necessity was avoided of digging deep holes for the palisades, or of building a rampart of earth about them, and the only danger to which such a structure was exposed, that of fire, was much lessened by the inclined position of the palisades. Still a wall of this kind would perish in no very great number of years, even if it escaped destruction by fire; and if not renewed would soon leave no trace behind. The poles for such a fortification must have been very similar to the poles of the Swiss lake habitations, and like them they were probably cut and pointed with the aid of fire. I have, however, in my collection a portion of a large tree which has been partially cut across with a thin chisel, probably of copper, which must have been driven in by mallets or hammers. In this way thick trees of the softer kinds of wood could easily be divided.

Vessels for collecting provisions and cooking food are primary requirements of man in every stage of civilization or barbarism. Here again the material is not characteristic of particular stages so much as of opportunities, and may be perishable or the reverse. In Central America the Spaniards found some nations not very far advanced in civilization whose ordinary utensils were of gold. On the other hand, many tribes had merely earthen vessels, and some were destitute of these, and used baskets or bark vessels only. The latter were especially characteristic of nomadic tribes, and of parties making long expeditions. People without beasts of burden or conveyances of any kind other than canoes, could not safely or conveniently transport with them heavy and fragile vessels. To them, therefore, the potter's art was unsuited; but so soon as such tribes became settled, they would adopt earthenware as the most cheap and convenient vessels. A tribe, therefore, of roving habits, or living in a region where it was necessary to make periodical migrations, might be destitute of pottery, though they might have vessels of wood, basket-work, or bark, more neatly and artificially constructed than the clay pots of more settled tribes. Still, the latter would leave a monument of their art in the *débris* of their pottery, which would be wholly wanting in the case of the former. Further, the pottery of primitive tribes is of a sort which speedily becomes disintegrated in a wet soil or ground up by attrition, so that river-side tribes might leave no sign of it, when it might be met with abundantly in the old residences of cavern and upland tribes.

The Hochelagans were potters, and, as we know to

have been the case with other tribes, this art was probably practised by the women, and the vessels, formed by hand, without the aid of a wheel, were imperfectly baked in a rude oven or fireplace constructed for the purpose. Their process for preparing the clay was that which seems to have been practised anciently all over the world, and is still vindicated by experience as the best to form vessels intended to stand the fire.

Fig. 21.—Earthen Pot found on the Upper Ottawa, and now in the Museum of the Natural History Society of Montreal (Reduced).

The clay was first mixed intimately with sand, usually a coarse granitic sand, different from that near Montreal, as the clay is also different from the ordinary brick-clay of Montreal, which being calcareous is not well fitted for the purpose of the potter. The mass was then kneaded out and doubled in pastrycook style, so as to give it a tough, laminated texture, and then was fashioned into the vessel desired. Specimens from an ancient British barrow given to me by Professor Rolleston have been made of precisely similar materials, and in the same way; and as their ornamentation is nearly the same, they show nothing, did we not know their origin, to prevent the belief that both might have been made in the same place and by the same hand.

The usual shape was that of a pot, round in the bottom and curving upward into a cylindrical neck. In some, however, the neck was square or octagonal, and in this case there were sometimes projecting ornaments or hooks at the corners for suspension. This primitive Hochelagan pot is of the type of those used by all ancient nations, from the old "Reindeer Epoch" of Belgium and France, down through all antiquity to our own round metal pots. Perhaps the earliest known example is that found in the palæolithic cave of the Trou de Frontal, by Dupont, which closely resembles the native American pots in form and material, except that it is not ornamented and that the projections for suspension are on the sides instead of at the rim. The Hochelagan women, however, had a very ingenious contrivance for hanging their pots over the fire, which deserves notice. They had no doubt found by experience that when an earthen pot was hung over the fire by strings or withes tied to the outside, the flames would sometimes reach the perishable means of suspension, and, burning it, allow the pot to fall, and its contents to be lost. Hence they contrived a mode of fastening the cord within the throat of the vessel, where the fire could not reach it. This hook for suspension was made in the shape of a human head and neck, the hole for the cord being left behind the neck (Figs. 14, 15, 18, 19). Many of these heads were found detached, and their use was not known until the fragment in Fig. 15 was found. Earthen heads of this kind are often figured on American vessels, and perhaps indicate guardian "manitous," but their peculiar use in the Hochelagan vessels seems unique.

Some of these earthen vessels were large enough to hold four gallons. Others would hold a quart or less, and the smaller are usually thinner and of finer clay than the others. All are very neatly made, and uniform in thickness, and wonderfully regular in form when we consider that they were fashioned without the potter's wheel. Many are elaborately ornamented with patterns worked with a pointed instrument, with rings made with a stamp, and with impressions of the finger-point and nail around the edge. (Figs. 16, 17, 22). This last kind of marking, still practised by pastrycooks, is common both to American and early British and Swiss pottery, in which we can distinctly see rows of impressions of the small finger-point of the lady-artificer with the print of the finger-nail. Fragments of pottery from a long barrow near West Kennet, in Wiltshire, figured by Lubbock, are remarkably near to a common Hochelagan pattern, and finger-prints as an ornament occur on vessels from the pile-villages of the Lake of Zurich. Examples have also been found of a potter's graving implement for forming these patterns. It was a small, neatly polished conical bone, sharp at one end and hollowed at the other, so that it could be used either for drawing lines or for stamping circles, precisely like those on some of the specimens of pottery.

The patterns on the pottery are not merely capricious. They are imitations, and of two distinct styles. One evidently represents the rows of grain in the ear of Indian corn, and may be called the corn-ear pattern. The same device is seen in specimens of Indian pottery from New York figured by Schoolcraft, and it still occasionally re-appears in our common earthenware pitchers. The second may be called the basket-and-bead pattern, and imitates a woven basket ornamented with beads, or, as in modern Indian baskets, with pendant rings. To this class belong the so-called chevron and saltier patterns, and it is possible that they may be originally traced, both in the old and new worlds, to the aboriginal practice of moulding pottery in woven grass baskets, subsequently removed by the process of baking. Many and elegant modifications of this pattern occur, and imply that the potters were familiar with the modes of basket-making still in use among the Indians. This basket-pattern appears, though in a rude form, in some specimens of early British pottery, and akin to it are the impressions, common both in American and European clay vessels, of twisted thongs or cords. A third pattern, which is confined to the round bottom of some of

THE REMAINS OF CITIES OF THE STONE AGE.   91

the larger vessels may be styled a net-pattern. It is formed by square or rhombic indentations, regularly arranged, so as to form a reticulated design. Similarly baked and ornamented pottery is found in all old Indian sites in Eastern America. Among the Mic-

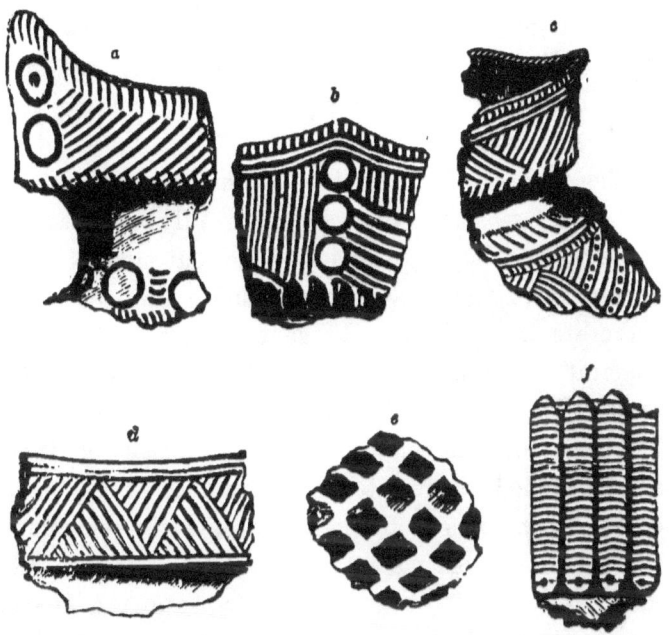

Fig. 22.—FRAGMENTS OF POTTERY (REDUCED). (*Site of Hochelaga.*)
(*a, b, c, d*) Basket patterns.   (*e*) Net pattern.   (*f*) Corn-ear pattern.

macs and New England tribes it is usually ruder than that of Hochelaga, corresponding to the supposed oldest types of the European caves and barrows. The Iroquois, Hurons, and Eries had the same types with those of Hochelaga. The old Alleghans, or mound-builders, made, at the same or possibly a still earlier period, finer and more gracefully ornamented vessels, and the art was carried to still greater perfection by the Mexicans and Peruvians. Many of the smaller pots are blackened with fire, and are encrusted near the neck with a black paste, evidently the remains of the pottage of Indian corn-meal formerly cooked in them. The large pots are usually clean, and may have been used as water-pots or for holding dry articles of food.

The highest skill of the Hochelaga potters was bestowed on their tobacco-pipes. They possessed stone pipes of steatite, or soapstone, but none of these of elaborate form have been found. One somewhat elaborate example seems to have been formed of the celebrated red pipestone, or catlinite, from the far west. The great number of fragments of clay pipes, however, and the manner in which some of them are blackened, testifies to the prevalence of the habit of smoking. In one Hochelagan pipe the remains of the tobacco-leaves were recognised when it was disinterred. It had been filled, perhaps, on the eve of the final assault of the town, and the smoker had thrown it down unused to rush to the last battle of his tribe. The use of tobacco was found in full force by Cartier. It was probably cultivated both at Stadacona and Hochelaga, as it still is by the Canadian "habitants." I have, indeed, seen a well-grown patch of tobacco growing beside a noble crop of wheat on the Laurentian hills, behind Murray Bay, on the

Lower St. Lawrence, in latitude 47° 40″, and at a height of 1000 feet above the sea level, though physical geographers place the northern limit of wheat at the sea level far to the south of this. The Indians could, therefore, easily cultivate this plant on the warmer soil in southern exposures along the St. Lawrence; but they also used wild plants designated as *petun* and *kinnikinick*. The habit was new to the French. Cartier says : " They have an herb, of which they store up a large quantity for winter, which they esteem very much, and the use of which is confined to the men. They use it in the following way. The plant having been dried in the sun, they carry suspended to the neck a little bag of skin containing the dried leaves, along with a little pipe ('cornet,' perhaps alluding to the trumpet-like shape usual at Hochelaga) of stone or wood. Thus prepared, they place a little of the powder of the herb in one end of the pipe, and placing a live coal on it, draw their breath through the other end until they fill themselves with smoke, so that it issues from their mouth and nostrils as from a chimney. They say that it keeps them healthy and warm, and never go without it." Cartier's men tried the weed, but found it too hot and " peppery " for their taste. This practice of smoking tobacco, as well as lobelia and other narcotic weeds, was universal in America, and is one of the few habits which men calling themselves civilized have thought fit to borrow from these barbarous tribes. It may have originated in the attempt to repel mosquitoes

94   FOSSIL MEN.

and other noxious insects, or to allay the pangs of hunger; or perhaps, as Wilson thinks, its narcotic fumes were supposed to aid in divination, and in

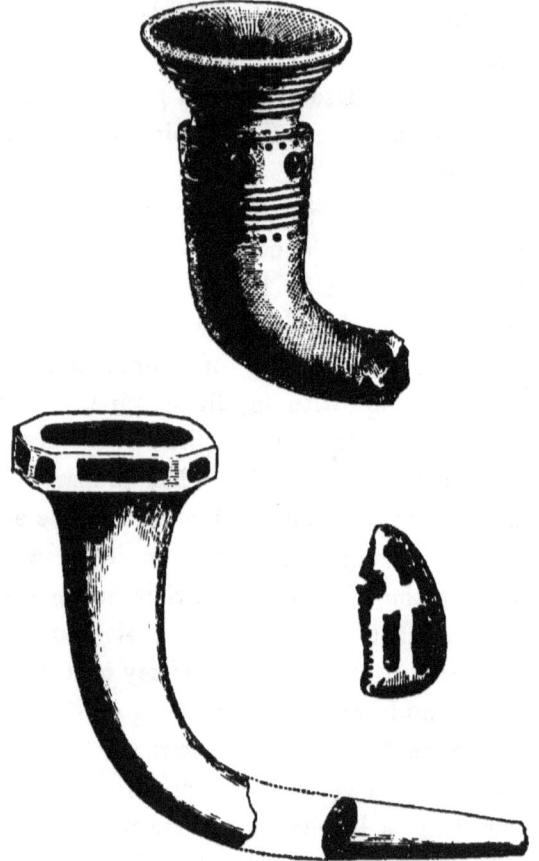

Fig. 23.—EARTHEN PIPES, HOCHELAGA (REDUCED).

communion with those spiritual beings whom the American firmly believed in as holding intercourse with man. Thus it may have become an appropriate sacrifice and means of invocation, even with reference to the Great Spirit. In any case, its use was interwoven with all the religious usages of the people, and as the "calumet of peace" with their most solemn social and political engagements. From this high place it has descended among the civilized imitators

Fig. 23a.—RED PIPESTONE PIPE.

of the red man to be merely the solace of their idle hours.

That the usage of smoking should have prevailed throughout America, and should have been connected with the religious and social institutions of all its tribes, and that it should not have existed in the old world till introduced from America, seems singular, yet the belief at one time entertained that the "elfin pipes" found in Britain indicate ancient usages of this kind, and that smoking is an old institution in

Tartary and China, where one species of tobacco is native, seems now generally discredited. Still it is not impossible that there may be some foundation in fact for the conclusion of Pallas, who argues from the general use of tobacco by the Mongol tribes, the primitive and original forms of their pipes, and the similarity of their modes of using the plant to those of the Americans, that the custom must be indigenous among them. If so, it would not be surprising that even the Palæolithic man of Europe, in his dark cavern abodes, enjoyed the solace of the fragrant weed, smoked the calumet of peace with his former foes, and, like his American brethren, fancied that he saw spiritual beings—

"In the smoke that rolled around him,
The punkwana* of the peace-pipe."

Archæologists should keep this in view in searching for the relics of the Stone period.

Certain clay tubes, suspiciously resembling tobacco pipes, are figured among the remains obtained by Schliemann on the site of ancient Troy; and on the other hand, a figure of an owl's head, remarkably like those found in the ruins of Troy, occur on many Huron pipes. Flinders, in his "Voyages," refers to a habit of smoking, or of puffing smoke through tubes, as existing among a tribe of Papuans. It is to be observed, however, that tubes of bone, clay, and stone were used by medicine-men for applying smoke to the

* The fumes or rising smoke.

bodies of the sick. On the other hand, the Micmac Indians of Nova Scotia sometimes used tobacco pipes made of birch-bark rolled in the form of a cone, and which of course are perishable.

The pipes of old Hochelaga were mostly of clay, and of many and sometimes elegant patterns. Some were very plain and small, others of elegant trumpet or cornucopia form, and some ornamented with rude attempts to imitate the human face. While the men were the smokers, the women seem to have exhausted their plastic skill in furnishing their lords with the means of indulging their taste for the narcotic. Schoolcraft has figured pipes used by the Iroquois and Eries precisely similar to those of the Hochelagans. Those of the mound-builders were peculiar (Fig. 10, p. 54), but it is curious, and probably an evidence of ancient intercourse, that stone pipes of the mound-builders' type are occasionally, though rarely, found in Canada. I have seen a broken specimen from Hopkins Island, near St. Regis, where many Indian remains are found. In addition to jars and pipes, the only frequent objects of earthenware are small discs, perforated in the centre and crenated at the edge. They may have served as an inferior kind of wampum, or beads, or perhaps for the playing of some game of chance. Similar clay beads found in Sweden are described by Nilsson as belonging to the pre-historic times of Scandinavia.

It has been said of the oldest Stone age, or Palæolithic age of Europe, that no remains of earthenware

are found in connection with its deposits; or to put it more broadly, in the words of a recent writer, Palæolithic man was "ignorant of pottery"—a very bold statement of a negative, when it is considered how little we know of the said men, and which might be contradicted at once could we discover the site of one of their villages instead of mere cave shelters and drifted implements in river gravels. The theory might, however, prevent any such discovery, for if the site of a village of the men who used the Amiens flint implements should be discovered, and if it contained fragments of pottery and polished hatchets, we might be told that it belonged to the Neolithic age, and it should be separated by countless centuries from the Palæolithic period. We shall see in the sequel how this applies to the remains of a "Palæolithic" village discovered at Soloutré, in France. If, however, it should appear that neither Palæolithic man nor his wife actually did make pottery, this would prove not so much their barbarism as their nomadic mode of life, and they may have made and used, like the North American hunter tribes, the most beautiful baskets and bark boxes, which would serve their purposes better than rude pottery.

It must not, however, be lost sight of that Fournal and Christie have recorded the discovery of fragments of pottery in caverns in the south of France, in mud and breccia containing bones of man mingled with those of extinct animals, among which are mentioned the hyæna and rhinoceros. As the material had been

THE REMAINS OF CITIES OF THE STONE AGE. 99

washed into these caves, we have no absolute certainty that the association may not have been accidental. Still the evidence is quite as good as that relied on for the association of so-called Palæolithic implements with bones of extinct mammalia in river gravels and in other caves filled by water driftage. Fragments of pottery have also been found by Dr. Fraas in the cave of Hohlefels, in Swabia, amidst the *débris* left by a Palæolithic people who fed on the cave bear, the extinct rhinoceros, and the reindeer; and the vase found in the Trou de Frontal, in Belgium, has already been mentioned. The fragments of pottery found in the *débris* from Kent's cave may perhaps be rejected as uncertain.

The bill of fare of ancient Hochelaga was somewhat varied. Bones are found of nearly all the wild mammals of the country, and of many birds and fishes. Those of the beaver, however, largely predominate, and remains of the bear, more especially lower jaws, are quite numerous. The dog seems to have been used as food, and the variety kept was that small breed seen among many Indian tribes, and sometimes called the fox-dog. The dog was no doubt the only domesticated animal. Grains of Indian corn are not infrequent, and fragments of the charred ear are also found. The variety cultivated was similar to the smaller kinds of early corn now used in Canada. More rare are cotyledons of the bean, *Phaseolus vulgaris*. The specimens of these preserved are of course only those which had been accidentally charred in the fire. In one spot was found a cache of charred acorns, probably those of the white oak, which after being buried in the ground for a time become edible. Stones of the wild plum are very abundant, and it has been observed that this tree grows abundantly on the sites of most old Indian villages. The stones of wild cherries and the shells of the butternut have also been observed. All this fully accords with Cartier's narrative and with those of the other early French explorers, who inform us that while the semi-civilized Indian tribes cultivated the ground, they also made tributary to their use all the wild animals and fruits of the country. It is instructive, however, to observe how little remains to indicate the somewhat extensive agriculture of these people, even in their central town, while it is obvious that in the remains of their hunting encampments nothing would be preserved except bones and weapons belonging to merely savage life.

One fragment obtained from a heap of kitchen refuse suggests some strange questions. It is a portion of the lower jaw of a human being, evidently broken before being imbedded. It has belonged to a very aged person, and from its size and proportions probably a woman. It is also remarkable for the narrowness and thickness of the bone, the smallness of the chin, and the forward projection of the sockets of the teeth. In these respects it more nearly resembles the celebrated jaw described by Dupont from the pre-historic cave of Naulette, in Belgium, than any other I have seen. Is it an indication of cannibalism?

and if so, did it belong to a captive from some distant and perhaps more barbarous tribe, or to an aged woman slain to prevent the death of her relatives by starvation? Unhappily, instances parallel to both of these are on record among the American tribes. We read in Champlain's narratives, of the bodies of slain enemies cut up and carried off for triumphal feasts, and even in more modern times there have been instances of parties of roving Indians being driven by the pangs of hunger to devour each other. If such things occurred in Hochelaga, they must have been rare, for this one bone alone raises the question. Even it may admit of a different explanation. It may have belonged to a victim of the final capture of the town; it may have been accidentally disinterred from some old grave in digging the fire-hole of a new lodge; it may be connected with the fact that the Hochelagans had the custom, like our own heathen ancestors, of using the skulls of their enemies for vessels. Two examples have been found of human parietal bones trimmed round the edges, evidently for the purpose of being used as cups or bowls. One of them has a hole pierced, probably for a means of suspension, and may have been carried by some warrior at once as a trophy of victory and as a drinking-cup. The old races of the two hemispheres may claim kinship in their cruelties and barbarisms, as well as in higher traits. I believe, however, that no certain instance is yet on record either of cannibalism or of the use of human bones as implements or vessels among the men of the Mammoth age in Europe, so that perhaps these are later practices of more degraded tribes.

In closing this chapter, let us reflect for a moment on the picture which it presents. The apparently flourishing town of Hochelaga, surrounded with its fields, and probably for long ages the residence of a settled and semi-civilized people, disappears suddenly from view. In a century or less its site is covered with a dense and tall young forest. This is cleared, and again becomes cultivated fields, showing no trace of former occupation. In three centuries the remains, when disinterred, are veritable fossils; everything perishable, even hair and the animal matter of bones, has disappeared. Nothing remains but stone and pottery and charcoal, and the mineral matter of bones, which underground might remain unchanged for a hundred centuries as well as for one. Nothing but Cartier's visit of a few hours' duration prevents us from being in a position to attach to these remains the longer date with as much show of reason as the shorter.

These considerations apply in various ways to the interpretation of European pre-historic remains. First, as to their antiquity. Owing to the entire disappearance of Hochelaga, Cartier's narrative has actually been discredited by some modern writers as a fiction, and only the recent discovery of the remains of the town he describes, has established its truth. But Cartier's narrative alone enables us to fix the date of the remains. Were it not for this, there was actually nothing to prevent us from referring them to any antiquity that any hypothesis as to their origin might demand, even as far back as the emergence of the bank of Post-pliocene sand, about 100 feet above the level of the St. Lawrence, in which they are found, from the sea of the Glacial age. Secondly, as to their evidence of culture or barbarism. Though the Hochelagans were an agricultural people, dwelling in houses in a walled town, the indications of this are so slight that they might easily have been overlooked, while the abundant bones of wild animals might lead us to suppose that we had to do merely with hunters, and these undoubtedly of a Stone and Bone age, in which some implements, at least, of the rudest type were used. Yet these relics are those of a central town. The indications left by the same people at their occasional camping-places, when on expeditions to obtain fish, game, furs, or maple sap, would indicate a far more primitive condition, and might be referred to a still older date.

In the old world, the now celebrated lake-towns, or Pfahlbauten, of Switzerland, present a type of civilization near akin to that of Hochelaga, and like it forgotten until accidentally disinterred as recently as the year 1854. They were laboriously and with some engineering skill built on platforms over the water supported on piles, originally by men with no better implements than those of stone. They afforded a comparatively secure retreat to simple and probably peaceful and industrious tribes, driven out of the plains and lower river valleys by the encroachments of wild and savage enemies, and obliged for safety even to forsake the dry land and pitch their abodes over the waters. When these lake villages were accidentally burned, quantities of the property of the inhabitants were lost in the waters, and have in modern times been recovered by the diligent search of antiquarians;* attention having first been called to these singular abodes by the unusually low state of the water in the Swiss lakes in the year 1854.

The lake settlements were inhabited from an early period of the Stone age down to the Roman period, and it is not impossible that they furnished some part of the Helvetian tribes with whom the Roman power came into conflict in the time of Cæsar. The earliest sites belong to the Stone age, and the successive introduction of bronze and iron can be distinctly traced in their remains. It is possible, however, that a Stone period continued in eastern Switzerland after bronze had been introduced into the west, and there are sufficient traces of bronze in the oldest of the villages to show that elsewhere there must have been peoples more advanced. In the Stone period the inhabitants were already skilful builders, constructors of boats, cultivators of grain and flax, weavers and potters. They had domesticated cattle, sheep, goats, and hogs; in which respect they were far in advance of the village Indians of America. But like them they sub-

* More especially Dr. Keller.

sisted largely on fish and on wild animals, and laid under contribution all the wild fruits of their country. So far as known, their physical characteristics were not materially different from those of the more modern inhabitants of Switzerland.

Unlike the Hochelagans, these lake-dwellers disappeared or changed their mode of life at so early a period that no mention of them occurs in written history, nor was it suspected that such remains existed until they were accidentally discovered. Yet the fact that their remains, submerged and covered with lake mud, and in some instances with peat, were removed from all destroying or disturbing agencies, has led to their preservation and recovery in a more perfect state than can be the case with similar villages built on the land, which may have been contemporary with them. Thus semi-civilized village-dwellers may have lived in Europe before the dates of the lake habitations, without our having any knowledge of their existence.

The mode of life of these people was not without example in America. Washington Irving has quoted from the narrative of Amerigo Vespucci an account of an Indian town named Coquibacoa, in the Bay of Venezuela, which consisted of twenty large houses, like bells in shape, and supported on piles driven into the bottom of the lake-like bay. From a fancied resemblance to Venice in these structures, the bay is said to have received the name of Venezuela. The *débris* of such a town would undoubtedly be in the main similar to that of the Swiss lake-villages. The remarkable edifices of stone, no doubt of the nature of communistic homes, or pueblos, found by the United States surveyors of the Western Territories,* hung like swallows' nests on the sides of almost inaccessible cliffs and ravines, though different in detail, belong to a condition of society akin to that of the lake-dwellers of Europe, and dependant on the efforts of a weak or peaceful people to escape the attacks of enemies, and possibly also to secure more salubrious abodes. Habitations built on piles existed in the time of Herodotus on Lake Prasias, in Thrace, and it is believed that some still exist there.† The same mode of building was practised in ancient times in Ireland, Scotland, and Italy, and it still exists in Borneo and elsewhere in the Austral Islands.

On the one hand, it would scarcely be reasonable to credit a practice of this kind to an instinct like that of the beaver. On the other, it can scarcely have been an invention communicated by one tribe to another. It is more likely to have been a modification of the primitive village communism suggested to the ingenuity of man by special local wants or dangers, and carried out in the same way by peoples widely separated geographically.

The facts above detailed may aid in the explanation of what seems to be a village site in Europe of far

* "Bulletins of United States Geological Survey of the Western Territories."
† Lubbock, "Prehistoric Times."

greater antiquity than the Swiss lake-villages, and which may be a veritable "Palæolithic" antediluvian town. It occurs at Soloutré, near Macôn, in eastern France, and has given rise to much discussion and controversy. As described by Messrs. De Ferry and Arcelin, the site is a mound or hillock near a steep rock or precipice. Judging from the great number of hearths and heaps of refuse, it was obviously a place of residence, and it was also a place of sepulture; and there is some reason to believe, from the distribution of the materials, that it may have been enclosed, perhaps by a palisade. The dead, mostly very aged people and children, are buried in an extended position, and always apparently in such relation to the hearths or fire-places as to show that they were interred under or over them. Either, therefore, these people, like the Greenlanders, some South American tribes, and Australians, buried their dead under their domestic hearths, or like the ancient Canadians they built funeral fires and held feasts for the dead over their remains. But the most remarkable thing about this village site is its relative antiquity, as indicated by the animal remains found in it, which belong to that Post-glacial time in which the land animals of Europe were very different from those at present inhabiting it. It would seem that these include the wild horse, of which enormous numbers occur, the mammoth, the cave-lion, the cave-bear, the saiga,* the cave-hyæna, the wapiti, etc. Bones of some of these animals are

* An antelope still extant in Eastern Europe.

actually found buried with the dead, and the others mixed with the *débris* of cookery. The remains of the horse are in such abundance, and the whole skeleton is so often present, that it is inferred that they were not killed in hunting like the other animals, but that they must have been driven over the face of the precipice behind the village in battues, or lassoed and led home as captives,* or that they were actually kept in herds as domesticated animals, and slaughtered for food, as amongst the Tartar Khirgis at present. The great depth of the beds of *débris* at Soloutré, and their stratification in layers, indicate a long term of residence, and it would seem that the remains of the mammoth and other extinct animals extend throughout the whole, and that only implements of stone and bone occur, except in the mere surface soil.

If, as seems most probable, this remarkable deposit at Soloutré indicates a truly Palæocosmic † village, it is probably the only instance of this kind extant; and it destroys utterly the pretension that the men of the Mammoth age were an inferior race or ruder than their successors in the later Stone age. Further, the condition of the objects found carries with it no evidence of that extreme antiquity often claimed for the earlier Stone age, and its relations to neighbouring river deposits do not indicate, according to some of

---

* It would seem, however, that this would necessitate that the captors should be horsemen.

† This term was proposed as a substitute for Palæolithic in a previous publication of the author.

its explorers an age exceeding 7,000 or 8,000 years. We are informed in the Book of Genesis, that in antediluvian times, Jabal initiated the nomadic mode of life. He was the father of those who dwell in tents. This would seem to imply the domestication at that period of some swift-footed beast of burden, probably the horse or the ass. A tribe of such wandering Jabalites might be expected to leave just such a deposit as that of Soloutré. Thus we have here a curious connection between this deposit and sacred history. On the other hand, it has been remarked that the most abundant "totem" engraved by the "Palæolithic" cave-men of France on their bone implements is the horse; and this would so far connect these cave-men with such a station as Soloutré. Lastly, many of the flint weapons of Soloutré are of the Palæolithic type characteristic of the river gravels, and the bones found with them are the animals of the gravels; while other implements and weapons are as well worked as those of the later Stone age.* Thus this singular deposit connects these two so-called ages, and fuses them into one. But in doing this, as explained above, and more fully illustrated in subsequent chapters, it does precisely what a village

* Recent discoveries by M. Prunieres in caves at Beaumes Chaudes, seem to show that the older cave-men were in contact with more advanced tribes, as arrow-heads of the so-called Neolithic type are found sticking in their bones, or associated with them. This would form another evidence of the little value to be attached to the distinction of the two ages of Stone.

site might on American analogies be expected to do, as compared with cave shelters and river gravels, where only special remains, not showing the whole conditions of a race, could be supposed likely to occur.

CHAPTER V.

IMPLEMENTS AND WEAPONS OF THE STONE AGE.

So much has recently been written on chipped and worked flints, and their familiar forms appear in so many popular works, that readers may well be tired of the subject. I shall try, however, in the following pages to avoid as much as possible its trite and hackneyed aspects.

As Nilsson well remarks in his excellent work on the primitive inhabitants of Scandinavia, it is well to begin the consideration of stone and bone implements by examining the tools with which they were made. Stone hammers at Hochelaga, and generally throughout pre-historic North America, were of three kinds: (1) discs, (2) hand-hammers of elongated forms, (3) handled hammers. From the latter the transition is easy to the pogamaugan, or skull-cracker, and to the tomahawk, or hatchet; and it will be the easier to remember these uncouth words if we bear in mind the affinity of the first to the Indo-European *poke, pugme, pugnus,* and Semitic *paga,* and that the latter is derived from an Algonquin root (*tem* or *tum*—to cut). The same with the Greek *Temno* and, perhaps, Hebrew *Taman.* These are at once mnemonic aids and examples of a vast number of widespread verbal analogies between the languages of Eastern America and Western Asia and Europe, the nature of which may in the sequel engage our attention.

Disc-hammers are in their rudest form merely flat pebbles, suitable to be held in the hand, for driving wedges or chisels, or for breaking stones, bones, or nuts. In their more finished forms they are carefully fashioned of quartzite or greenstone, with one side convex and the other flat, or even slightly hollowed, and the edge neatly and regularly trimmed. Stones of this kind are found all over America on old Indian sites, and are almost equally common in Europe; and there can be little doubt from the habits of the modern Indians as to their ordinary uses. They were probably hammers, pounders, and polishers. Held with the convex side in the palm of the hand, they could be used to drive wooden stakes or to split wood with stone chisels, or to crack nuts or to bruise grain and fruits, or to grind paint on a flat stone. With sand or earth they made efficient polishers for dressing skins, and held edgewise they served to trim flint weapons or to crack marrow-bones. One of these hammers must therefore have been an indispensable utensil in every household, and a well-made one of durable stone may have been an heirloom handed down for generations.

These hammers should not be confounded with the stones having deep hollows in their sides, and which were mortars for grinding pigments, or sockets for fire-drills; nor should they be confounded with the discs hollowed on both sides, and used for playing the almost universal game of the Indians, which was to them what croquet has recently been to us, and which was named *chunke,* or *tshung-ke.* The game was played on a flat rectangular space of ground prepared for the purpose, and often enclosed. It consisted in one player rolling a disc along the ground, while others tried to throw spears or poles in such a manner as to be near to the disc when it came to a state of rest. The chungke yards figure largely in old Indian sites, especially in the south, and the stones are often found. It would seem that both paint-mortars and chungke-stones occur among pre-historic human remains in Europe, even among those which belong to the Palæolithic period. Stones referable to these uses are figured by Christy and Lartet, and by Nilsson and by Keller. It is to be observed, however, that among rude nations stone implements are often in case of need applied to uses different from those for which they were intended. Hence it would not be wonderful if round hammers were sometimes used for chungke stones, and the reverse. Stones with similar hollows were also used as drill-stones, to obtain fire by the rapid revolution of a wooden stake. In the collection of Mr. Jones, of Brooklyn, I have lately seen chungke discs of large size and most elaborately cut in hard quartzite. The work of forming them must have been that almost of a life-time; perhaps it was perfected in successive generations.

The second kind of hammer is of elongated form,

round or oval in cross-section, and suited to be held in the hand, though, perhaps, in some cases lashed to a wooden handle. It much resembles the ordinary stone axe or celt, but differs in having a blunt end, indented with blows, instead of an edge. This almond-shaped hammer was employed to chip stones, to drive wedges, and to break nuts and bones. One example from Hochelaga has a rough depression on one side, which may have been produced by hammering wedges with the side instead of the end, or may have been intended to give a better hold to the end of the handle. Hammers precisely of this kind are found in the caves of Perigord and in Sweden. The savages of all countries seem to have discovered that dioritic rocks, from the toughness of the crystals of hornblende which they contain, are specially suited for the formation of these hammers, so that wherever greenstone can be found it is employed.

The third and most artificial kind of stone hammer is that with a groove around it, by means of which it could be attached to a handle or slung upon a tough withe. Such a hammer is sometimes merely an oval pebble with a groove worked around it, but some examples, especially those of the old mound-builders, are elaborately grooved and carefully shaped; and there are some with two grooves, the working of which must have cost much labour. Some specimens are so small as to weigh only a few ounces, and one from the ancient copper mines of Lake Superior, now in the museum of the Geological Survey of Canada, is $11\frac{1}{2}$

IMPLEMENTS AND WEAPONS OF THE STONE AGE. 115

inches long, and weighs more than 25lbs. The larger end of it has been much bruised and broken, and it was evidently a miner's sledge-hammer. Grooved stones of this kind occur on pre-historic sites in Europe, though they have sometimes been regarded as plummets or sling-stones. In America similarly-grooved pebbles are often found in circumstances which lead to the belief that they have been sinkers for nets. These are, however, usually of stone too soft to have been used for hammers, and have no marks of use on the ends. The ordinary sinker for lines and nets is, however, on both sides of the Atlantic a pear-shaped or drop-shaped stone, with a groove for the line at the sharp end.

Sling-stones, properly so called, we probably have not in North America; but there are two kinds of stones used as weapons, and which resemble what have been regarded as sling-stones in Europe. The first is grooved, and fastened to a cord the other end of which is attached to the right arm. This stone, Carver tells us, was used as a weapon with deadly effect by certain tribes west of the Mississippi. The other was a sort of slung-shot. As described by Lewis and Clarke, and as appears from specimens in collections, it is a pear-shaped stone, sheathed in leather or hide, and attached by a thong two inches long to a stout handle, with a second thong by which it can be fastened to the wrist. Champlain found a similar weapon in use among the nations of Western Canada, and stones of this kind are used by the South

Sea Islanders. I have a very fine one of calcareous spar from the New Hebrides, and very neatly formed and effective specimens made of heavy iron ore are found on American Indian sites. They occur also among the relics of the Stone age in Scandinavia. If slings properly so-called were used by European prehistoric men, it is likely that, like David of old, they contented themselves with smooth stones from the brook, and did not waste their labour in shaping round stones to be lost the first time they were thrown. The American Indians were, however, in the habit of heaping stones in the inside of their forts to be thrown at their enemies either by hand or by a sling, and it has been suggested that some of the heaps of chipped flints noticed by Foster and by Squier as found in Ohio and Illinois may have been collected for this purpose, though it is perhaps more likely that they were magazines of unfinished weapons.

One implement of the Flint age which has recently attracted much attention, and which has been elaborately discussed in the beautiful work of Messrs. Lartet and Christy, is the pogamaugan, or striker, an absolutely universal weapon of the rude hunter and warrior in all ages and countries. One of its earliest forms is that of an antler trimmed into the shape of a sort of pick or hammer, and this, still in use among the Western Indians, occurs under precisely the same form in the cave deposits of the Reindeer period in France. The primitive hunter well knows the effective use of the antler by the deer at bay, and nothing is more natural than that he should adapt this weapon to his own use, so that perhaps the antler is the oldest of all strikers or war-clubs. But the implement has other forms. A stick with a clubbed end was a usual form in America, and corresponds to the waddy so effectively used by the natives of Tasmania and other Austral savages. This was rendered more deadly by a sharp bone or antler, or a chipped flint, firmly socketed in the wood and bound with thongs. Sometimes a row of flints was set along the edge of the handle, as described by Captain Gray in the case of Australian savages, and a saw-edged sword of this kind used by the Mexican tribes, and fitted with very Palæolithic obsidian or flint blades, was much dreaded by the early Spanish adventurers. Schoolcraft and Catlin figure many strange and grotesque forms of these weapons, and they abound in museums. Those of a more modern date have a metal blade instead of a sharp stone. If the so-called Palæolithic axes of Western Europe were used as weapons in the state in which they are now found, they must have been handled in this way, by being attached with thongs or cement to pieces of wood or of bone.

To this class of weapons undoubtedly belong most of those strangely-shaped stone axes and picks, with a socket for a small handle, which are found in primitive graves both in the Old and New World (Fig. 24). They are generally of so small size and weight, and the socket for the handle of so small diameter, that antiquaries are disposed to regard them as ornaments, or "batons of command," or sceptres, rather than as weapons. And this impression is strengthened by the fact that they are sometimes made of comparatively soft stone. In most cases, however, they were probably made for actual use in striking men or animals, except where they were intended as mere models of weapons to be buried with the dead or offered in

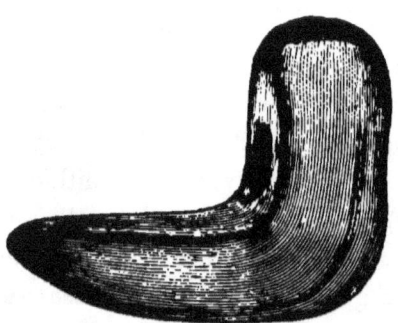

Fig. 21.

sacrifice. The theory of the implement is that it enables the blow of the arm to be delivered on a limited spot, so as to pierce or fracture the skull of an enemy or a wild animal. For this purpose the weapon does not need to be large or heavy. On the contrary, lightness is necessary to portability, and to that rapidity of stroke which is everything in combat and in hunting. Hence many of the American pogamaugans and tomahawks are so small and light as not to appear at all formidable; but, guided by a quick eye and wielded by a rapid hand, they were really most deadly weapons, and they were often thrown with great precision and effect. Champlain has depicted a Huron warrior armed for the fight, his small war-hatchet contrasting strangely with his great shield and long bow. To the light and agile Indian or his European prototype, the heavy mace of a mediæval warrior would have been as great an incumbrance as his ponderous coat of mail. On this subject an interesting letter from Mr. Anderson, published in the "Reliquiæ Aquitanicæ," well deserves perusal. Among other facts, he mentions that a small skull-cracker is carried by the Western Indians in their canoes to kill fish when caught. Specimens of them, recently obtained by Dr. G. M. Dawson in the Queen Charlotte Islands, are so elaborately and elegantly carved that they might be regarded as sceptres, though intended for no more noble use than that of killing halibut or seals. The European aborigines who speared or angled for large fish would have equally needed such weapons; and it is not unlikely that some of the elaborately carved objects from the French caves, dignified with the name of "batons of command," are nothing else than fish-clubs or skull-crackers.

While on this subject, it may be as well to remark that it is a mistake to suppose that heavy stone axes or large spears would be required to slay such large game as the urus, the woolly rhinoceros, or the mammoth. The American hunter for such purposes used the arrow and the javelin, and his object was to have these as sharp and slender as possible, that, urged with the bow or from the arm, they might pierce the vital parts of the animal. We read in the narratives of the early adventurers in America of the rapidity and accuracy with which the Indian could launch his arrows or javelins. Slender arrows of cane, with points hardened in the fire or tipped with small flints or pointed bones, were thrown with such force that they have been known to pierce through the body of a horse or a buffalo from side to side. I have seen the war-arrows of a Western Indian which had actually been used in fight with Europeans armed with firearms, and which were tipped with thin flints less than an inch long and half an inch wide. If the aborginal European really derived any considerable part of his subsistence from very large animals, we may be assured that he did not kill them with stone celts or huge hatchets and so-called spears of chipped flint, but with points as small as those of the smallest flint flakes or bone javelins; and he probably pursued these animals, like the American Indian, during winter, when their action was impeded by the deep snow. We also learn from American examples that a very rude chipped flint may be fitted into an elaborately ornamented handle or shaft, and when the latter has perished by decay, the flint may afford a very imperfect idea of the skill of the artificer.

The most primitive of all cutting instruments of stones are flakes chipped or pressed from quartzite, jasper, agate, chert, or flint, any of which stones will serve the purpose, and used at once without any other preparation. Such flakes occur in millions in the old European caves and kitchen-middens, in the vicinity of the chalk districts, where excellent flint nodules are so abundant that the old savages could be prodigal of knives. They are also very abundant on ancient Indian sites in America, though it is often impossible to distinguish those intended for use from those thrown away in the preparation of more elaborate chipped implements. Nor can they always be distinguished from the chips broken by frost from siliceous rocks untouched by human hands. Such flakes, while the first, are probably also the last, stone implements used by man. The Mexican barbers at the time of the conquest shaved their customers with such flakes, and the old Egyptians and Jews used them in surgical operations at a time when their general civilization had attained to a very high pitch of advancement.

But flint is susceptible of much higher uses. Chipped by the skilful hand of the practised arrow-maker, it took the form of triangular, tanged, and leaf-shaped arrows and spears, of saws and knives. The forms of these are of the same plan throughout America with very little variation, and these forms are those also of Europe—so much so that a tray filled with European arrrow-heads cannot be distinguished from a tray of American ones. It will be quite unnecessary, therefore, to enter into any description of them. I may content myself with noticing a few points known as to America which may help to explain European facts.

One of these is as to the mode of their manufacture. Some persons seem to think that when a certain stage of civilization or semi-barbarism had been attained, any one could make neat flint arrows and spears. This is a great mistake. Alike in the ruder and more advanced American tribes, there were professional arrow-makers, whose skill was acknowledged often over wide districts. In pre-historic times, also, the tribes inhabiting the mountains and rocky districts were especially arrow-makers, and traded the produce of their skill with the tribes of the plains and valleys. We are even told that the travelling merchants of flint weapons were privileged persons, allowed to go from tribe to tribe without molestation. No doubt, any one could in an emergency manage to tip an arrow in some way, but it required long practice to make well-shaped arrow-heads, and it was not every district that could afford the best material for their manufacture. In some modes of making them, indeed, it required two skilled persons, one to hold the stone, the other to strike off small pieces with rapid and dexterous blows of a hammer and chisel.

It results from this that the rudeness or skill of the manufacture of flint weapons may be no test of age. One tribe had often more skilful makers or better material than others, and a party out on a hunting or military expedition might be reduced to the necessity of making arrows under disadvantageous circum-

IMPLEMENTS AND WEAPONS OF THE STONE AGE. 123

stances. Hence in the same sites very different kinds of arrow-heads may be found. Thus it happens that on the old Indian sites arrow-heads of the most varied character are found, and that when we succeed in discovering the places where arrows were made, we find that various and often distant places had been resorted to for the material of the manufacture. A conclusive evidence of the contemporaneous use of so-called

Fig. 25.—STONE ARROW-HEADS, MODERN. (*From Hopkins Island, Canada.*)

Palæolithic and Neolithic weapons appears to be afforded by the caverns of Beaumes Chaudes, in France, where skeletons of the old type of cave-men are found under circumstances which show that they were slain with arrows of small size and neatly made, portions of which are found actually imbedded in their bones. Thus the "Neolithic" men of Europe must have fought with the "Palæolithic," a fact which American analogies would quite prepare us to expect. In illustration of this I have before me three Canadian arrowheads from the collection of a friend (Fig. 25). They are of two types, the long and short, and are made of similar kinds of dark quartzite. They are from Hopkins Island, in the St. Lawrence, a place to which the Indians resorted in pursuit of wild fowl, in killing which these arrows, larger than those commonly employed in war, were probably used. These specimens were selected from a large number, showing all sorts of gradations from the rudest to the most perfect, and yet all probably made and used by the same tribes at the same time and in the same circumstances. The southern Indians are shown by Jones to have used large arrow-heads with chisel-shaped ends for striking off the heads of small birds, and some of their arrowheads which at first sight seem rude and misshapen are found to have been bevelled with opposite slopes on the sides, so as to give a rotatory motion, constituting as it were rifled arrows.

In America the rudest of all rude implements, similar to the Palæolithic type of the European archæologists, were used not by the ruder tribes but by the more settled and civilized agricultural nations. They are found most abundantly in the river valleys occupied by the southern tribes of the United States, and in the valleys of the Mississippi and Ohio. It is the opinion of most American archæologists that they were hoes or spades, and this is probably the most rational explanation of their use. The more civilized American tribes, from the gulf of Mexico to the valley of the St. Lawrence, were agriculturists, and their culture of maize, beans, pumpkins, and tobacco, was all carried on by manual labour, with hoes made of wood, or headed with bone, shell, or stone, which were used in great numbers in the spring, and then cast away or laid by in heaps, or buried in the ground until again required. Hunting tribes had no need of such tools. Even the more highly civilized nations of the Mississippi valley, who possessed copper implements, and were skilful artists in many ways, have left behind them vast numbers of rudely-chipped discs and flat flints, probably used in their agriculture.* They are found in caches, or deposits of many together, as if quantities were used at one time. This would agree with the idea of their agricultural use. They would be prepared in large quantities for the planting time, when the whole tribe mustered, like the South Africans described by Livingstone, to till their fields; and when the work was over they would be gathered and hidden in some safe place till the next season, or perhaps buried as an offering to the god of the harvest. Abbott, in his "Stone Age in New Jersey," figures one example found with 149 others in a ploughed field. They were buried in the ground with the points up, and he remarks that such implements are not met with

* Rau, "Smithsonian Report for 1868," describes several forms of stone hoes; some having notches for attachment to a handle, others oval in form. Thin, flat, sharp-edged stones of various forms, found on old Indian sites, may often have been agricultural implements.

singly; like arrows, hatchets, and other weapons. In the museum of the Historical Society of Brooklyn I saw a hoe similar to those described by Abbott, and which had like them been found with many others arranged in a circle under the ground; and Mr. Jones, of the same city, the author of an excellent work on the antiquities of the Southern Indians, showed me some of these hoes with the edges evidently worn by use, and pointed out to me that Carver refers to the care and secrecy with which the Indians were in the habit of hiding their stores of stone implements and weapons. Squier describes large deposits of these in Ohio. He also states that at a place called Flint Ridge, in the same state, where certain concretions of chert suitable for these implements are found, countless pits, dug for these flints, occur for many miles. These excavations are often ten or fourteen feet deep, and acres in extent.

In connection with this, it is be observed that in localities where flint weapons or implements were fabricated, great quantities of imperfectly made specimens were left behind, as well as of chips. Further, it was a well-known practice of American tribes to carry off from the quarries roughly-shaped implements, to be afterwards more carefully shaped at leisure. These facts may account for many deposits of so-called Palæolithic weapons, as well as for the occurrence of so-called "transition" deposits, in which imperfectly and well made flint objects are found mixed together, as in the celebrated pre-historic flint mines of Cissbury,

IMPLEMENTS AND WEAPONS OF THE STONE AGE. 127

in England. In one of the mounds of Ohio, Squier and Davis discovered an immense number of rudely-shaped flint discs placed on end. They are on the average six inches in length, and weigh about two pounds each. They are evidently unfinished implements, and Rau regards this as a depôt or magazine from which supplies of flint could be obtained as required, and where the material could be kept damp, so that it might be the more easily chipped.

A somewhat similar place is described by Leidy in a recent report on the geology of the Western Territories. It is at the base of the Uintah Hills, in Wyoming, where vast quantities of jasper, agate, and other stones suitable for implements, have been swept down upon the plain. Immense numbers of these have been chipped and broken into angular fragments, whether by art or nature does not seem evident; but from the number of arrow-heads and other definitely-formed objects, it is evident that the place was for ages resorted to as a quarry and manufactory. Nor need we wonder at this when we consider the dense agricultural population evidenced by the mounds and earthworks of the old Alleghans in all the alluvial plains of the West, and that thousands of industrious flint-chippers and migratory traders must have been constantly employed in working the agates and jaspers of the hills, and transporting them to the towns and villages of the plains, where they are still found in great numbers.

I suggested many years ago, when writing of a visit

to the celebrated gravel-pits of St. Acheul, that these may have been worked in pre-historic times like the American flint-beds, and I find that Mr. Belgrand, in his recent report on the Paris Basin, which solves so many difficulties as to the French river gravels regards these beds, and also those of Hoxne in England, as sites of manufactories of implements, though he thinks the manufacture was carried on when the water flowed at the height of these gravels. Rau has described in the Smithsonian Reports hoes from Illinois $7\frac{1}{2}$ inches long and 6 inches broad, neatly chipped, and with two notches in the upper part for the attachment of a handle. Foster has figured two specimens from the same State, of rude form and without notches. One of them is no less than 13 inches long. They show in the lower part an abrasion attributable to long use in digging. Many of these American hoes, of the ruder forms first mentioned, are scarcely distinguishable from the broader styles of so-called Palæolithic implements found in Europe, while there is a sharper and narrower European type sometimes also found in America, and which may have been used as a pick rather than a hoe. It is quite true that in our ignorance, born of too great civilization, it is often difficult for us to distinguish hoes from spears, tomahawks, or scrapers; but this renders all the more futile any attempt to assign these to distinct ages from one another, or from more polished implements. In any case, American analogies would lead us to refer some of the larger forms of Palæolithic chipped implements to agricultural populations, and we should expect to find such implements in great numbers in the vicinity of alluvial grounds or near to river valleys, and unmixed with the household utensils and weapons of war and hunting, which might remain in connection with habitations or fortresses. Their abundance in the European river gravels gives countenance to the supposition that in Europe, as in America, the earliest pre-historic peoples were agricultural, though there may, no doubt, have been contemporary hunting tribes in the districts less suited for cultivation.

In connection with these facts, it may be pertinent to inquire whether we have formed any definite conceptions of the habits and implements of the dense agricultural populations implied in the narrative of the antediluvian period in Genesis. Had they domesticated the horse or ox to plough their fields, or was all done by manual labour, as in America? Is it likely that they possessed metallic tools in sufficient quantity for agricultural use, even after the date, the seventh generation from Adam, assigned to the discovery of the metals? Is it not likely that their agriculture was carried on principally with primitive stone hoes? If so, we may expect to find in the river valleys of Western Asia vastly greater quantities of Palæolithic flints than those which the gravels of Europe have afforded, and it would not be wonderful if millions of these rude implements should be recovered without our meeting with any other evidence of civilization or of human agency. There must also have been quarries and excavations of great magnitude, out of which the demand for flints among this primitive population was supplied. It is much to be desired, in the interest alike of scientific and biblical archæology, that thorough explorations should be made of those lands which are historically the cradle of our species, to ascertain what traces remain of the prehistoric people who must have swarmed on the tablelands and river valleys of Asia, before they were swept away by the diluvial catastrophe which is recorded alike in the pages of Moses and the clay tablets of Assyria, and the dread memory of which survives in the traditions of nearly every family of mankind. It is well known that all over Asia and Northern Africa implements and weapons of chipped flint were used in historic times along with those of metal; but it is doubtful if we know anything of the antediluvian agricultural populations. American analogies would lead us to suppose that their only remaining traces might be the roughly-chipped flints which they probably used in cultivating the soil. Should these be found, however, they would be assumed by most archæologists to be the implements of a rude and savage race, scarcely elevated above the brutes.

Chipped-stone scrapers, knives, and borers exist among the American tribes, of similar patterns to those of pre-historic Europe; but we must now pass on to the polished stone implements made of quartzite, diorite, and other hard rocks. Those in

America do not belong to a different age from those of chipped flint, nor is it conceivable that they could have done so. The makers of chipped implements must have possessed at least stone hammers; and in districts where cleavable flints could not be found, the primitive men must have had recourse to other stones; and the use of the teeth, antlers, and horns of animals must from the first have led to imitations in stone and bone. In the oldest cavern deposits of Europe there is abundant evidence of the use of teeth and antlers as cutting implements, and it is absurd to suppose that the men who made the bone spears and other implements of Kent's Cave and the French caves could not, if necessary, have made implements of polished stone. If they did not do so, it was because they lived in a region where the abundant supply of excellent flint rendered unnecessary the laborious operation of polishing fragments of more refractory stones. Axes, chisels, and celts of polished stone run in parallel series to the hammers already mentioned; corresponding to the grooved hammers we have grooved axes. The hand hammers have correspondingly shaped celts and chisels, and the hammers with handle holes have their corresponding "Amazon axes," as they have been called in Europe.

I shall here merely make a few remarks on one or two of the kinds. The chisels show in their broken and battered heads the marks of the hammers with which they were driven in splitting wood. The axes for handling, on the other hand, are smooth and sometimes pointed at the top, or have a groove or grooves worked round them to give a more firm attachment by thongs or withes. In most cases the stone axe has not been furnished with a socket, but was fastened into a hole or cleft in the handle, or was merely tied to it with thongs. Those with holes or sockets were usually small, elaborately worked, and often made of soft kinds of stone. There is no good reason, however, to believe that they were merely ornamental. They were, no doubt, unsuited for cleaving wood, but they could as already explained, be used as tomahawks for killing fish and small animals, or even in war, and the Indian had the art of throwing them with great force and precision. They were, in short, to the American what the boomerang is to the Australian. Sir John Lubbock conjectures that such axes were not used till after metallic tools were introduced; but this will not apply to America.

The hollow chisel, or gouge, is a very common implement among the Northern Indians, but less common apparently in the south. It was always long, smooth, and often broken by hammering at the upper end; but some specimens have the upper end worked into a sharp edge. Like the hoes already referred to, these chisels are often found in groups or nests, indicating that they were used by parties or companies of people. This accords with the prevalent belief already mentioned, that they were the implements for tapping the maple-tree in spring to extract its sap.

This seems to have been universally used among the Northern Indians, and is highly valued as the first and most delicious gift of nature in the opening of spring. In the east the sugar maple and white maple are tapped, and in the west the allied *Negundo,* or ash-leaved maple. The juice was then boiled into syrup, but Charlevoix states that among the Canadian Indians at least, it was not crystallized into sugar until after the arrival of the Europeans.

In Europe these gouges are supposed to have been used for hollowing canoes, but it is precisely in those regions in America where bark canoes, and not those of hollow logs, were used, that these hollow chisels most abound. In some cases also, the hollow is cut the whole length of the chisel, so that it forms a spout which might be used to collect the sap as well as to make the incision. These gouges were, however, probably used to hollow wooden troughs to contain the juice, an operation which the modern backwoodsman performs with an adze or a chisel. The modern Scandinavians make sugar or syrup from the birch, and as, according to Nilsson, the hollow gouges of that country are found in nests or groups, they may mark the sites of sugar camps. In that country, however, it is probable that canoes were principally made from trunks of trees, and the Polynesians who used hollow stone chisels, must have employed them in making such canoes. No hollow chisels appear as yet to have been found in connection with so-called Palæolithic remains, so that we do not know whether the oldest European tribes tapped trees or dug out troughs or canoes. Still, as these hollow chisels, if they existed, would be found by themselves and not associated with chipped implements, the inveterate prejudice which regards polished and chipped implements as of different ages would probably dissociate them from the contemporary remains.

Bone was extensively used in America as in Europe, for a great variety of purposes, but the perishable nature of bone implements causes them to be difficult of recovery even from sites so modern comparatively as that of Hochelaga. Fortunately, however, some of these implements may still be found in use among our western tribes. The American bone fish-spear or harpoon is constructed on the same plan with that of pre-historic Europe, and the visitor to the British Museum may see bone harpoons from the caves of the reindeer folk in France, so like those in the same collection from Greenland and Terra del Fuego that all might have come from the same workshop. As Rau has pointed out, they have even the little grooves cut in the barbs to allow the blood of the wounded animal more readily to flow, a requirement not found in some of the American harpoons, or in those of more modern times, though attended to in the arrow-shafts of the Plain Indians who hunt the buffalo. The fish-spear was always an important means of subsistence with the American savage. In the south large fish were killed with spears made of canes, with the point sharpened and hardened in the fire. In the north

IMPLEMENTS AND WEAPONS OF THE STONE AGE. 135

barbed bone spears were used, and also little unbarbed bones with two elastic pieces of wood at the sides to hold the body of the fish between them when pierced with the spear. Even in winter the Indian cuts a hole through the ice, and sitting beside it spears the fish that are attracted by the light. Pointed bone implements, explicable as spears, arrow-heads, bodkins, piercers, and potters' stamps, are not uncommon in the kitchen-middens of old Hochelaga, though often

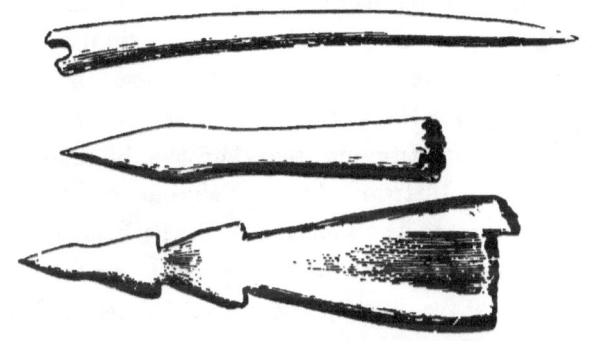

Fig. 26.—Bone Needle and Spears, Hochelaga.

softened and impaired by decay. Their appearance may be learned from the figures which I give of a few of them, and which will recall the pre-historic European bone implements which the reader may have seen either in museums, or figured in books, and many of which date back to the oldest deposits in caves of the Mammoth age. The simplest form of spear is that with notches along one side, though even this implies some thought and skill in the arrangement of its barbs, and the plan of these seems to have been nearly alike in all times and places. I figure in illustration (Fig. 27) four examples: one modern, from Terra del Fuego; three ancient, from Nova Scotia, from Denmark, and from Kent's Cave in Devonshire. All of them were probably used for capturing fish.

One very neat little bone implement found at Hochelaga has on one end a round stamp to make rings on pottery, while the other end is pointed, and may have been used for drawing lines. Others are explained, by the habits of the modern tribes, as needles for weaving snow-shoes, and others are similar to the piercers to this day used by the Northern Indians in making holes for the *watep*, or cord of spruce or larch roots, used for stitching together the birch-bark of their canoes. Instruments very similar to these are figured by Lartet and Christy from the French caves, and by Dupont from those of Belgium.

The ancient pre-historic people of France and Belgium made, according to Lartet and Dupont, very neat and serviceable sewing-needles of bone, and similar, though coarse, needles were used in Canada. One of them in my collection from Hochelaga is flattened and bent like the collar-needles used by saddlers, and has an eye large enough to receive pack-thread (fig. 26). It may have been used in sewing skin garments with sinews of deer. We can easily imagine the surprise of women accustomed to such rough handiwork when they were first introduced to the French fashions of those days, as seen on the persons of Cartier and his gentleman volunteers.

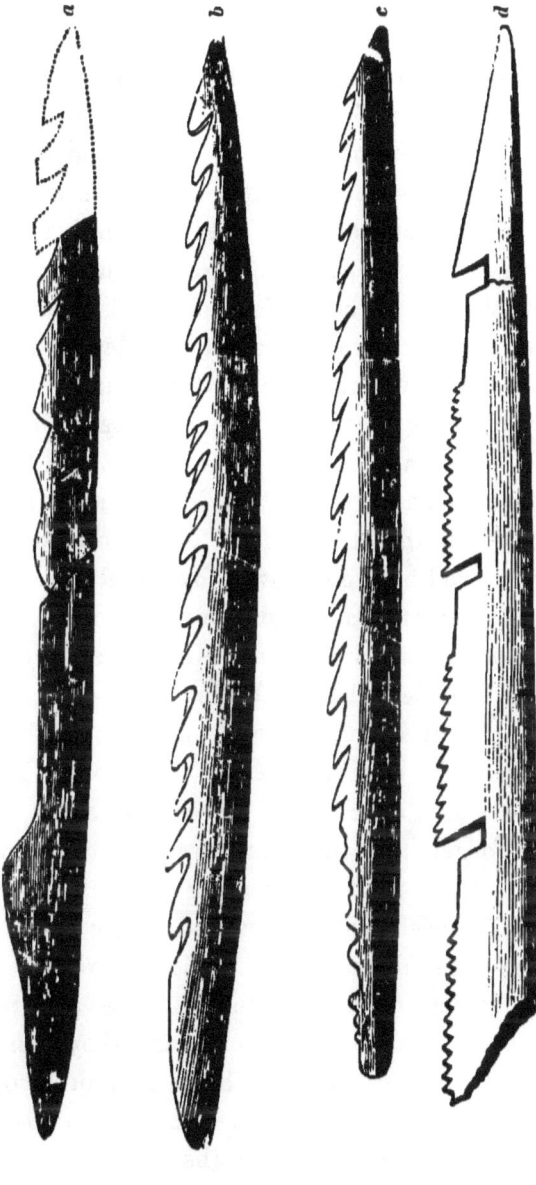

Fig. 27.—Bone Harpoons.
(a) Kent's Cavern—Palaeocosmic.
(b) Ancient Danish—Neocosmic.
(c) Fuegian—Modern.
(d) Micmac, Nova Scotia.

They crowded around them, touched their garments, and wept, as he says, for joy, but perhaps merely because they were thoroughly overcome by the contemplation of such rare and inimitable woman's work, the like of which they had not seen, nor had they heard of such things except in the vague and uncertain rumours of the cotton-clad Mexicans and mound-builders, which may have reached the valley of the St. Lawrence. Bone needles much finer than those above figured were used by the Esquimaux, and also by the American Indians. They abound in the caves of the "Reindeer period" in France, and that they were used in the still earlier "Mammoth age" seems to be proved by the discovery by Dr. Rivière of needles in the Mentone Cave, and also by the character of the ornamental head-dress of the Mentone skeleton. Pengelly has also described a needle from below the upper stalagmite of Kent's Cave, belonging therefore to the period of the cave hyæna and mammoth. He regards it as too delicate to pierce the skins of animals, but forgets that the skins sewed with it may have been those of small fur-bearing quadrupeds, or that it may have been used for embroidering with hair or with vegetable fibres. We shall find, however, in the sequel, reason to believe that by the ancient Europeans, as well as by the Americans, they were used to sew skin bags made to hold pemmican or preserved meat, and that this may account for their association with cracked bones in the caves. Their use among the Americans was not only to sew together their skin garments with the sinews of the deer, but to embroider them with patterns, and to attach to them the beads and perforated shells with which they were ornamented. They were also used in making nets, and in weaving the network of snow-shoes. There is no reason as yet to believe that the earlier pre-historic peoples of Europe could make textile fabrics. These appear for the first time in the Swiss lake-habitations, but there are figures of human arms apparently with embroidered sleeves, in Lartet and Christy's collections, and which are sufficient to show the same love of needlework which is observed among the modern Esquimaux and Indians, and which was so conspicuous among all early historic nations of the Old World. If the people of the Mammoth age already practised the art of embroidery, this fact would imply the careful tanning of skins, the manufacture of needles, the preparation of thread from animal or vegetable fibres, and probably some knowledge of vegetable dye-stuffs; and some proficiency in all these arts is so widely diffused that there seems no improbability in their being even thus ancient.

According to Cartier, the most valuable of all the possessions of the people of Canada and Hochelaga was that which they called "Esurguy," the same known more familiarly to us by its New England name of "wampum." The great original wampum of America was probably that which still stands at the head of all kinds of beads, the pearl, which seems to have been collected by the Southern Indians, and is mentioned by the early Spanish adventurers as an abundant and valued possession of the chiefs. Next to this came polished and perforated pieces of the shell of the pearl oyster and of other shells. The solid columella of the great Strombus, and other large univalves, was used by the Indians of the south. The New England Indians used the hard shell of the "Quahog" (*Venus mercenaria*), the purple spot at the posterior end of the shell forming the more precious blue wampum. The more northern coast tribes sometimes used the shells of the great Clam (*Mactra solidissima*). The inland nations purchased wampum from those of the coast, and, like the Coast Indians, they used small shells perforated with holes. The wampum of the Iroquois, and also of the Hochelagans, was made of freshwater univalves, probably the *Melania*. They also ground into perforated discs for beads the pearly shells of freshwater Unios. The Indians of the west coast use the long tubular shells of the *Dentalium*. Copper beads and long bugles were worked out of the native metal, and a cheaper kind of bead was made of clay, moulded into ornamental discs and baked. (Fig. 28.) Whatever the form or material, wampum was in universal use for ornament or dress, and as necklaces, bracelets, and anklets, both among men and women. It was also a medium of exchange, and was buried with the dead as a possession valuable even in the world of spirits. Champlain informs us that the Huron girls accumulated strings of wampum for their dowry, and lavishly adorned themselves with it on occasions of festivity. In another chapter I have reproduced (P. 156), in illustration of this, his drawing of a Huron belle dressed for a dance.

That it was carried to great distances is shown by the discovery of tropical shells far to the north, in the interior of America. I have seen the remains of a necklace found in a grave at Brockville, on the St. Lawrence, composed in part of shells of *Purpura lapillus* from the distant coast of New England, and in part of rude beads of native copper from Lake

Fig. 28.—SHELL AND TERRA COTTA BEADS, HOCHELAGA.

Superior. When Cartier left Stadacona with Donnaconna as his prisoner, the people brought twenty-four strings or necklaces of wampum as a ransom for their chief, no doubt thinking that even in the distant country of the stranger so large a quantity of treasure would be a fortune too tempting to be refused. So when a great chief died, treasures of wampum were placed with him to enrich him in the other world; and even the infant had strings of it twined around its little corpse, to secure a welcome in the happy fields of the west.

In his universal use of wampum the American was but kin to all men from the beginning. If we turn to the pages of Genesis, we find the gold, pearls, and agate of Havilah as the riches of primitive man. If we turn to those old graves of the Mammoth age, which reveal to us the habits of the oldest men known to geology, wampum appears to be the universal treasure. Perhaps one of the most curious illustrations of this is the skeleton discovered by Dr. Rivière, in a cave at Mentone, on the borders of France and Italy. This and some companion caves are situated in a rocky cliff bordering a narrow terrace overlooking the sea, and which seems to have been a highway, or pass, from pre-historic times to those of modern railways. Among the earliest lodgers to whom these caves afforded a resting-place in their wanderings, and a place of sepulture, were some of those tribes who are believed to have used only roughly chipped implements, and to have been contemporary with the now extinct mammoth and woolly rhinoceros of the Post-pliocene period. A man of one of these tribes had been buried here, having probably died from wounds while on the march. As we shall find when we come to consider physical characters, this man was essentially in face and frame an American, as were also his contemporaries in other parts of Europe, and their habits and modes of sepulture were American as well. His head had been covered with a cap or chaplet, ornamented with the perforated shells of a Nassa, thickly plaited into the network of the head-dress. Around the edge was a fringe of perforated canines of the deer; two flint arrows—trophies, perhaps, of war—were fixed on the back, and in front was a bone pin, which had probably supported his long hair. Bracelets and anklets of similar shells adorned his stalwart limbs, and to complete the resemblance, a little oxide of iron was placed in front of his face, the "war paint" wherewith to appear in presence of his ancestors. Could this old brave of Mentone, belonging to a tribe whose very name is unknown to history, spring again into life, he would, in garb, arms, and appearance, have shown no marked difference from the tribes that inhabited the St. Lawrence valley three hundred years ago. This is not an isolated case, for we find that the same customs with regard to wampum prevailed throughout Western Europe in the oldest pre-historic times known to us, and that shell beads were transported by trade or migration to great distances, exactly as in America. There is no good reason to assign to these pre-historic men of Europe the fabulous antiquity claimed for them by some; but they carry back the customs of America to a time as old as any known to us by human remains and works of art.

In America the wampum had a still higher use. Woven into belts of various patterns, into which dates and histories and national treaties were "talked," it formed the records of the American tribes; committed to the care of "wampum-keepers," it was handed down from one generation to another, and regarded in the same light as that in which we view our most precious national archives. The treaty of the Lenni-Lenape with Penn in 1682 is commemorated by a great belt of white and purple wampum, still preserved in Philadelphia, and probably made of the Venus shell. The great charter of the Iroquois league, according to Morgan, was made of fresh-water univalves, and in the early records of New France we constantly read of belts or strings of wampum as being presented in confirmation of engagements or claims. Wilson well states the analogy of all this with the quipus, or knotted strings, which formed the records of the Peruvians, and which, like the wampum of the north, were sometimes buried in their graves as records of their lives and deeds. Of this use of wampum as a substitute for letters we have, I believe, as yet no trace in Europe; but may we not hope yet to find the buried quipu or historic wampum of some pre-historic man or tribe?

Among the most mysterious of the objects found among the ancient relics in European caverns, are slender bones, marked with notches or scratches in variable number. They have been held to be tallies, or aids to memory, and it has even been suggested that they make a rude approach to the beginning of historical writing. This may be so; but of the American objects which they resemble, the most striking are the gambling sticks used by the Western Indians. In the Queen Charlotte Islands, for example, the Haida carries a leather bag containing, perhaps, fifty small rods, a few inches long, and made of wood, ivory, or the leg-bones of birds. They are marked with rings or notches, differing in number on each piece, and giving them different values in the games played with them. They appear to be dealt like cards, and each player throws down in turn the pieces he may have, which are rated according to their marks. If such games were in use among the old cave-men of Europe, this would account for the frequency of the tallies, or gambling sticks, in their former habitations.

The strange and ghastly custom of preserving portions of the bodies of slaughtered enemies as trophies of victory, belongs to the American in common with some of the races of the Old World. In scalping the slain he agrees with the ancient Scythians as described by Herodotus, and with the modern aborigines of Formosa, according to the reports of missionaries to that country. Our own heathen forefathers made drinking bowls of the skulls of the dead, and two specimens illustrative of this have been disinterred in Hochelaga. They are human parietal bones, trimmed around the edges so as to form flat bowls, and one of them has a hole at the edge, probably for a string to suspend it. That customs of this nature were prevalent in antiquity we have evidence even in the monuments of civilized nations; but as yet, I believe, no traces of them have been found among human pre-historic remains. Perhaps such practices were as yet unknown to pre-historic men, and belonged to the moral degradation of historic times alone.

CHAPTER VI.

LOST ARTS OF PRIMITIVE RACES.

NOTHING is more clearly shown by American analogies than the illusory nature of the popular modes of reasoning as to the progress of pre-historic races in the arts, from the remains which they have left in the soil. Chipped stone as distinguished from polished stone may depend altogether on the material accessible. The rudest and most savage tribes of hunters may chip or grind their weapons more elaborately than tribes far higher in general civilization. When metal tools begin to come into use, the more elaborate and costly kinds of stone implements cease to be made, though some of the ruder ones may still be employed. As tribes adopt settled habits and become agriculturists, they may have less need for the carefully made flint implements used in hunting, and less time to make them. Long-continued peace and prosperity will enable a tribe to accumulate stores of well-formed weapons; sudden attacks or military reverses may oblige them hastily to manufacture the rudest kinds in order to resist their enemies. Arts long pursued and carried to much perfection may, by the introduction of new objects of trade, or from other causes, perish and become forgotten in a single generation. Thus, as we have already seen, the potter's art, in itself the germ of many others, has perished from the Indian tribes of North America, and the art of making gold jewellery from the Indian tribes of Central America, while many important arts practised by the old mound-builders are now wholly extinct among their successors in the same regions.

Perhaps few illustrations of this are more striking than those afforded by what is known as to the art of drilling, perforating, and carving hard stones, as practised by nations not acquainted with the use of metals. This art was universal among the primitive people of the northern hemisphere, as evidenced by the stone hatchets with sockets for handles found both in Europe and America, and by the marvellously carved and bored pipes made of the hardest stones by the American Indians. Professor Rau, of New York, who has given much attention to this subject, has shown that the means employed to bore round holes was either a hollow cane or a solid round stick, supplied with sand and water, and rotated with a drill bow, either of the kind called the "pump-drill," and used by the Iroquois and other tribes, or of the kind now commonly employed by artisans, and which was known to the Alleghans and other primitive nations. This zealous and judicious observer further tried the experiment of boring in this way, and found it most tedious work.

"The deeper the drill penetrated into the stone, the more difficult the work became, which induced me,

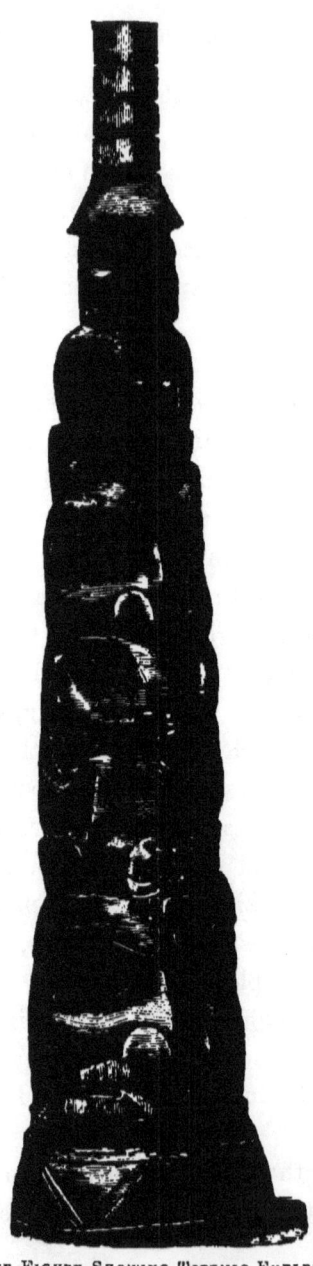

Fig 29.—GROTESQUE FIGURE SHOWING TOTEMIC EMBLEMS CARVED IN BLACK ARGILLACEOUS STONE BY NATIVES OF THE QUEEN CHARLOTTE ISLANDS, WESTERN AMERICA. (*From a Photograph by J. C. Weston, Geological Survey of Canada.*) (*Reduced*).

after having drilled through half the thickness of the stone, to begin another bore at the opposite side. In due time it met the first exactly in the middle. It was originally my intention to drill a hole of about three-quarters of an inch in diameter; but I had not made sufficient allowance for the lateral friction of the sand, and hence it happened that the two conical cavities forming the perforation acquired, much against my wish, greater proportions than I expected, measuring, in fact, an inch and a quarter in their widest diameters. They would have become narrower, as well as more cylindrical, if I had used a drill half as thick as that which served in the operation; but when I made this discovery the work was already too far advanced to be commenced again."

With regard to the process of manufacturing pipes of hard stone, he writes as follows:—

"The manufactures of stone which evince the greatest skill of the former inhabitants of North America, are by no means their pierced axes, but those remarkable pipes, often made of the hardest stones, that have been found in the so-called sacrificial mounds of the Western States, but more especially in Ohio. These 'mound-pipes' usually represent bowl and tube in one piece, thus differing from the modern Indian pipe, which consists of a bowl and a long wooden stem, and bears a distant resemblance to the chibouk of the Turks. A great number of pipes of the above-mentioned antique shape were disentombed by Messrs. Squier and Davis during their survey of the ancient earthworks in the Mississippi valley, and are described and figured in their work, which forms the first volume of "Smithsonian Contributions to Knowledge." The accompanying cut (Fig. 30) presents the outline of the mound-pipe in its simple or primitive form. The drawing is about half the size of the original, which was exhumed with many similar articles from a mound near Chillicothe, Ohio. It will be seen that the bowl

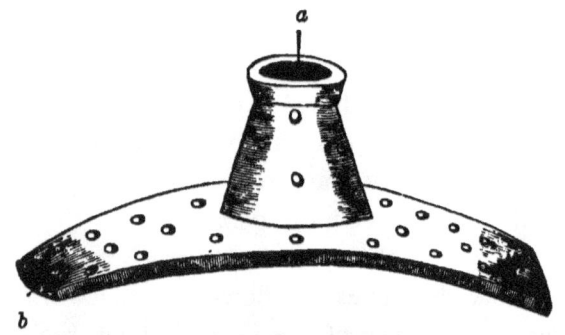

Fig. 30.—Pipe Carved out of Hard Porphyritic Stone by the Alleghans of the Ohio.
  a. Bowl drilled down to the base.
  b. Hole drilled through the base to the bowl. The bowl and base are covered with small drilled holes for ornament.

rises from the middle of a flat and somewhat curved base, one side of which communicates by means of a narrow perforation (*b*), one-sixth of an inch (about four millimetres) in diameter, with the hollow of the bowl (*a*), and represents the tube, or rather the mouth-piece, of the pipe, while the other unperforated end forms the handle by which the smoker held the implement and approached it to his mouth. Bowl and base are ornamented with small cup-shaped holes.

This pipe consists of hard porphyry, and is wrought from a single piece, like all others of a similar character. I have already stated that it may be considered as the simple or typical form of this class of implements. In the more elaborate specimens the bowl is formed in some instances in imitation of the human head, but generally of the body of an animal, and in the latter cases the peculiar characteristics of the species which have served as models, comprising mammals, birds, and amphibia, are frequently expressed with surprising fidelity; a modern artist, indeed, notwithstanding his far superior instruments, would find no little difficulty in reproducing the more finished of these objects, especially when carving them from porphyry, which was the kind of stone chiefly employed by the manufacturers."

What wonder is it that time, which "antiquates antiquities, and hath an art to make dust of all things, hath yet spared these minor monuments;" and how strangely does it illustrate the religious fervour of the old mound-builders that they could sacrifice hundreds of these precious trophies of skill and labour in the fires of their altar hearths. Whatever the objects of their worship, or the ends they hoped to attain, they could give no costlier offerings unless they had offered their own lives on the altar. Lafitau informs us that the shaping and perforation of a tomahawk was sometimes the work of a lifetime, and might be left unfinished by the patient artist whose life-work it had been. It is said that perforated pieces of rock-crystal, worn by the chiefs of some South American tribes, cost the labour of two men's lives. It is not surprising that arts like these perish immediately on the introduction of the implements of more civilized races, and drop out of the memory of the successors of the artists in a few generations.

It is only under peculiar circumstances that arts implying so much labour as well as contrivance can flourish. The man whose whole energies are occupied in providing for the ordinary wants of life cannot take time to select particular kinds of stone, to construct drills, and to work patiently for months or for years in order that he may possess an unusually perfect or finished implement. Hence, of two peoples similarly constituted, and in a similar stage of culture, one may be quite unable to indulge in such luxuries of art, while another more favourably situated may abound in them.

It is interesting also to observe that under certain conditions of external influence, the arts of a people may change without any corresponding advance in general civilization. For example, the natives of the Queen Charlotte Islands, on the west coast of British America, are remarkable, like other tribes on that coast, for strange and grotesque carvings in a black argillaceous stone, and which sometimes remind one of Chinese carvings in agalmatolite. Yet some of these tribes, since they have come into contact with Europeans, and have found their carvings capable of being made into articles of merchandise, have invented or borrowed new patterns. A little further progress of civilization will probably turn the attention of this people into new channels, and their later works, as well as their own earlier grotesque figures, will become obsolete and forgotten; and if exhumed by antiquaries, might give very false impressions as to the history and progress of the tribe, unless some historical account of the circumstances were preserved.

The case of the Queen Charlotte Islanders might be made to indicate even a change of religion as well as of art, for their grotesque carvings are their *penates*, the tokens or signs of their guardian manitous (Fig. 29), to which their more modern carvings, often copied from European models, bear no relation.

The Haida Indians of the Queen Charlotte Islands, when first visited by Europeans, dwelt in villages composed of large houses, laboriously constructed of wooden planks, and in front of each house was an immense obelisk or pillar of wood, often so large that the doorway was cut through its substance. This pillar was elaborately carved with great labour, from top to bottom, with totems or armorial bearings of the family. They used vessels of wood and of the horns of the mountain sheep and goat, which were in like manner adorned with carvings of animal and grotesque forms. Their masks, rattles, and maces, used in their dances, were all highly finished pieces of carving, and often inlaid with pearly plates of the shell of the *Haliotis*. Their canoes, constructed out of a single large tree, were beautifully modelled, carved and inlaid with mother-of-pearl. In short, these people had made great progress in decorative art, or had brought such art from Asia, or received it through occasional Japanese junks wrecked on their coasts. All this primitive art is now rapidly perishing, and will soon be replaced by European arts and manufactures, though the manner of life and subsistence of the people remains in the main the same as before. The Haida is still a fisherman, though tin pails may replace the carved wooden dishes of his fathers, and his house may want altogether the grand carved posts, replaced perhaps by a flag-staff.

Agriculture may be extensively pursued by primitive tribes, and if these tribes perish, or if they are driven by reverses to adopt a nomadic life, their culture of the earth may leave no appreciable remains behind, and so far as antiquities are concerned, they may appear to be a ruder people than one that has lived by hunting or fishing. Tribes living in rock shelters, or obliged to build with stone or earth, may leave remains altogether exceptional in amount compared with those which commemorate the existence of comparatively cultivated people living in wooden houses and tilling the soil. The introduction of new tools by foreign trade may indicate the very reverse of any progress in culture or civilization in the rude tribes who receive such new objects.

Cartier, in 1535, found around the town of Hochelaga "goodly and large" cultivated fields, and he speaks of the Mountain of Montreal as tilled round about—

implying a large amount of cultivated land. This culture, too, must have been of long standing; for the removal of the "goodly great oaks" that originally cumbered the ground was a work of time, especially to people without iron implements, and who must have destroyed each tree by laboriously girdling it, or by scorching its bark with fire, and must have carried on their culture amidst the tall, scathed trunks, until these were broken down by the winds, aided by decay; and then they must have removed them by burning. All these processes had long ago been complete, else the French narrative could not have spoken of goodly and large fields. But what was cultivated in these fields? Cartier mentions as the principal crop maize, or Indian corn, and with this there were beans, different, he says, in appearance from those cultivated in France, great cucumbers or melons—by which he probably means pumpkins,—and probably tobacco. He mentions also several kinds of fruits, but whether wild or cultivated he does not say. The wild Canadian plum, the choke-cherry, a hawthorn producing edible fruit, and the wild grape, still abound in the vicinity of the ancient Hochelaga, and may have been cultivated or cared for and collected by the Hochelagans. It was shortly after harvest when Cartier visited the town, and they then had great store of all the productions of their fields. They had on the tops of their houses granaries, or possibly corn-cribs, for preserving the Indian corn, probably to secure dryness and prevent the attacks of vermin. For keeping

FIG. 31.—GROUP OF HURON WOMEN, FROM CHAMPLAIN'S VOYAGES, REPRESENTING THEIR STYLE OF DRESS, AND MODE OF GRINDING MAIZE IN A WOODEN MORTAR. The left-hand figure is a girl dressed for a dance, showing beads, or wampum, as employed for ornament. These figures show the aboriginal costumes before intercourse with Europeans.

the smoked fish of which they laid in quantities for winter use, they had large bins or vessels probably made of wood or bark. Their corn was ground in wooden mortars, as was usual with the Canadian and neighbouring tribes (see Fig. 31), and baked in cakes or made into various kinds of pottage. What a picture we have here of agricultural plenty! and this was, no doubt, repeated in all the villages along the St. Lawrence, and thence to the southward.

Let us further note that of the plants cultivated as field crops at Hochelaga, all belonged to species not found wild north of the Gulf of Mexico, more than a thousand miles to the southward. Yet these plants had found their way from tribe to tribe to the banks of the St. Lawrence, and were at the time of Cartier cultivated as far north as the climate will allow them to be cultivated now. These plants are indigenous to America, and their properties and uses must have been discovered or recognised by the people living where they are native, and from them transmitted, either by migrations or by commercial intercourse, to the far north. Further, the culture of these plants in Canada is attended with much greater difficulty than it is at the south. Early varieties require to be selected, and I have evidence that the variety of corn cultivated at Hochelaga three hundred years ago was similar to one of the early varieties cultivated still in Canada. More careful tillage and manuring also are needed, and precautions to avoid the effects of late frosts in spring. Yet all this was known to the old

Hochelagans. Similar agricultural towns, some of them on a larger scale, existed among the Hurons and Iroquois. Gaensera, a town of the Iroquois, destroyed by the French in 1687, is described as built of wood and bark, with granaries of bark, in the form of towers, fifteen feet in diameter. Besides this, there was a detached and fortified granary on a neighbouring hill. The French reported that in this town, which, judging from the number of fighting men, must have been inhabited by three or four thousand people, they destroyed 100,000 minots of corn in the granaries, and 150,000 standing in the fields, or perhaps 750,000 bushels in all. Yet this and other cities destroyed in the Indian wars were not rebuilt, the Iroquois being disheartened and reduced in numbers, and they now exist only as mounds and old earthworks, many of them with no written history.

Cartier tells us that the women were the principal agriculturists. The men were hunters, fishermen, and warriors. The women tilled the ground and carried on most of the domestic manufactures. This was the case generally among the semi-civilized Americans, and, according to our modern notions, it gives the women a more advanced place than the men; and as women were often taken prisoners in war, it might be a means of spreading the arts of life among the more barbarous tribes. On the other hand, it allowed a very speedy relapse into the condition of barbarous hunters when a tribe was driven from its ancient abode.

Let us now ask what trace of this ancient culture remains? The cornfields of Hochelaga, not even ridged with the plough, would be overgrown with tall trees within fifty years of the abandonment of the site. The corn-cribs and wooden mortars had been burned or have mouldered away. The plants cultivated were too tender to survive in a wild state. The wooden hoes which Cartier tells were the ordinary agricultural implements, have long ago perished, and if, as was probably sometimes the case, they were tipped with a flat stone, this was so roughly shaped, if shaped at all, that when found it would scarcely be recognised as even a Palæolithic implement. May not, then, the whole tale be a myth, its materials furnished by the narratives of more southern voyagers, and intended to exalt the new country in the opinion of the French Government? For all that could be proved by any but a few slight indications, the search for which was prompted by Cartier's narrative, it might have been so, and Hochelaga might have been inhabited by a tribe as rude as the Palæolithic people of Europe are supposed to have been. The microscope shows traces of charred corn-meal encrusting the necks of some of the earthen pots; and after sifting a cartload or two of the kitchen-midden stuff through wire sieves, I became the possessor of a dozen or two of charred grains of corn and a cotyledon and a half of the bean. Another collector found a charred "corn cob." Besides this, I found evidence that the wild plum and cherry, and even the acorn, had been used as food. Let it be observed, further, that a grain of corn or a bean could not have escaped decay unless it had happened to be accidentally charred, and some accident of this kind, occurring in connection with cookery, alone provided this slight confirmation of the story of the agriculture of Hochelaga.

Perhaps in no respect is it usually supposed that primitive man is more to be contrasted with modern races in an imperfect state of civilization, than in his knowledge of distant regions and the intercourse which he carries on with them. In this respect, according to Dupont, there is evidence that the Palæolithic men had more extensive commerce than their successors of the Reindeer age, and perhaps both of them more than the peasant of mediæval or modern times. Just as we find evidence in the French caves, and the older dwellings built on piles over the Swiss lakes, that their inhabitants had communication with the Mediterranean and the Atlantic, and could procure the sacred and useful jade of the far east, the coral of the Mediterranean, the amber of the Baltic and the improved wheat of Egypt,* so was it in pre-historic America. The Hochelagans who accompanied Cartier to the summit of Mount Royal, and the ancients of Stadacona with whom he conversed after his return, concurred in informing him that the great river of Hochelaga, which he called the St. Lawrence, extended many days' journey beyond the point to which he had penetrated, and that it issued

* Keller, "Report on Swiss Lake Habitations."

from great lakes or seas of fresh water so vast that they knew little of their farther shores. That the river which we now call the Ottawa, from the name of an Algonquin tribe inhabiting its banks, ran from a western land which they called Saguenay, a name now applied to a river far to the east of Quebec, from a geographical confusion arising from the fact that the Saguenay river was one of the outlets in ancient times of the more western land of that name. It was from this western land that their copper implements came, and this not by the St. Lawrence route, but by that northern line of communication from Georgian Bay to the Ottawa, which the modern Canadian Government has, so far unsuccessfully, been endeavouring to open out, and which enabled the old Hochelagans to trade with Lake Superior through the domains of friendly tribes. Further, they knew that to the south were countries where the people were clad in woven fabics, where delicious fruits and spices, unknown to Canada, were produced, and where there was no frost or snow, even in winter. These countries could be reached by the Richelieu river, or from the great western lakes; but unfortunately there lay between, tribes of people fierce and warlike, who in recent times had cut off all communication between the nations of the St. Lawrence and the sunny lands of the south. Still it was from these southern lands that their ancestors, in older and happier times, had procured the seeds of the maize, beans, pumpkins, and tobacco, which they still cultivated, and whose culture they had extended as far to the north as it yet reaches.

Similar facts occur even among the ruder hunting tribes. The Micmacs of Nova Scotia seem scarcely if at all to have cultivated the soil. But as hunters and fishermen they had explored all the natural riches of their country and its neighbouring waters. They knew the haunts and habits of every useful animal of the land and of the sea, and had devised means for its capture at the appropriate season; and their graves, and the heaps left by their makers of stone weapons, show that they had discovered all its treasures of greenstone, jasper, agate, and native copper, and habitually turned them to account. Shortly after the first French colony had settled at Port Royal,* some alarm was caused to them by a visit of 800 Micmac warriors who encamped near the little settlement. But it appeared that they were engaged in an expedition against some tribe inhabiting the coast of what is now New England, and for this purpose they crossed the Bay of Fundy in their bark canoes. These same adventurous savages carried on naval and military expeditions far up the St. Lawrence, and were acquainted with the names and distribution of the tribes on that river, and even farther west. Cartier heard of them, or of the allied Malicetes, at Quebec, as dangerous and predatory savages, under the name of Tudemans. Their traditions told of a primitive people whom they had driven from Nova Scotia, and

* Now Annapolis.

the remnants of this people, the Red Indians, they pursued into Newfoundland, crossing the stormy sea which separates this island from Cape Breton, in their bark canoes. As the opposite coast could rarely be seen, they were in the habit of kindling large fires upon the northern point of Cape Breton which they called Sakpeediah, the Smoky Cape, and steering from these in the direction of Newfoundland. Such adventures, though perhaps not comparable with the voyages of the islanders of the Pacific, show us what primitive man can do, and how rapidly he may overspread the earth.* The present condition of the Micmacs, reduced to pauperism and destitute of any spirit of progress or adventure, tells how readily the life and spirit of rude peoples can be crushed out by oppression.

The learned archæologist, Rau, has, in a memoir on Ancient Aboriginal Trade,† collected a great number of interesting facts showing the remarkable extent to which in pre-historic times the productions of North America had been utilized and conveyed from place to place. He shows that the produce of the copper mines of Lake Superior had been dispersed over the whole continent to the Gulf of Mexico and the Atlantic coast. In like manner, the celebrated red pipestone

* The Micmacs seem also to have a tradition of the Northmen who visited their coasts in the tenth century, in a people whom they call Chenooks, who are said to have had hearts of ice, a terrible war-whoop, to be of immense strength, to sail in canoes of stone, to possess magical powers, and to use weapons of brass. Rand has preserved this tradition.

† " Report of Smithsonian Institution, 1872."

of the Coteau des Prairies, on the head waters of the Missouri, had been distributed as far as the State of New York, and I believe one of the pipes found at Hochelaga to be made of it. Plates of mica quarried in the metamorphic districts of the Appalachians, have been abundantly diffused over the plains of the Mississippi and the Ohio, and were used as ornaments and perhaps as mirrors. The chert from the "Flint Ridge" of Ohio is shown to have been transported at least 400 miles from the quarries; and Rau holds, with good reason, that the flint was first formed into flattish or disc-shaped pieces, and in this state transported to distant places, where it was stored up till required to be fashioned into arrowheads or other weapons. These stores of partly formed objects were also buried in the ground in order that they might not be injured by the drying influence of the air. It is in this way that we account for the "caches" or buried deposits of imperfectly formed flint implements which are often discovered; and no doubt many of the deposits of the so-called Palæolithic implements in Europe admit of a similar explanation. Sea shells also, pearls and wampum beads, used as ornaments, objects of religious veneration, or media of exchange, were distributed in pre-historic times throughout the length and breadth of the continent. All this internal trade is now as much a thing of the past as that carried on by primitive man in Europe; but its evidence remains to show how much can be done even by men despised as savages.

It is a remarkable fact that our researches on the site of Hochelaga have disclosed so few relics of this trade and intercourse which existed between the nations of distant parts of America, and of which, as we have seen, we have evidence in the narrative of Cartier, as well as in the objects found elsewhere. Of this the relics of Hochelaga show little except a few copper beads; and, beside the two small pieces of metal already referred to, nothing of the numerous tools and trinkets left by Cartier himself. Yet one of these fragments—the little piece of brass mentioned in a previous paper—may have been a part of one of Cartier's crosses, which it is not unlikely were cut up into small pieces and distributed to different persons, or disposed of in trade with less fortunate tribes. This absence of evidence of commercial intercourse may be accounted for in one of two ways. At the time of Cartier's visit, the people of Hochelaga, owing to the hostility of the Hurons on the west, and of the Iroquois on the south, were very much isolated, and may for a long time have lost the intercourse with foreign nations which they had once enjoyed. Changes of this kind tending to isolate tribes, often reduce them to great scarcity or absolute want of foreign commodities, and may account for such remarkable differences as have been observed in this respect between the people of the older and more recent Palæolithic ages in Europe by Dupont and others, the oldest European race being evidently better supplied with foreign objects than that which succeeded it. Again, at the destruction of Hochelaga, its treasures may have been thoroughly plundered by the conquerors, a fate which has no doubt befallen many of the old haunts of primitive men in the Old World.

I fear such considerations are too often overlooked by observers who study such remains, and who may reach the most opposite results from the investigation of different localities occupied contemporaneously by tribes precisely in the same stage of civilization. Thus of three or four sites occupied by different sections of a tribe, simultaneously or at times not very remote from each other, one may have been destroyed and plundered by an enemy; another may have witnessed the hurried manufacture of a quantity of rough weapons for an emergency; another may have been only abandoned from slow decay. Each of these would be so dissimilar from the others that it might be regarded as having belonged to times remotely distant.

But a careless or too enthusiastic antiquary might commit still graver errors of this kind. A village like Stadacona or Hochelaga had its outlying stations. Its pottery would be made at some clay-bed, probably distant from the town. It must have had its mines or quarries of flint and other useful stones, perhaps far away within the confines of friendly tribes on the Ottawa. Its hunting and fishing parties had their places of resort, where in spring, autumn, or winter, they may have spent weeks together in the pursuit of particular animals requiring special kinds of tackle or weapons. Many tribes on the sea-coasts had their summer stations near to oyster-beds, on the produce of which, along with sea-birds and fish, they subsisted during a part of the year, though we know that in winter the same tribes dwelt inland, and hunted deer and other large animals. After the extinction of the tribe these different stations would present the most diverse appearances. One would yield a great collection of mis-shapen and half-made implements, difficult to understand, and rude and primitive in aspect. Another would apparently be the shelter or station of a tribe provided only with implements for hunting, and leaving behind it abundance of the bones of deer and other large game. Another would show a people living solely on fish, and with implements of entirely different form, and mostly of bone. Another would present gouges for tapping maple-trees, and kettles of pottery broken in the boiling of sugar. Another on the coast might show little beyond heaps of oyster-shells, and a few of the stones used in opening them for use. The main town would have the aspect, in its kitchen-middens and stores of pottery, of the settlement of a far more advanced people. I do not say that all of our modern archæologists have failed to appreciate the meaning of these differences, but it is impossible to overlook the fact that many of their researches have been vitiated to some extent by neglect of considerations so simple, that the most ordinary observers of the pre-historic monuments of America scarcely think them deserving of mention.* It must, however, be confessed that American writers also, taken by the infection wafted from the Eastern Continent, have sometimes allowed their fancy in such matters to get the better of their judgment.

In Scandinavia, Prof. Steenstrup deserves great credit for the constancy with which he has maintained the identity of age between the shell-heaps, or Kjökken möddings, of the coast, and the inland tumuli of the Stone age, though the one contain scarcely anything else than rude implements, useful in opening shells, and the others well-formed implements of polished stone. He has shown conclusively that even a few exceptional implements of the latter class found in the shell-heaps are enough to redeem them from the imputation of being the deposits of an earlier and ruder people.

Even among hunting tribes, culture and the arts are not wholly dormant. In the ancient Acadia † the immense abundance of deer, water-fowl, and fish, enabled the Micmac to live in plenty on the produce of fishery and the chase, each season having its appropriate animal, while the rocky character of many parts of the country was not favourable to agriculture.

* This has been markedly shown in the attempts which have been made to assign the deposits of different caves in the valley of the Vézère, in France, to widely separated ages, and in the foregone conclusion that the rude implements of the river gravels indicate a very barbarous people.
† Now Nova Scotia and New Brunswick.

Hence the Micmac was almost wholly a hunter, and the arts of life had reference mainly to the implements for the chase, and for fishing, or for the preparation of meat and skins; and as he must necessarily move from place to place according to the seasons for different kinds of fish and game, he dwelt in tents, or *wigwams* (his *oik* or *wick*), made of birch bark, and could easily pack his family and property in his bark canoe, or transport his whole house and furniture on the backs of his party, or on a tobogan drawn over the snow. Mambertou, a celebrated Micmac Sachem, and one of the first converts of the French missionaries, when taught the petition, "give us this day our daily bread," which, by the way, was practically a mistranslation on the part of the missionaries, objected, "Why is no mention made of our fish and venison?" and very properly, since these two in his former creed were gifts of the Great Spirit, and were to him much more than bread. Yet the Micmacs were not only adepts in the more delicate and difficult parts of the art of chipping flints, but as we have seen, were geographers and travellers of no mean intelligence, and made their name and power known and felt widely over the American coast, both to the north and to the south; and this, perhaps, just for the reason that they were hunters rather than farmers.

Another illustration may be taken from the now extinct Red Indians of Newfoundland. McCormick, in his expedition to discover this people, found that they had built across the country long fences of wood to arrest the migrations of the reindeer, and determine them to certain points where a deer battue on an extensive scale might give them a supply of food for months. One such erection he traced for forty miles across the country. It appeared to be intended to force the herds of deer towards a lake, and oblige them to take to the water, where they could be easily killed by the natives in their canoes. Similar plans were used by the Indians on the great Canadian lakes, though it does not appear that they executed so great public works to contribute to this end as the Red Indians. I may add, that in the Hudson's Bay districts, immense numbers of cariboo are killed in the spring when crossing certain rivers, where they are waylaid by the natives. Such facts serve to explain some of the deposits of bones of the reindeer found in France. When, by such means as those above mentioned, a tribe had succeeded in killing several hundreds or thousands of deer, there would not only be a great feast and much cracking of marrowbones, but a long time would be occupied in drying and preparing the flesh and skins, and working the antlers up into implements. In these processes multitudes of flint knives and scrapers would be used, and when the tribe left the place, a deposit of remains of the reindeer period would be left. This might recur year after year at the same place, till the tribe might be driven from the country by some enemy, or till the deer became exterminated, or were obliged to migrate in some other direction. At other seasons of the year the reindeer hunters might be living as fishermen on the coasts, or even as farmers in particular valleys. Even if the people in question were merely rude hunters, they could not have lived on reindeer all the year, and must have left elsewhere deposits indicating their mode of life at the seasons when deer could not be had.

I may connect these illustrations of perished arts with a reference to a now obsolete implement—the grooved hammer, noticed in the chapter on imple-

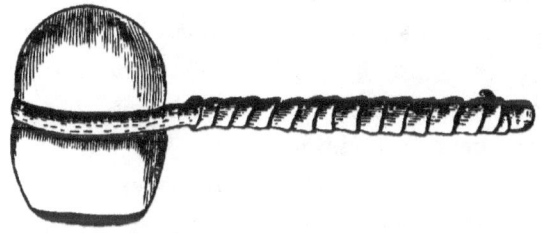

Fig. 32 — GROOVED HAMMER, WITH HANDLE OF WITHE AND THONG, AS USED BY ARICKAREE INDIANS FOR BREAKING MARROW-BONES OF BUFFALO. From a paper by Morgan, in the Report of the Regents of University of New York.

ments. Such hammers were the common tools of the ancient copper miners of Lake Superior. Evans informs us that they are found in ancient copper mines in Wales, also in Staffordshire and in the north of Ireland, and in Scandinavia, as well as in ancient mines in Spain and in Saxony. They also occur in the old Egyptian turquoise mines of Wady Meghara, in Arabia. In North America they are not limited to the mining districts. I figure a specimen with its handle of tough wood and raw hide

(Fig. 32), as now, or lately, used by the Arickarees, a people of the western prairies. Morgan, from whom the illustration is taken, states that it is used to drive stakes, and for cracking buffalo bones to extract the marrow. I have seen similar hammers brought by Dr. Bell, of the Canadian Survey, from the country of the Dakotas or Sioux and other western tribes, who constantly use them for breaking marrow-bones of the buffalo. Thus, the grooved hammer may be equally a relic of the civilized Egyptian or Alleghan miner, or of the rude hunter of the plains. But, even in the case of the latter, it may not be a token of absolute barbarism. The American hunter does not merely use it to break bones, that he may at once devour their marrow. On the contrary, he often breaks up the marrow-bones of his game, that he may refine and preserve the precious oil for future use, or may employ it as an ingredient of his carefully 'prepared pemmican, which is his dependence in his long journeys, and one of his most valuable sources of income. As he says, the agricultural white man may have plenty of bread, but he is "hungry for buffalo meat," while the Indian, with plenty of pemmican, may be "hungry for bread," or may be desirous of the goods of the European trader. What if some of the old cave men of Europe were not merely savage gorgers on flesh and marrow, but industrious preparers of pemmican, for future use or trade, and if the caves were their temporary workshops at the season of preparing this valuable product, and the implements therein their knives for cutting up the flesh, their hammers for breaking the bones, and their bodkins and needles for sewing up the skin bags in which it was finally put up for the markets of the Stone age. If we take this view, so accordant with American analogies, it will explain why the greater part of the chipped bones in many cave deposits bear no traces of cooking; and will relieve the cave men from the suspicion which has been cast upon their memory, that they habitually ate raw venison.

In a previous chapter I referred to the old quarries of flint in the Flint Ridge on the Ohio, and to the mines of the ancient Alleghans in the copper districts of Lake Superior. These mining arts, like the agriculture of many of the more settled tribes, have become lost to the modern Indian, and in the case of his flint mines, even to the white men who have succeeded him, and who, while they have at a comparatively recent time reopened his copper mines, have found that in all the more important of these they had been anticipated by the Indians. In like manner there are obsolete mines of the flint age in Europe. Evans describes those of "Grimes Graves" at Brandon, where 250 flint mines have been found. They are shafts sunk through chalk, in some cases to the depth of thirty-nine feet, to reach a layer of specially good flint. Galleries had been run out from them horizontally in this layer. The miners had worked with picks and chisels of deer's antlers and basalt; and the traces of their sagacious industry are now only traditional "graves" to the agricultural peasants who have succeeded them. Still more extensive ancient mines of the flint period exist in Belgium. That the men who made these excavations were industrious and ingenious we cannot doubt, yet their flint knives and arrows are to us the indices of a still ruder stage of humanity than that to which we would refer their antler-pointed picks and basalt chisels.

It should perhaps somewhat moderate our pride of higher civilization when we find that, with the exception of a few "flint Jacks," we have not only lost the art of fabricating the beautiful chipped implements of the flint age, but that throughout the east, and even among the peasantry of western Europe, they are, when found, regarded as the work of supernatural beings; and as "elfin bolts," and under other names, have strange talismanic virtues ascribed to them, at which their ancient makers would have smiled. Still these fancies have a venerable origin. Among the flint folk themselves a flint-headed arrow was a type of efficiency, as compared with one tipped with bone, horn, or hardened wood. Hence, in the traditions of the Micmacs, as collected by Mr. Rand, and in old Norse Sagas referred to by Nilsson, it is always a flint arrow that is used in slaying the giants and other monsters of their tales. Such stories would readily, after flint weapons fell into disuse, lead to the belief in their magic powers; nor is a great lapse of time necessary to effect such results. Already, in some districts of America, the Indian has so lost the tradition of the arts of his ancestors, that when questioned as to their implements, he says the Great Spirit alone knows by whom and for what they were made.*

Thus, even if we confine our attention to the one subject of lost arts, it can be shown that changes, many of them tending rather to degradation than to elevation, have taken place in America since its discovery, which are comparable in amount with those extending in Europe from the Palæolithic age to the present day. That they occurred as rapidly in Europe I do not affirm, yet there is no good reason to doubt that many of those diversities to which vast periods have been assigned, were either not successive, or required for their production times not much greater than that which has elapsed since the voyages of Columbus. It may be asked, If this is so, what reliance can be placed on archæological investigations? I answer:—Much, if observers will carefully study facts, and compare them with their modern analogues, and will avoid hasty generalisations, and the common error of making the facts conform to preconceived hypotheses. Geologists require also to learn that the methods which apply to the succession of formations, in which we have to do only with

* An interesting discussion of this subject will be found in Tylor's "Researches into the Early History of Mankind," Chapter VIII.

physical causes, and with the structures and instincts of irrational animals, will not suffice when we have to deal with the results of the many-sided intelligence of man, which, even in his most primitive and rudest states, gives him a god-like supremacy over many external conditions to which mere animals succumb, and vastly complicates all his relations with nature.

NOTE.—The facts in this chapter, and elsewhere, relating to the inhabitants of the Queen Charlotte Islands, are from unpublished notes of Dr. G. M. Dawson, F.G.S., who, while engaged in the geological survey of these islands, in 1878, made large collections of works of art, photographs of buildings, etc., and memoranda as to customs and superstitions. (1882) These observations have been published with illustrations in the Report of the Geological Survey of Canada for 1878–9, and afford many interesting facts as to the manners and arts of a very primitive and secluded people.

CHAPTER VII.

PHYSICAL CHARACTERISTICS OF PRE-HISTORIC MEN.

THE part of our subject on which we now enter may well be compared to the prospect presented to the prophet Ezekiel when he was introduced to a valley filled with bones, and observed that they were " very dry." Yet if the reader will bear with a little disquisition on the dry bones of pre-historic humanity, we may promise him that in the end we shall find that these bones will come together and be clothed with flesh, and that their owners will fall into the ranks of the great army of mankind as known to us in our more modern times.

The attempts which have been made to draw such lines of distinction as would serve for race characters between the different varieties of man have necessarily been only partially successful, since these race characters shade into each other, and this in several directions, depending on the particular lines of comparison followed. More particularly, when we have merely bones to rely on, classification becomes less satisfactory; and though it is easy to divide any number of skulls into dolichocephalous, or long-headed, and brachycephalous, or short-headed, and these again into those that are orthognathous or prognathous, that is, with more or less prominent jaws and retreating forehead, yet these pass into each other by imperceptible gradations, and the differences are not altogether coincident with those of race as established on other grounds.

I have long thought that this matter of comparison of skulls and skeletons requires to be placed on a somewhat different basis, which is well indicated in the note furnished by Professor Huxley to Sir Charles Lyell in connection with the pre-historic skulls of the Belgian and Neanderthal caves. He contents himself with a broad distinction between skulls of the low and high types; that is, of the ruder and the more civilized nations, and informs us that even in rude and homogeneous races like the Australians there is great cranial variety; while it is well known that any skull, ancient or modern, except those that have been artificially flattened, may find its counterpart in a large collection of European skulls.

The practical point, therefore, is to ascertain what cranial characters are necessarily or generally connected with those other characters which we perceive in different races, and so to apply the whole as to obtain definite information regarding the state of civilization and general habits of life which they indicate. From this point of view the mere length or shortness of skulls does not seem a very important feature, except locally. There are rude and uncivilized races with both forms of cranium. The Laps are a rude people, somewhat comparable with the

Greenlanders, and, like them, of small stature, but they have short orthognathous heads, while those of the Greenlanders are dolichocephalic and prognathous. Of the most ancient skulls taken from caverns, as we shall see, some are long-headed, others very short. Those of the more northern American Indians tend to a lengthened form, but in the south they become short and broad. Of modern civilized races, the Germanic race seems to have shorter and more broadly oval heads than the English and Swedish, and these than the purely Celtic peoples. The greater or less prominence of the jaws or recession of the forehead is, on the other hand, more an indication of lowness of culture and civilization than of difference of race. In civilized countries the ruder peasantry present most of this prognathous character, and it belongs to nearly all the more barbarous nations. A similar statement may be made respecting breadth and prominence of the cheek bones and of the angles of the lower jaw, though these probably have reference rather to the constant use of coarse and tough food than to want of mental culture. Small capacity of the brain-case is also a mark of an inferior race, though some highly intelligent people have small heads. On the whole, the smaller development of the anterior and upper regions of the cranium, and the greater proportionate development of the face and jaws, are marks of the lower races. Habits of life may have mechanical connections with skull forms. Independently of the attempts made by some tribes to modify the skull artificially, modes of carrying infants may have an effect. Wilson has pointed this out in the case of the connection of the American cradle-board with a flat form of occiput. So there is some reason to believe that severe work on the part of the mother tends to produce long heads in the children, and that less constant work, as well as nomadic habits, tends to shortness of head.

Let us sum up these remarks in a few general statements, and then proceed to inquire how they apply to the American Indians and to pre-historic men in Europe. First, then, forms of skulls are often merely individual, and much variety thus exists in the skulls of one and the same race. Secondly, when a sufficient number of skulls are compared, certain general characters for a race, at any given time of its history, can be obtained. Thirdly, the cranial characters of races being dependent on external circumstances and on culture, may vary in the lapse of ages. Fourthly, cranial characters are thus of even more importance in determining the low or elevated condition of a people than the race from which they have been derived. Fifthly, the small development of the frontal and superior regions of the skull, and the large size of the jaws and facial bones, are marks of low type. Sixthly, long heads with low frontal region generally belong to the lowest race; short and broad heads often to an intermediate stage of culture; and regularly oval heads to the highest type.

If we connect these different forms of skull

PHYSICAL CHARACTERISTICS OF PRE-HISTORIC MEN. 181

with what is known of the functions of the brain, we should infer that a large brain would be correlated with great muscular energy; and since experiment shows that the lateral portions of the cerebral hemispheres are those connected with motor nerves influencing the limbs, we might infer that heads relatively broad would indicate active and powerful limbs. Again, since it is probable that the frontal part of the cerebrum is more especially employed in correlating the impressions of the senses with the actions, heads long and prominent in front should be connected with general intelligence. Lastly, as the posterior part of the brain seems to minister more largely to the emotional nature, length posteriorly would indicate active passions and emotions. These criteria, if applied to pre-historic skulls, would indicate great cerebral powers of all kinds in the earliest European race, inferior powers, but relatively greater bodily activity, in the second race. The artificial flattening of the head, if it had any effect on the functions of the brain, would tend to subdue speculative and emotional energy, and to develop activity of limb. The distortion of the skull is said not to diminish the intelligence; but Paul Kane* remarks that the infants whose heads are subjected to pressure never cry or moan, and seem to be more dull and torpid than usual, which would agree with what is known of the functions of the front and back regions of the head, as above stated. Possibly the accidental

* Quoted by Wilson in "Pre-historic Man."

discovery of facts of this kind may have led to the practice.

Dr. Wilson, of Toronto, has devoted much study to American skulls, and the American race is to form our term of comparison in this chapter. We may begin therefore with his description of the typical head of Eastern America. It is short and broad, or somewhat elongated, with largely developed maxillaries and zygomata, prominent superciliary ridges, a comparitively narrow and poorly developed frontal region, and flattened or truncated occiput, great facial breadth, both at the cheek-bones and in the square massive lower law, and prominence in the nasal bones. To this we may add as a consequence of the widening of the face, a somewhat elongated or less round form of the orbits, and that in many tribes the occiput is by no means flattened. According to the same careful observer, the Esquimaux of North America have long heads, resembling in form those of the Tschuktchi of North Asia, and also those of the northern tribes of Indians, differing, however, from the proper Indian type in smaller nasal bones and more projecting jaws. In regard to mere length of head, the American Indians proper divide themselves into two groups: the Algonquin, Iroquois, and Lenapé races, extending across the northern and eastern regions, being long-headed; and the southern and south-western races, including the mound-builders, being short-headed. The two types graduate into each other, and among long-headed tribes occasional short heads occur; while on the other hand, short-headed races present occasional long-headed specimens. These varieties sometimes depend on the presence of captives, or on conquests and intermixture of tribes, but they show at least a primitive identity with modifications. Further, some of the short heads and flat occiputs seem to have been at least aggravated by the use of the cradle-board to which the "papoose" is strapped in infancy among all the migratory tribes. Among some western tribes, as well as among some now extinct peoples of the south, the forehead was flattened by pressure in infancy, a practice which obtained also among some Turanian tribes of the Old World. It would also seem that a remarkably short form of head was characteristic of the ancient Alleghan race, and that some of their heads were high in front, while others had remarkably retreating foreheads.* It is curious to notice this indication of low intellectual capacity in this old semi-civilized race; but if it really indicates the position of these people, it may readily be accounted for. Living undisturbed for ages in a rich alluvial region, with stationary and fixed institutions, and with the energies of the individual cramped by a system of tribal communism, their intellectual powers may well have been reduced to a lower point than that

* On the monuments of Central America we find representations of men with high, almost conical, heads. These resemble in outline the form at present produced among some tribes on the coast of British Columbia by artificial pressure, and were probably of this character; as were also the elongated Peruvian skulls, and perhaps also those of the old Alleghans.

of the rude hunter tribes, except in the case of those men of higher caste who had to manage public affairs. Men may become degraded by too great peace and prosperity, along with unvarying routine, quite as much as by the exigencies and hardships of savage life. These mound-builders, with their peculiar, yet American heads, are perhaps the oldest men of the Western Continent known to us, if we except some stray bones found under circumstances which have been supposed to indicate a still greater antiquity. One of the most remarkable of these, the " Calaveras" skull from California, is stated by Professor Wyman to be of somewhat larger capacity than those of modern Indians of that country, but of the same type. We thus find in America a characteristic type of head, but under this a great many varieties of long and short, straight and prognathous, natural and distorted forms; and this American type of skull on the whole resembles that known as Turanian in the Old World. Further, the possessors of these American heads were found in the most varied stages of civilization and barbarism; though, as stated in a previous chapter, the more ancient and civilized peoples had more delicate and refined forms of face and head than the ruder tribes.

Nothing is more distinct in the intimations, both of tradition and of monuments, than the existence in the Old World in pre-historic times of two types of men representing respectively the American Indian and the Esquimaux—the one of large stature and powerful frame, the other comparatively small and feeble. Nilsson well argues that all the northern tales of giants, dwarfs, and elves, arise from this source, and he refers, as parallel cases, to the terror of the Israelites at the gigantic size of the Anakim, and of the Romans when informed of the bulk and strength of the Germans. In the oldest historic times of Scandinavia and of Britain of which we have any certain information, there seem to have been contemporary races of small and large men, and the latter seem to have been encroaching on the former. In the various mixtures and movements which have taken place, races of these different types sometimes remain distinct and sometimes have been blended. In Scandinavia, the Laps are still a very distinct people from the Swedes, just as the Esquimaux are distinct from the eastern American Indians; but in Scotland the little men of the north and the gigantic men of the west speak one language, and are regarded as equally Celts, and in western America the Esquimaux and Indians graduate into each other.

There is nothing to prevent our believing that races thus distinct in stature, and to some extent in form of head, may be of common origin. Unfavourable circumstances and deficient food may depauperate races of men, and there is no reason to think that the stunted Fuegian is of different race from the gigantic Patagonian, or the feeble Hare Indian of the north from his better-developed brethren who feed not on hares but on deer. Still, such differences mark at least long continuance of the different modes of life, and they necessarily lead to hostility of races, one of which prides itself on strength and power, the other on *finesse* and cunning.

It was at one time difficult to say whether in America and Europe the large or the small races were the earlier, or whether there is any difference in this. It used to be maintained that in Europe generally, as the Scandinavian antiquaries still believe with reference to that country, the smaller short-headed race was the earlier; but recent discoveries in the French caves and rock shelters seem to negative this, and to show that a race of great stature and large cranial development had the precedence. So while in historic periods the Indians of eastern America have been destructive to the Esquimaux, and have been at least restricting their range, there seems no certain evidence that, on the western coast, where the two races graduate into each other, they may not have been contemporaries from the first, and some have regarded the Esquimaux as the later of the two. In any case, the graduation of the one race into the other in the west, while they are markedly distinct on their confines in the east, is an important fact. Just as, even in antediluvian times, there were Nephelim, or men of strength and of violence as distinguished from the rest of the world, and as in ancient Palestine there were certain races noted for their stature, and as the same differences obtain at the present day, so they may have always existed both in Europe and America, and may have fluctuated in their boundaries and extent. Changes in physical character may also have occurred,—as feeble races driven to the more bleak and unproductive districts became for that reason more feeble, or as the less muscular races succeeded by superior energy and sagacity in overcoming and reducing to subjection the stronger, as the Hebrews did in Syria, the Romans in Germany, and the Normans in England. Further, all such movements and conquests lead to intermixtures of these divers races.

In any case we have these parallel facts, that while the Esquimaux are a small race corresponding to the Laps, and to the extinct elves and dwarfs of other parts of Europe, the American Indians are men of large stature and of great muscular development, corresponding in this to the pre-historic men of Mentone and of the Perigord caves in Europe. This stature, and the great development of muscular processes in the bones of the limbs, are consequences of abundant food and a temperate climate, and of roving habits in a wild country, and without beasts of burden. Cartier mentions on several occasions the stature of the Indians as compared with his Breton sailors; and in his visit to Hochelaga, when his men were tired with a long walk, the savages took them up like children and carried them on their shoulders. This accords perfectly with the great power of limb of the American Indian, and with his known capability of carrying immense burdens over portages. The strongly carinate thigh-bone, the flattened tibia, and large fibula, observed in the oldest pre-historic skeletons of Europe, show that they belonged to men possessing similar power.

The beautiful work of Lartet and Christy has vividly portrayed to us the antiquities of the limestone plateau of the Dordogne—the ancient Aquitania—remains which recall to us a population of Horites, or cave-dwellers, of a time anterior to the dawn of history in France, living much like the modern hunter-tribes of America, and, as already stated, possibly contemporary, in their early history at least, with the mammoth and its extinct companions of the later Post-pliocene plains and forests. We have already noticed the arts and implements of these people; but what manner of people were they in themselves? The answer is given by the skeletons found in the cave of Cro-magnon. This is a shelter or hollow under an overhanging ledge of limestone, and excavated originally by the action of the weather on a softer bed. It fronts the south-west and the little river Vézère; and having originally been about eight feet high and nearly twenty deep, must have formed a cosey shelter from rain, or cold, or summer sun, and with a pleasant outlook from its front. All rude races have much sagacity in making selections of this sort. Being nearly fifty feet wide, it was capacious enough to accommodate several families, and when in use it no doubt had trees or shrubs in front, and may have been further completed by stones, poles, or bark placed across the opening. It seems, however, in the first instance to have been used only at intervals, and to have been left vacant for considerable portions of time. Perhaps it was visited only by hunting or war parties. But subsequently it was permanently occupied, and this for so long a time that in some places a foot and a half of ashes and carbonaceous matter with bones, implements, etc., was accumulated. By this time the height of the cavern had been much diminished, and instead of clearing it out for future use, it was made a place of burial in which four or five individuals were interred. Of these, two were men, one of great age, the other probably in the prime of life. A third was a woman of about thirty or forty years of age. The other remains were too fragmentary to give very certain results.

These bones, with others to be mentioned in connection with them, unquestionably belong to the oldest human inhabitants known in western Europe. They have been most carefully examined by several competent anatomists and archæologists, and the results have been published with excellent figures in the "Reliquiæ Aquitanicæ." They are, therefore, of the utmost interest for our present purpose, and I shall try so to divest the descriptions of anatomical details, as to give a clear notion of their character. The "Old Man of Cro-magnon" was of great stature, being nearly six feet high. More than this, his bones show that he was of the strongest and most athletic muscular development—a Samson in strength; and the bones of the limbs have the peculiar form which is characteristic of athletic men habituated to rough walking, climbing, and running : for this is, I believe, the real meaning of the enormous strength of the thigh-bone, and the flattened condition of the leg in this and other old skeletons. It occurs to some extent, though much less than in this old man, in American skeletons. His skull presents all the characters of advanced age, though the teeth had been worn down to the sockets without being lost, which again is the character of some, though not of all, aged Indian skulls. The skull proper, or brain-case, is very long, more so than in ordinary modern skulls, and this length is accompanied with a great breadth, so that the brain was of greater size than in average modern men, and the frontal region was largely and well developed. In this respect this most ancient skull fails utterly to vindicate the expectations of those who would regard pre-historic men as approaching to the apes. It is at the opposite extreme. The face, however, presented very peculiar characters. It was extremely broad, with projecting cheek-bones and heavy jaw, in this resembling the coarse types of the American face; and the eye-orbits were square, and elongated laterally. The nose was large and prominent, and the jaws projected somewhat forward. This man, therefore, had, as to his features, some resemblance to the harsher type of American physiognomy, with overhanging brows, small and transverse eyes, high cheek-bones, and coarse mouth. He had not lived to so great an age without some rubs, for his thigh-bone showed a depression which must have resulted from a severe wound, perhaps from the horn of some wild animal, or the spear of an enemy.

The woman presented similar characters of stature and cranial form, modified by her sex, and must in form and visage have been a veritable squaw, who, if her hair and complexion were suitable, would have passed at once for an Indian woman, but one of unusual size and development. Her head bears sad testimony to the violence of her age and people. She died from the effects of a blow from a stone-headed pogamogon or spear, which has penetrated the right side of the forehead with so clean a fracture as to indicate the extreme rapidity and force of its blow. It is inferred from the condition of the edges of this wound that she may have survived its infliction for two weeks or more. If, as is most likely, the wound was received in some sudden attack by a hostile tribe, they must have been driven off or have retired, leaving the wounded woman in the hands of her friends to be tended for a time, and then buried, either with other members of her family or with others who had perished in the same skirmish. Unless the wound was inflicted in sleep, during a night attack, she must have fallen, not in flight, but with her face to the foe, perhaps aiding the resistance of her friends, or shielding her little ones from destruction. With the people of Cro-magnon, as with the American Indians, the care of the wounded was probably a sacred duty, not to be neglected without incurring the greatest disgrace, and the vengeance of the guardian spirits of the sufferers.*

* Prof. Boyd Dawkins, in "Cave Hunting," has thrown some doubts on the antiquity of the skeletons of this type. A

The skulls of these people have been compared to those of the modern Esthonians or Lithuanians, but on the authority of M. Quatrefages, it is stated that while this applies to the probably later race of small men found in some of the Belgian caves, it does not apply so well to the people of Cro-magnon. Are, then, these people the types of any ancient, or of the most ancient, European race? We have already noticed the remarkable skeleton of Mentone, in the south of France, found under circumstances equally suggestive of great antiquity. Dr. Rivière, in a memoir on this skeleton, illustrated by two beautiful photographs, shows that the characters of the skull and of the bones of the limbs are precisely similar to those of the Cro-magnon skeleton, indicating a perfect identity of race, while the objects found with the skeleton are identical in character.

The ornaments of Cro-magnon were perforated shells from the Atlantic, and pieces of ivory. Those at Mentone were perforated Neritinæ from the Mediterranean, and canine teeth of the deer. In both cases there was evidence that these ancient people painted themselves with red oxide of iron; and as if to com-

comparison, however, of all the cases of their discovery in France and Belgium fully vindicates the opinions entertained on this point by Continental geologists; and some of the more recent discoveries in the French caves, and especially in that of Laugerie Basse, where traces of the mammoth also occur, place this beyond doubt. The comparison by Dawkins of these people with the Esquimaux applies to some of their implements and weapons, but not to their physical characteristics.

plete the similarity, the Mentone man had an old healed-up fracture of the radius of the left arm, the effect of a violent blow or of a fall. Skulls found at Clichy and Grenelle in 1868 and 1869 are described by Professor Broca and Mr. Fleurens as of the same general type, and the remains found at Gibraltar and in the cave of Paviland, in England, seem also to have belonged to the same race. The celebrated Engis skull, believed to have belonged to a contemporary of the mammoth, is also of the same type, though less massive than that of Cro-magnon; and, lastly, even the somewhat degraded Neanderthal skull, found in a cave near Dusseldorf, though, like that of Clichy, inferior in frontal development, is referable to the same peculiar long-headed style of man, in so far as can be judged from the portion that remains. (See Fig. 33.)

Let it be observed, then, that these skulls are probably the oldest known in the world, and they are all referable to one race of men; and let us ask what they tell as to the position and character of Palæolithic man. The testimony is here fortunately well-nigh unanimous. Huxley, who well compares some of the peculiar features of these ancient skulls and skeletons to those of Australians and other rude tribes, and of the ancient Danes of Borreby, a people not improbably allied to the Esthonians and Fins, remarks that the manner in which the individual heads of the most homogeneous rude races differ from each other "in the same characters, though perhaps not to the same extent with the Engis and Neanderthal

o

skulls, seem to me to prohibit any cautious reasoner from affirming the latter to have necessarily been of distinct races." My own experience in American skulls, and the still larger experience of Dr. Wilson, fully confirm the wisdom of this caution. The figures given in this chapter will show this in the case of two

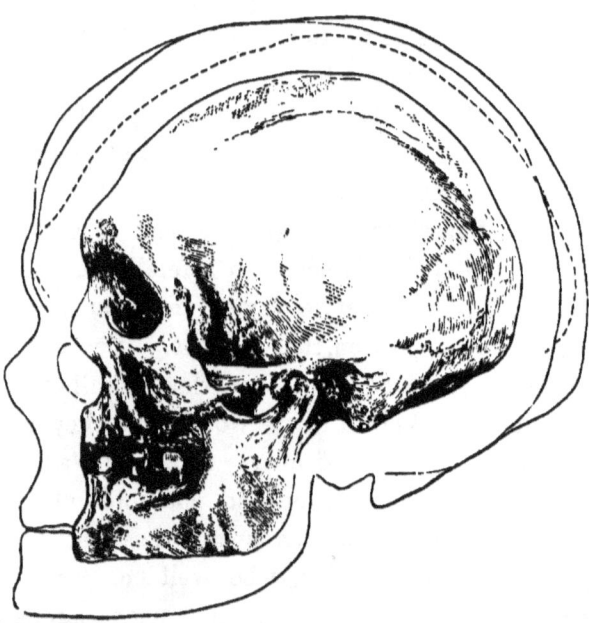

Fig. 33.—OUTLINES OF THREE PRE-HISTORIC EUROPEAN SKULLS COMPARED WITH ONE FROM HOCHELAGA. Outer outline, Cro-magnon skull; second outline, Engis skull; third outline (dotted), Neanderthal skull; inner figure, Hochelagan skull on a smaller scale.

skulls, both from the ancient cemetery of Hochelaga. He adds:—"Finally, the comparatively large cranial capacity of the Neanderthal skull, overlaid though it may be by pithecoid bony walls, and the completely

PHYSICAL CHARACTERISTICS OF PRE-HISTORIC MEN. 195

human proportions of the accompanying limb-bones, together with the very fair development of the Engis skull, clearly indicate that the first traces of the primordial stock, whence man has been derived, need no

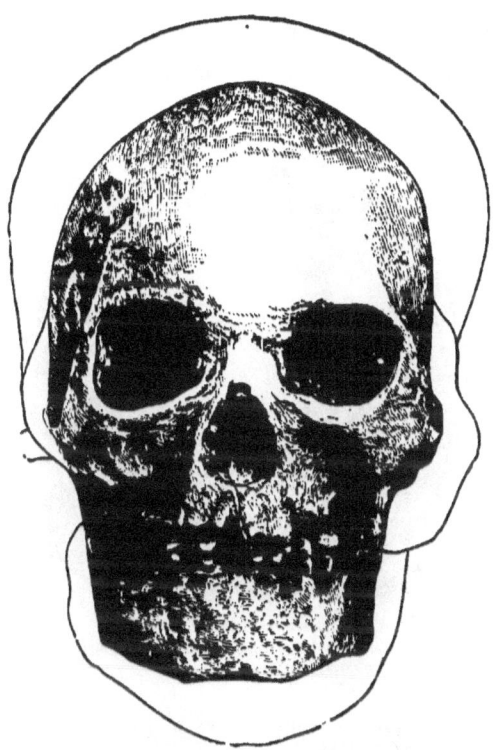

Fig. 34.—OUTLINE OF A CRO-MAGNON SKULL AS SEEN IN FRONT, AND HOCHE-LAGAN SKULL ON SMALLER SCALE. The resemblance of the two skulls would appear greater but that their attitude is not precisely the same.

longer be sought by those who entertain any form of the doctrine of progressive development, in the newest tertiaries, but that they may be looked for in an epoch more distant from that of the *Elephas primigenius*, than that is from us." If he had possessed the Cro-magnon and Mentone skulls at the time when this was written, he might well have said immeasurably distant from the time of the *Elephas primigenius*. Professor Broca, who seems by no means disinclined to favour a simian origin for men, has the following

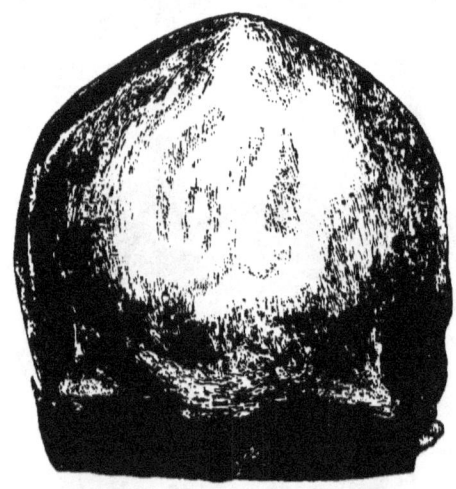

Fig. 35.—FRONT VIEW OF ANOTHER HOCHELAGAN SKULL OF A SIMILAR TYPE BUT OF HIGHER CRANIAL DEVELOPMENT, CLOSELY RESEMBLING THE MENTONE SKULL AS PHOTOGRAPHED BY DR. RIVIERE.

general conclusions which refer to the Cro-magnon skulls :—" The great volume of the brain, the development of the frontal region, the fine elliptical profile of the anterior portion of the skull, and the orthognathous form of the upper facial region, are incontestably evidences of superiority which are met with usually only in the civilized races. On the other hand,

PHYSICAL CHARACTERISTICS OF PRE-HISTORIC MEN. 197

the great breadth of face, the alveolar prognathism, the enormous development of the ascending ramus of the lower jaw, the extent and roughness of the muscular insertions, especially of the masticatory muscles, give rise to the idea of a violent and brutal race."

He adds that this apparent antithesis, seen also in the limbs, as well as the skull, accords with the evidence furnished by the associated weapons and

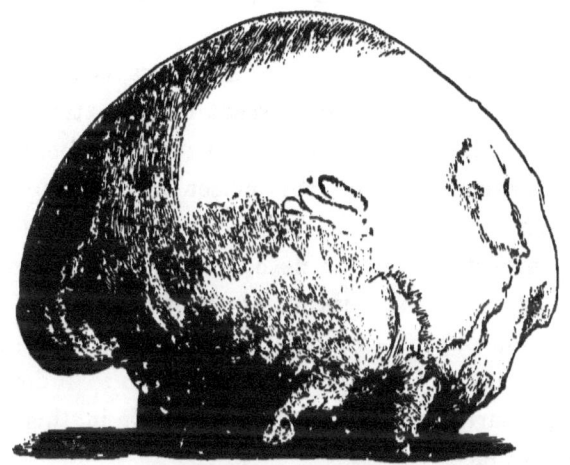

PROFILE VIEW OF SAME SKULL.
Both the Hochelagan skulls are from photographs by Henderson, of Montreal.

implements of a rude hunter life, and at the same time of no mean degree of taste and skill in carving and other arts. He might have added that this is precisely the antithesis seen in the American tribes, among whom art and taste of various kinds, and much that is high and spiritual even in thought, co-existed with barbarous modes of life and intense ferocity and cruelty. The god and the demon were combined in these races, but there was nothing of the mere brute.

Rivière remarks, with expression of surprise, the same contradictory points in the Mentone skeleton. Its grand development of brain-case, and high facial angle, even higher apparently than in most of these ancient skulls, combined with other characters which indicate a low type and barbarous modes of life.

Another point which strikes us in reading the descriptions, and which deserves the attention of those who have access to the skeletons, is the indication which they seem to present of an extreme longevity. The massive proportions of the body, the great development of the muscular processes, the extreme wearing of the teeth, among a people who predominantly lived on flesh, and not on grain, the obliteration of the sutures of the skull, along with indications of slow ossification of the ends of the long bones, point in this direction, and seem to indicate a slow maturity and great length of life in this most primitive race.

The picture would be incomplete did we not add that in France and Belgium, in the immediately succeeding or Reindeer age, these gigantic and magnificent men seem to have been superseded by a feebler race of smaller stature and with shorter heads; so that we have, even in these oldest days, the same contrasts, already so often referred to as occurring in the races of the north of Europe and the north of America in historical times.

It is further significant that there are some indications to show that the larger and nobler race was that which inhabited Europe at the time of its greatest elevation above the sea and greatest horizontal extent, and when its fauna included many large quadrupeds now extinct. This race of giants was thus in the possession of a greater continental area than that now existing, and had to contend with gigantic brute rivals for the possession of the world. It is also not improbable that this early race became extinct in Europe in consequence of the physical changes which occurred in connection with the subsidence which reduced the land to its present limits, and that the dwarfish race which succeeded came in as the appropriate accompaniment of a diminished land surface and a less genial climate in the early Modern period. Both of these races are properly Palæolithic, and are supposed to antedate the period of polished stone; but this may, to a great extent, be a prejudice of collectors, who have arrived at a foregone conclusion as to the distinctness of these periods: its validity will be discussed in our next chapter. Judging from the great cranial capacity of the older race, and the small number of their skeletons found, it would be fair to suppose that they represent rude outlying tribes belonging to races which elsewhere had attained to greater numbers and culture.

Lastly, both of these old European races were Turanian, Mongolian, or American, in their head-forms and features, as well as in their habits, implements, and arts. To illustrate this, in so far as the older of the two races is concerned, I have figured from photographs two Hochelagan skulls of the extreme types found there, and have placed in connection with one of them tracings in outline of the forms of some of the oldest European crania above referred to (Figs. 33–35). One may be fairly compared in its characters with the Mentone skull, and the other with those of Cro-magnon, Engis, and Neanderthal; and so like are these and Huron, Iroquois, and other northern American skulls to these ancient European relics and others of their type, that it would be difficult to affirm that they might not have belonged to near relatives. On the other hand, the smaller and shorter heads of the race of the Reindeer age in Europe may be compared with the Laps, and with some of the more delicately formed Algonquin and Chippewyan skulls in America. If, therefore, the reader desires to realize the probable aspect of the men of Cro-magnon, of Mentone, or of Engis, I may refer him to modern American heads. So permanent is this great Turanian race, out of which all the other races now extant seem to have been developed in the milder and more hospitable regions of the Old World, while in northern Asia and in America it has retained to this day its primitive characters.

The reader, reflecting on what he has learned from history, may be disposed here to ask: Must we suppose Adam to have been one of these Turanian men, like the old man of Cro-magnon? In answer

I would say that there is no good reason to regard the first man as having resembled a Greek Apollo or an Adonis. He was probably of sterner and more muscular mould. But the gigantic Palæolithic men of the European caves are more probably representatives of that fearful and powerful race who filled the antediluvian world with violence, and who re-appear in post-diluvian times as the Anakim and traditional giants, who constitute a feature in the early history of so many countries. Perhaps nothing is more curious in the revelations as to the most ancient cave-men, than that they confirm the old belief that there were "giants in those days."

And now let us pause for a moment to picture these so-called Palæolithic men. What could the old man of Cro-magnon have told us, had we been able to sit by his hearth, and listen understandingly to his speech, which, if we may judge from the form of his palate bones, must have resembled more that of the Americans or Mongolians than of any modern European people? He had, no doubt, travelled far, for to his stalwart limbs a long journey through forests and over plains and mountains would be a mere pastime. He may have bestridden the wild horse which seems to have abounded at the time in France, and he may have launched his canoe on the waters of the Atlantic. His experience and memory might extend back a century or more, and his traditional lore might even reach to the times of the first mother of our race. Did he live in that wide Post-pliocene continent which extended westward through Ireland? Did he know and had he visited the nations that lived in the valley of the great Gihon, which ran down the Mediterranean valley, or that nameless river which flowed where the German Ocean now lies. Had he visited or seen from afar the great island Atlantis, whose inhabitants could almost see in the sunset sky the islands of the blest? Or did he live at a later time, after the Post-pliocene subsidence, and when the land had assumed its present form? In that case he could have told us of the great deluge, of the huge animals of the antediluvian world, known to him only by tradition, and of the diminished strength and longevity of men in his comparatively modern days. We can but conjecture all this. But mute though they may be as to the details of their lives, the man of Cro-magnon and his contemporaries are eloquent of one great truth, in which they coincide with the Americans and with the primitive men of all the early ages. They tell us that primitive man had the same high cerebral organization which he possesses now, and we may infer the same intellectual and moral nature, fitting him for communion with God and headship over the lower world. They indicate also, like the mound-builders who preceded the North American Indian, that man's earlier state was the best, that he had been a good and noble creature before he became a savage. It is not conceivable that their high development of brain and mind could have spontaneously engrafted itself on a mere brutal and savage life. These gifts must be remnants of a noble organisation degraded by moral evil. They thus justify the tradition of a golden and Edenic age, and mutely protest against the philosophy of progressive development as applied to man, while they bear witness to the identity in all important characters of the oldest pre-historic men, with that variety of our species which is at the present day at once the most widely extended, and the most primitive in its manner and usages, the great Turanian or Tartar race of Northern Asia and America.

We have seen, or shall see in subsequent chapters, that this race underlies in Europe and Asia, and probably in Africa as well as in America, the older historic peoples, and that it presents throughout an animistic religion, a great and marked devotion to the doctrine of immortality in connection with certain forms of sepulture, the classificatory system of relationships, a permanent and unchanging temperament, and great constructive and artistic tendencies. In this division of the human family also, we find—as in the Peruvians, the Natchez, and the Flatheads in America, and in the ancient Macrocephali and more modern tribes in Asia—the singular practice of artificially distorting the head. In other words, we find in that post-diluvian, or historic race, which most nearly coincides with the ante-diluvian or palæocosmic type of man, and which is the most widely diffused of all, characteristics which indicate its place as the main stem of humanity in historic times, from which the Semitic and Aryan civilizations budded out, and to which can be traced back the rudiments of their arts, their science, their literature, and not a little of their religion. Here, again, America has preserved the oldest and most unchanged type of humanity, even if in many cases much degraded.

Note.—As confirmatory of some of the views stated in this chapter, I have much pleasure in quoting the following, from the address of Dr. Tylor, F.R.S., at the Meeting of the British Association in 1879:—"There appears no particular reason to think that the relics from the drift-beds or bone-caves represent man as he first appeared on the earth. The contents of the caves especially bear witness to a state of savage art, in some respects fairly high, and which may possibly have somewhat fallen off from an ancestral state in a more favourable climate. Indeed, the savage condition generally, though rude and more or less representing early stages of culture, never looks absolutely primitive, just as no savage language ever has the appearance of being a primitive language. What the appearance and state of our really primæval ancestors may have been seems too speculative a question, until there shall be more signs of agreement between the anthropologists, who work by comparison of actual races of man toward a hypothetical common stock, and the zoologists, who approach the problem through the species adjoining the human." Other points in this address, and in recent papers by Dawkins and others, received when these pages were in type, may be noticed in an appendix.

CHAPTER VIII.

ANTIQUITY OF MAN.

It is difficult to arrive at any conclusion as to the duration of the human period in America. If we were to accept without question the statements which have been made as to the finding of flint implements and a human skull in the ancient gold gravels of California, we might carry back the human occupancy of America even into the Pliocene age, or further than any authentic remains have yet carried it in Europe. But these reports so require confirmation that we cannot rest on them. The same remark may be made with regard to the discovery of implements and human bones in those more modern estuarine and lacustrine deposits in which the bones of the mastodon are entombed, though a sufficient number of probable indications appear to make it not unlikely that man had reached America before the disappearance of the mastodon. If so, there was an ancient American population little known to us, and coeval with the oldest cave-men of Europe, and who possibly, like these old cave-men, may have been swept away before the advent of the more modern races. It is remarkable, however, that some of the indications relied on as evidence of this early race, would go to show a degree of culture equal to that of the more civilized modern tribes. Of this kind are the beautiful polished plummet or ornament, and polished spear heads, found in the California auriferous gravel at great depths, and the baskets and pottery described by Hilgard and Fontaine from the salt-beds of Petite Anse. To the same effect is the fact stated by Professor Wyman, that the Calaveras skull from the gravels of California is of the ordinary American type, and rather larger in cranial capacity than those of the modern Indians of the same region. Still, the probability is that all these remains are of somewhat modern date.* This applies, for example, to the discovery in California of polished implements and stone mortars in the auriferous gravels, which also contain bones of the mastodon. Some of these objects are stated to have been found at depths exceeding 300 feet in gravel, capped by beds of lava and tufa, and attributed to the Pliocene age. They would go to prove that the "polished stone age" had been established in California at that somewhat early Tertiary period. Unfortunately, however, they occur in deposits known to have been worked by the Mexicans for gold, and in which deep shafts of ancient date have been found, and as the mortars and other objects are those likely to have been used in the search for gold, this would seem to afford the most probable explanation of their presence. In the more northern part of America no remains what-

* Whitney's Memoir (1879) must be noticed in an appendix.

ever have been found to connect man with any of those terraces and raised beaches which mark the elevation of the land out of the glacial seas.

The actual American race can make no monumental pretensions to a great antiquity, for its oldest remains, those of the ancient Alleghan nations, situated as they are on the modern alluvium of the western rivers, claim no greater antiquity than the similar mounds on the banks of the Tigris, and possibly are much less ancient. The only actual evidence of great age known in connection with them—that afforded by the growth of forest trees—would not carry them back farther than the earlier centuries of our era, and the decayed condition of the bones in the burial mounds is well known to be a criterion of very uncertain value. The languages, customs, and religions of the Americans, as well as their physical characters, are allied to those of Post-diluvian nations of the Old World, and though they indicate migrations belonging to an early part of the historical period, while the Turanian race was still dominant, go no farther back than this. The American traditions of the Atlantis, of the Deluge, and of the huge extinct quadrupeds, can scarcely be held as proving anything more than a common inheritance. Thus our primitive American men seem to fall short in interest of those pre-historic races in Europe with which we have been comparing them, and which are by many believed to reach backward to a time enormously exceeding that to which any history, sacred or secular, extends. The real interest of the

American peoples depends, as we have already seen, on their reproducing to us the conditions of these ancient men, and showing us that under the eyes of Europeans the same people, with the same usages, have been living in America, and are still living in some remote parts up to our own time. The American tribes thus bring near to us the living picture of the almost forgotten men of the pre-historic time of the Old World, while their rapid disappearance in the presence of European colonisation shows how those rude peoples of the Old World may also have perished. But may they not aid also in settling some of the still disputed questions respecting the antiquity of pre-historic man in Europe? This will be best ascertained by summing up the evidence for that antiquity, and, as we proceed, noting the points where American facts may aid us.

We have already, in the introductory chapter, inquired as to the import and validity of the ages of Iron, Bronze, and Stone, now so strenuously insisted on by European archæologists. At the time of the discovery of America it was the age of Bronze and Gold in Peru, of Copper in Mexico and the valley of the Mississippi, and of Stone and Bone everywhere else. Possibly even then the Greenlanders may have had some weapons of native iron, and some few iron and steel implements may have found their way to the west coast by means of wrecked Japanese junks. In less than four centuries the Iron age had established itself in all except a few remote localities.

The progress in the Old World was slower, and has been already noticed. If we rely on the narrative in Genesis, it was but the seventh generation from Adam when the greatest of all discoveries in the mechanical arts was made, and an artificer arose in copper and iron. At the date of the Exodus iron was widely used; and though bronze was still more abundant and cheaper, the Phœnicians, and the tribes of Canaanites trading with them, had enough of the metal to enable them to arm their war-chariots with it. Yet we also find that stone implements were used in Assyria and Egypt up to a late date, along with those of metal. In Europe, in the Homeric poems, we can trace the age of Bronze, then beginning to decay among the Greeks, though there were soldiers in the army of Xerxes, long after, who used stone weapons; and the discoveries of Schliemann show that on the site of Troy a people using stone implements succeeded one using bronze, while in Santorin we find the indications of an early Greek people using stone implements. In the ancient Greek tombs at Mycenæ stone arrow-heads are found along with the richest and most artistic objects of gold, and throughout Europe there is in ancient tombs and battlefields a most inextricable mixture of bronze, and even iron, with stone. The Roman age was one of iron everywhere, so that even the Britons who fought with Cæsar used iron weapons; still stone lingered much later in remote places, in Britain and in Scandinavia, for there seem to have been stalwart Saxons at Hastings who smote Norman skulls with

P

lignis imposita saxa, probably stone-headed clubs, or stone battle-axes.* Such facts, of which any number are furnished to us by history, show that in any absolutely general sense we cannot rationally divide the pre-historic time into ages of Stone and Metal. The only sense in which such classification can be accepted is locally, and even then with some reserve. Admitting, then, a certain local value of the Iron, Bronze, and Stone ages in western Europe, with such modifications as the American and other facts already discussed require, it remains to satisfy ourselves as to the possibility of distinguishing separate ages of chipped and polished stone, or Palæolithic and Neolithic ages, and as to the nature of the line of separation between these supposed periods and the times to which they belong.

In America the age of polished and chipped stone, used together, and with some intermixture of copper and bronze, existed unchanged up to the discovery by Columbus. In Europe the Stone age is usually supposed to have given place to that of Bronze almost before the dawn of history, except in certain remote places. If we inquire what were the causes which at so early a date caused the introduction of bronze and iron in northern Europe, the answer is not difficult. It was foreign trade with the more civilized nations inhabiting the Mediterranean—nations which had possessed these metals from a still earlier period,

---

* "William of Poictiers." A different meaning has been attached to this by some; but stone weapons were used in Ireland and Scandinavia to quite as late a date.

and were to these people of northern and western Europe what the latter in modern times have been to America. It is evident, however, that in the dawn of history, in Egypt, Syria, and Greece, the quantity of iron and bronze was scarcely sufficient for purposes of extensive foreign supply; and tin, an essential ingredient of bronze, was especially expensive. If we ask for an explanation of the spread of bronze into northern Europe, the most probable is that it dates from the time when the Phœnicians discovered the rich tin mines of Cornwall, yielding for the first time a large and cheap supply of the metal. We have no certain date for this, but cannot be far wrong in fixing it between 800 and 500 years before Christ. From this time the Phœnicians and Carthaginians were able to supply their customers in all parts of Europe with this beautiful and useful alloy of copper and tin at low prices; and as this alloy could easily be recast, even by rude peoples, and was not liable, like iron, to decay by rust, the implements and weapons obtained by the natives were retained, and when worn out recast into new forms; and the metal thus accumulated in sufficient quantity to replace to a great extent the old stone implements. At a later date, when the Carthaginian power was broken down, iron, supplied by the Roman traders, took the place of bronze. Any other view than this is negatived by the fact that tin could be obtained abundantly only in Cornwall, that this source of supply was in the hands of the Phœnicians, that the antique bronze of all parts of Europe is similar in composition, and the implements of similar patterns, and that there is no evidence that any of the pre-historic races of northern Europe could either smelt copper or tin.

We may therefore reasonably conclude that, except in the regions on the Mediterranean coasts, the Stone period extended unbroken up to the sixth century before Christ—in other words, to the time of the early kings of Rome and the decay of the Hebrew monarchy, and we know from history that it lasted in some places much longer. Thus in graves in Russia and Scandinavia, and even in Germany, France, and England, stone weapons are found associated with remains of the tenth and even of the twelfth century. It is also to be observed that in every country some objects of stone—as arrowheads, hammers, sling stones, and sharp flakes—were in current use long after the introduction of daggers, swords, and spears of bronze or of iron.

The question, How far back in time did the Stone age extend? is less easily answered, and we may consider it under three heads: 1st. The validity of a Palæolithic as distinguished from a Neolithic age. 2nd. The question of the contemporaneousness of the men of the earlier Stone age with mammals of the Post-pliocene period now extinct. 3rd. The physical revolutions which are proved to have occurred since the origin of man. Having considered these points, we shall be in a position to decide whether there is any reality in the idea of an extreme antiquity of man in the old continent, and more especially in Europe.

First, with regard to the reality of the two ages of Stone. The current doctrine is that there was an earlier age in which men were possessed only of rude implements of chipped flints, and in which they are supposed to have been ignorant of pottery and of the metals. This was succeeded by a later Stone age, in which polished stone implements were used, and which later age passed into that of Bronze. These statements are of course to be taken only locally, as referring to western Europe. They must also be taken with some limitations, as pottery has been found in at least one cave in France referred to this age; and the book of Genesis and all early history would lead us to infer that the metals gold and copper at least were known from the earliest times, though there must have been then as in more modern days extensive regions in which they were unknown.

There appears further, as we have stated in the last chapter, to be a twofold division of the earlier Stone age, into that of the Mammoth with the men of large stature, and that of the Reindeer with the men of small stature; and these ages were probably separated by considerable physical changes. Further, the latter of these periods evidently graduates into that of polished stone; while the carvings in ivory and the highly artificial bone implements which are traced back into the older age, and the probability that the people who chipped stones possessed stone or bone hammers for the purpose, renders the distinction of Palæolithic and Neolithic ages far less clear than it appears to be at first sight. In the Dordogne caves, for example, some supposed to be older than the others show roughly-made implements along with bones of extinct animals; but there are associated with them others, both of stone and bone, which could be referred to the Neolithic age; and the same is the case with the Aurignac cave, if of the great age originally attributed to it. Even Kent's Cavern, in England, has produced highly artificial bone implements from the bed of clay holding remains of extinct mammalia, and no reason can be shown why men capable of carving bone and ivory could not have polished stone. If they did not do so, it may have been merely because the plentiful supply of flints in their vicinity rendered it unnecessary. Further, our American investigations show us that people who used the best stone implements used also the rudest, and even naturally-shaped stones, for some purposes; so that out of any American village site we could pick out a collection of Palæolithic and of Neolithic implements. Besides this, in any place where the raw material abounded and where stone implements were made, we should necessarily find a very large preponderance of the ruder types. Again, a people living where the material was plentiful and easily chipped, would probably be in the habit of making rude implements and throwing them away carelessly, as they could be so easily replaced by others. After carefully going over the several deposits of remains ascribed to the Palæolithic time, as summed up by Lyell and Lubbock, I think we must exclude from the true Palæolithic period, as defined above, all the known cases, except those of the river-gravels and shore-gravels of the cretaceous districts of western Europe, because all the other repositories, even those containing bones of the mammoth, show implements of more advanced construction. It is further obvious that with regard to these gravels the exceptional conditions above referred to come into full force. First, the implements occur principally in those cretaceous regions in which flints well suited for chipped implements abound. Hence it is likely that rude tribes migrating from place to place might not care to take with them ordinary implements, but might make a new supply wherever they happened to be, and then abandon them. A very few such implements as those found at Amiens would be burdensome to a savage in his journey, and when he knew that at any place in the district he could procure flints and make a new supply in an hour or two, he would not fatigue himself with their weight. He would be more likely to carry a light hammer of stone or antler or tooth, with which he could chip flints as he required them. Secondly, independent of this, a region so abundantly supplied with flint might be visited by remote tribes who might spend weeks in the chipping of flints, and then leave the locality, taking with them those which were most suitable for use, or for further working into finer weapons. Resident tribes also, if sufficiently powerful to prevent others from visiting the gravel-beds, might manufacture or roughly block out weapons, and supply neighbouring tribes in the way of trade. A remarkable illustration of this is afforded by the fact that the numerous flint flakes found by Dupont in some caves of the Reindeer age in Belgium, are believed to have been imported from Pressigny, in France, where a variety of flint, known from the most ancient times for its excellence, exists, and where vast numbers of cores, or "nuclei," from which flakes have been struck off are found. We may imagine in the Reindeer age makers of nuclei and flakes at Pressigny, and itinerant traders carrying their productions into Belgium, or distant tribes making long journeys to reach the locality of such precious stone. We know from American examples that in this way the produce of the flint-beds might be conveyed for hundreds of miles into districts not naturally provided with so good material. Thirdly, another consideration comes in here, which has been strangely overlooked by some writers on the subject. The objects known as flakes, knives, scrapers, and cores, are unquestionably of natural or accidental origin far more frequently than artificial in the proper sense. My own limited experience in the chalk districts convinced me of this many years ago. I picked up in the flint-heaps by the roadside near Amiens and at Dover many broken flints of this kind, and some that even approached in perfection the implements of the gravel-beds, and Mr. Whitley fully establishes this view for large districts in England and France.*

* "Transactions of Victoria Institute."

Savages no doubt were in the habit of picking up and using such flakes, and even of carrying them to districts where they were less abundant, and of chipping them for themselves when natural ones could not be found; but no one can distinguish those which man has used from the vastly greater number which nature has produced and man has not touched, except when they are found in association with unquestionable human remains. Taking these considerations into account, it appears to me that the Palæolithic period, as a distinct age, fades away from view, and is rather a local phenomenon than one relating to time. It is, perhaps, rather a product of the imagination of overzealous antiquaries, whose fancies have too readily been accepted as facts by geologists. There is, indeed, no good evidence that the people of the earliest Stone age in Europe were materially different in grade of civilization from the aborigines of America at the period of its discovery, a conclusion confirmed by the fact that their skeletons were so remarkably similar in type, and that their brains were in no respect inferior. If, therefore, we are to make any twofold division of the people of the Stone age, it should be on some other ground than the quality of their implements. They may be divided into the men of the Mammoth age and of the Reindeer age, after the French and Belgian archæologists; or, as this is merely a local distinction,—the reindeer not being found in Italy, for instance,—we might regard them as men living before and after the last subsidence of the land, or as Antediluvians and Post-diluvians; or, to avoid committing ourselves to historical connections, I have elsewhere proposed the names *Palæocosmic* and *Neocosmic*. *

In any case, I think that American archæologists and geologists must refuse to accept the distinction of a Palæolithic from a Neolithic period until further evidence can be obtained. If, therefore, man in Europe was contemporary with the extinct Mammalia of the Post-pliocene, and existed there before the latest great physical revolutions of climate and surface, he did not belong to an imaginary rude and semi-simian race. He not only displayed a good physical organization, but had some knowledge of the arts of life, and by virtue of this was able to shelter himself from the severities of climate and to cope with the wild animals which surrounded him.

Of course we should not maintain that in the earlier Stone age there may not have been progress in civilization, as well as differences between the peoples of different localities. In the Cresswell caves, described by Dawkins,† we are informed that "in the lowest stratum implements of the rudest and roughest form, made of quartzite pebbles from the neighbouring Permian conglomerate, were the only tools left behind by the hunter. In the middle stratum, composed of red earth, he used better implements, of flint brought from a distance; while in the upper portion of

* "Story of the Earth and Man."
† "Journal Geological Society, 1877: Manchester Proceedings, 1877." See also Appendix.

the cave earth, and in the breccia, all his cutting implements were made of flint, and are of a higher order."
Here also are implements of bone and antler, and even specimens of artistic carving. This sequence may represent either a gradual elevation of one race, or a succession of races, or the first rude efforts of a small company of new settlers, as compared with their condition when more fully established and with a wider circle of intercourse, or the makeshifts of men cut off by war or accident from their usual supplies. The Micmacs resident in or visiting Prince Edward Island, often had to use rude arrow-heads made from the quartzite pebbles of the Triassic conglomerate, though in Nova Scotia they employed beautiful weapons of agate and jasper.

We can imagine even stragglers from civilization, destitute of metals and obliged to begin a rude manufacture of flints. Remarkable illustrations of this occur at a later time in the remains of those extraordinary villages built on platforms supported on piles in the Swiss lakes, and which have afforded so many curious relics. If the oldest of these villages, as described by the Swiss antiquaries, belong to an early part of the Stone age, they point unmistakably, by the presence of several kinds of grain, of woven cloth, and of a few objects of metal found in them, to a greater civilization existing to the south; and if the Danish shell heaps, which exactly correspond to our Indian shell heaps on the American coast, are contemporary, then they also point to a ruder people living in the north. Had a civilized traveller visited one of these Swiss villages in the Stone age, he would have been told of highly civilized agricultural countries to the south, and of rude tribes to the north, just as the Hochelagans could give similar information to Cartier.

This much being settled, we may enter on the consideration of the absolute antiquity of the age of Stone in Europe. The evidence of the high antiquity claimed for the early Stone age, extending even to 100,000 years, or as an enthusiastic advocate of human antiquity has recently inferred, possibly to 500,000 years, resolves itself into two theses which were held by Sir C. Lyell to be proved, or at least rendered somewhat probable, by the evidence obtained :—

1. Man existed in western Europe at the same time with the mammoth and its contemporaries, or in the later Post-pliocene period of geology.

2. Man existed in western Europe before certain great physical changes of denudation and elevation and subsidence, which must have required a vast lapse of time.

We may take these up in succession, premising that neither gives any positive date in years.

Long before the present inquiries into the antiquity of man began, it was known that certain animals contemporary with our ancestors in early historic times were now extinct, at least locally. In the British Islands, for instance, and over large portions of Europe, the beaver and the wolf, once plentiful, have disappeared. The urus, or great wild bull, and the reindeer, were found by Cæsar in the forests of Germany. The one is extinct, the other is now confined to Lapland. The aurochs, or European bison, existed in central Europe up to the twelfth century, but is now limited to a single herd artificially preserved in Lithuania. There is also reason to believe that the Irish deer (Megaceros), whose bones are found under bogs in Ireland, was contemporary with man. These facts are, however, precisely parallel to some known as quite recent in America; as, for instance, the entire disappearance of the wapiti, the noblest of American deer, and of the American bison, or "buffalo," from the regions east of the Mississippi, with the limitation of the latter to one narrow district at the foot of the Rocky Mountains,* and the rapidly approaching extinction of the reindeer or caribou in Nova Scotia and the neighbouring parts of Eastern America. These American facts relate to the comparatively short period since the discovery of America, and are connected with the introduction of fire-arms and the progressive settlement of the country. In Europe such changes were slower; but there can be no doubt that the introduction of bronze and iron, the migrations and conquests which have occurred, and the increase of population, have been instrumental in producing them.

More significant facts, as bearing on the antiquity of man, are those which seem to indicate his having

* It is estimated by Dr. G. M. Dawson, that the buffalo, at the existing rate of destruction, will be extinct in about fourteen years.

entered Europe before the extinction of the mammoth and other animals not known in history, and believed to have survived only to the close of the Post-pliocene period. These facts are now somewhat numerous, and give good ground for the inference that some of these creatures lived up to the human period, though they give no absolute date for the disappearance of the latest of them. They have been obtained chiefly from caverns, and these may be classed as caverns of drift-age, of interment, and of residence.

To the first class belong the remarkable caves on the banks of the Meuse and its tributaries near Liege, explored by Schmerling. These caves contain scattered skulls and bones of men, and occasional implements of bone and stone, mixed with bones of the mammoth and other extinct quadrupeds, and also of many modern quadrupeds, the whole imbedded in a confused manner in mud, and covered with stalagmite produced subsequently by the drippings of the cave. Such deposits cannot give absolute evidence of contemporaneity, because bones of very different ages may be huddled together in such places, and in a few centuries may all assume much the same coloration and chemical composition. To this extent, therefore, the geological evidence in the case of these and all similar caves is defective. Still, the coating of stalagmite,* and other circumstances, establish an antiquity at least

* Recent facts show that under favourable circumstances stalagmite may be deposited in a much shorter time than hitherto supposed.

pre-historic, and even the modern animals present are believed to indicate a somewhat colder climate than at present. Passing over this doubt, and regarding the bones as those of the contemporaries of man, three hypotheses may be suggested in explanation of their mode of occurrence. (1.) They may be the bones of dead men and animals lying unburied on the surface, or imbedded in alluvial banks cut away by streams. (2.) Sepulchral caves similar to some of those which Dupont has described in the same region, may have been scoured out by water, and their contents mingled promiscuously together. (3.) Men and animals may have been engulfed in open fissures and their bones scattered by subsequent floods of water passing through these caves. Either of these suppositions, and also the present position of the caves, would seem to imply, not merely time, but a large and irregular amount of diluvial force, the precise extent of which it is difficult to ascertain, and in reference to which Sir C. Lyell suggests changes of level and possible eruptions of the Eifel volcanoes, which are only sixty miles distant. In any case, a cutting or clearing out of the valleys into which these caves open, to the extent of 300 feet in some places, seems to be required, and the objects found in the caves show that this must, at least in part, have been effected by inundations.

With regard to the relative probability of the three suppositions above mentioned, the discoveries of M. Dupont in the neighbouring caves of the Lesse would attach some probability to the second. In some of these caves he found alluvial clay, with bones of the mammoth and what are supposed to be rude flint implements, and implements of reindeer-horn; a single jawbone being the only remains of man. Newer than this was the sepulchre of Frontal, referred by Dupont to the Reindeer period of the Palæolithic age, in which were skeletons, well-made flint weapons, wampum of fossil shells, a flint spear, and fragments of pottery. It is remarkable that the objects found imply art and extensive commerce, of which the supposed Neolithic or more modern graves of Belgium show much less evidence. Now, if one of M. Dupont's caves, containing drifted material below and sepulchral material above, were by a new inundation or cataclysm to be again traversed by water, so as to mix up its contents, and were then left undisturbed, it would present precisely the appearances described by Schmerling in the Engis cave.

Similar remarks apply to other caverns of driftage, except that in caves like Kent's Hole and Brixham, where only implements and not human bones are found, the facts have probably not been complicated with sepulchral arrangements. In any case, to apply to the explanation of such caves the continued operations of merely modern causes, without taking into account floods and other cataclysmic agents, is a stretch of uniformitarianism which the deposits in the caves themselves plainly contradict. Thus the calculations which we can make as to age, rather serve to bring the age of the mammoth up toward us than to throw man back in geological time, while the association itself in the Belgian caves and similar receptacles is encompassed with grave doubt as to its causes.

Caves of residence and caves of sepulchre are often associated with each other. It is so in those of the Dordogne and in the Mentone cave, and probably also in that of Aurignac. The latter, however, has been lately subjected to so many doubts with reference to its antiquity, that we may for the present leave it out of the account. The caves of the Dordogne and that of Bruniquel, all in the limestone districts of the south of France, indicate very clearly the fact that the ancient tribes which inhabited them hunted the reindeer in a region not inhabited by that animal in historic times, and also in all probability the extinct mammoth; and the testimony of these caves is not complicated with water driftage, except in the case of small deposits of sand due to land floods. The people who inhabited these caves were not abject savages, but well-developed men of what we may call the American type. They were well provided with implements of stone and bone, and were not inferior to some of the American tribes in the art of carving in bone and ivory. They must have inhabited their caves for a long time, and attempts have been made to subdivide the Dordogne cave-dwellers and their relics into distinct ages of great duration.

I agree with Sir C. Lyell, however, in believing that there is but slender and insufficient ground for this. The facts detailed by Lartet and Christy, and more recently by Mortillet, only imply such differences as might obtain among a hunting and migratory people, and the animals on which they relied for support, at different seasons or in the lapse of a few generations—differences much less than those which we know were occurring in almost every generation among the Indian tribes of America before the advent of Europeans. Such conditions would vary among the primitive people of the Vezère valley according to the " success of the hunters or the sojourn of migratory animals in the neighbourhood," and even more according to the relations of peace or war, victory or defeat, which they might sustain with neighbouring tribes.

To one of these caves of habitation and sepulchre, that of Cro-magnon, I have fully referred in the last chapter, and may now add a few remarks as to the lapse of time during which it may have been occupied. Such shelters, though now open in front, were probably, when inhabited, walled up on the outer side with logs, wattle, or boughs of trees; and it is most likely that they were the winter houses of the people.

The accumulation of ashes, bones, and other remains is in exact accordance with the want of cleanliness of the ruder American tribes, and also with the habits of a people who in summer live in the open air, or in temporary cabins or wigwams, and only in the colder months or in bad weather resort to more secure and permanent abodes. The accumulation of rubbish in such places, and especially at their mouths, is also a much more rapid process than would at first sight be supposed, more particularly as the remains of fir boughs, heather, rushes, and similar substances, taken in as bedding, and also the husks and other *débris* of vegetable food, may be added to the mass. Further than the accumulation of such *débris*, which may indicate several centuries of continued habitation, and the accumulation of fallen stones which may have been detached by frosts and earthquakes, there is nothing to indicate the great antiquity of these caves and shelters, except the want of metals, the presence of the bones of extinct mammalia, and the coating of stalagmite covering the remains.

A remarkable confirmation of this is the fact that, while the physical characteristics of the people of the Dordogne caverns, as well as of the man of Mentone, are essentially those which would indicate American or Turanian habits of life : they are also, according to the elaborate comparisons of Pruner Bey, as given by Christy and Lartet, similar in important points to those of the modern Lithuanians—that is, to an existing European race, and one inhabiting the only country where the otherwise extinct bison survives. These Palæolithic men are, therefore, not of an extinct species, nor even of an extinct variety of man, but identical with races still existing.

If, then, we have to deal, in the case of these ancient remains, with no extinct species of man, but with a variety allied to modern races ; if he was contemporary in the main with modern mammals; and if some of those that are locally extinct existed in Europe up to historic times, while the others present in the condition of their bones and mode of occurrence no evidence of greater antiquity, what geological evidence have we that the residence of man in Europe has been longer than 6000 years? The answer must be—Absolutely none, as far as the association of man with extinct animals is concerned. Further, when we consider the mode of occurrence and state of preservation of the remains, and their identity with the remains of modern American races, the very long periods assigned by some authors to the residence of man in Europe become ridiculous in their absurdity.

We may now proceed to consider the second chain of evidence for the antiquity of man—that derived from the physical changes which have occurred since his entrance upon the scene. Reference has already been made incidentally to the depth to which certain river valleys seem to have been cut since the caverns on their sides were filled. In the case of those near Liege, the depth is estimated at 200 feet in some cases, and it is stated as possible that the caves on opposite sides of certain deep gorges may correspond. If this could be proved, it would show that this great depth had been cut out of the solid limestone of the country. It may well be, however, that old valleys have only been emptied of *débris;* and in any case, if an elevation of the land had occurred, and there were floods or volcanic debacles, or a permanently swollen condition of the rivers owing to a more humid climate or a dense covering of forest, the time required for such cutting would be much shortened.

We shall be better able to judge of these probabilities when we shall have considered the next case presented to us, that of the river gravels containing implements believed to have been made by man. If we stand on one of the beds of gravel quarried at St. Acheul, near Amiens, we may see before us the broad flat valley of the Somme, with the little stream flowing between banks of alluvium 100 feet below us. But the ground on which we stand is a loess or river mud with fresh-water shells, and below this are many feet of river-gravel made up mainly of the flints which fill the underlying chalk, and in this gravel, at great depths from the surface, have been found numerous flint implements which it seems difficult to explain unless they have been wrought by man. Ancient miners, it is true, may have worked galleries, since fallen in, through these gravels; and in visiting this place in 1865, I believe I could perceive some indications of this; but the general impression conveyed is, that they were mixed with the gravel by the floods of a stream representing the River Somme, but straggling over the country at a height of 100 feet above its present bed. This implies that at the time in question the valley was either not cut out, or filled with some material since swept away, and that the water-flow of the river was going on in a manner not favourable to erosion of its bed. Such conditions evidently bring before us considerable changes of level which we must, I think, be prepared to face more boldly than has been customary with writers on this subject. To give such a state of things as that implied in these high-level gravels, we must suppose that the Somme valley was flat and filled up with detritus, presenting an alluvial plain over which the river, at times of flood, could spread itself with great ease, while the climate must have been sufficiently severe to allow ice to float in spring freshets large blocks of stone. This implies a lower level of the country than at present, and probably a very recent elevation out of the sea, followed by a condition of much greater rainfall and more severe floods. Now, at the mouth of the Somme there are beds of peat, the bottom of which is below the level of the sea; consequently this modern peat began to be formed at a time when the land was higher than it is at present; and the submerged forests with remains of man and modern animals, at several points along the coasts of France and England, give us the same indication. First, then, we learn from the peat that immediately before the historical period the Somme valley was higher than now, and the circumstances more favourable than at present to its rapid cutting. But the gravels must have been deposited before this in a previous time of lower level. Now, that man existed at this time of lower level, we have evidence elsewhere. Nilsson has described certain skulls found in beds holding marine shells on the coast of Sweden at an elevation of 100 feet above the sea, and infers that the men to whom they belonged were drowned when the sea was at that height on the land. It has long been well known to geologists that the coast of Scotland shows evidence that it was twenty-five feet, possibly forty feet, lower in the early human period than it is at present. Mr. Milne Home has very recently given some interesting illustrations of this in the valley of the Forth, where skeletons of whales occur in the carse of Stirling, at an elevation of twenty or thirty feet above the sea, and with them were found pointed instruments of deer's horn. In the West of Scotland, also, numerous canoes, cut out of solid logs of wood, have been disinterred from marine beds now twenty feet or more above the level of the sea. Human bones have also been found in Cornwall in elevated beds covered with marine shells; and in Sardinia there are said to be old beaches no less than from 230 to 234 feet above the level of the Mediterranean, with fragments of pottery associated with sea shells.*

We do not certainly know that these depressions were contemporaneous, but they all belonged to the early human period, and if this depression extended from Sweden to the Mediterranean, and amounted to from fifty to one hundred feet in the valley of the Somme, it would give precisely the state of things in which the lower part of that valley might be a sort of delta, with banks of gravel to which aborigines of the country might resort for materials for their implements, or into which their rejected or lost implements might be drifted, and these aborigines would be contemporaries of the drowned men of Stangeness, in

* Lyell, "Antiquity of Man," p. 115.

Sweden, and of the ancient Caledonians whose canoes and implements we find in the estuaries of the Clyde and Forth. Before their time there had been a continental period, in which the bed of the German Ocean and Irish Sea had been dry land, and men had been able to walk dryshod to Britain; their ancestors had witnessed a great, and probably sudden depression of the land, and in their day it was again slowly rising. In subsequent generations it rose still further, and what had been in their day under the sea at Abbeville, became a bog, while the Somme valley, raised to a higher level, became reduced to its present form, and the river shrunk into a deeper channel, its volume becoming greatly diminished by the increasing dryness of the climate and removal of the forests, changes which also extirpated the last survivors of those species of quadrupeds which had been suited for a wilder and more wooded country.

These changes are well summed up by Sir C. Lyell, in his "Antiquity of Man," pages 331 *et seq.*, and by tabulating his succession we may clearly understand the position of the supposed Amiens flint-chippers. (See Table on opposite page.)

All this leaves us, however, still in uncertainty as to the absolute time involved. Our estimate of this must depend on the rapidity or slowness of the oscillations in the Modern period (No. 4). If we adopt with Lyell a strictly uniformitarian method, and estimate the elevations and depressions of which there is geological evidence at thirty inches per century,

ANTIQUITY OF MAN. 233

Table of Physical Changes in Western Europe in the Later Tertiary and Modern Periods.
(See Lyell, "Antiquity of Man," p. 323).

POST-PLIOCENE.

1st. Continental Period. Land elevated. Climate mild . } Cromer Forest bed.

2nd. Period of Glaciation and Submergence. Land depressed 1,000 feet or more. Climate cold and much floating ice . . . . } Boulder deposits and marine Post-pliocene drift.

3rd. Second Continental Period. Land again elevated until much higher than at present, and British Islands united to mainland. Climate continental and surface densely wooded . . . . } Passage of German flora into England. Mammoth and Megaceros and Cave Bear etc., living in Europe. Advent of man? *

MODERN.

4th. Period of depression and oscillation, ending in re-elevation, and present geographical condition of Europe . . . . . . } Age of Amiens gravels and raised beaches, and close of Palæocosmic and beginning of Neocosmic age. Men subjected to great diminution of numbers by floods and subsidences. Several species of mammals become extinct. Stone age of antiquaries.

5th. Modern or historic age. Land slowly subsiding. . } Bronze and Iron ages of antiquaries.

* Pengelly, in a recent paper on the Flint Implements from Kent's Cavern, holds that man may have existed in Devonshire in or shortly after the first continental period. This conclusion, however, requires us to believe that the oldest deposit of Kent's Cavern is of this age, and that the flints found in it are really of human workmanship. Neither of these data can as yet be considered as established (see p. 348).

being the rate in modern subsidences now observed, we shall require periods in comparison with which the received chronology of historians shrinks into insignificance. This rate is, however, confessedly "purely conjectural," and there are many considerations which seem to show that it is based on insufficient data. Such modern elevations as are on record, as for example those in Italy, the Greek Islands, and South America, have been rapid and paroxysmal; and the raised beaches of western Europe and of North America show that this must have been its character in former times. Slow and gradual movement, even if interrupted, could not have produced these sharply defined terraces. Modern depressions have, with few exceptions, been gradual; but their rate is so unequal that we cannot reason with any certainty as to the past. While, therefore, it must be admitted that the physical changes of elevation and subsidence which have taken place since man's arrival may have occupied long periods, it cannot be said that they must have done so.

It is much the same with the arguments derived from aqueous erosion. This must have gone on simultaneously with the elevations and depressions, and must have been greatly modified by these. When we stand by the grassy and tree-clad slopes of a river valley, and consider that they have been just as they are during all the centuries of history, it is difficult to resist the prejudice that they must always have been so, and that vast periods have been required for their excavation at the slow rate now observed; but if we carry ourselves in imagination to the time when a plain was raised out of the sea, bare and bald, and a river began to run in it, we at once see our error. The river so running and beginning to cut a channel, and cutting back the falls which would occur in its course, must in a few years execute a stupendous work of erosion almost diluvial in its character; but in the course of centuries its work becomes completed, a state of equilibrium succeeds, and its banks, protected by vegetation, scarcely experience any modification. An elevation to a higher level, or a new depression succeeded by re-elevation, or forest fires or other causes laying bare the isurface, would at once initiate a new series of erosions; but until this occurs all things continue as they were.

It must also be observed that in the period No. 4 (p. 233), there were not only oscillations of level, but apparently a somewhat extreme climate, in which alternate frosts and thaws and violent river floods must have greatly aided the work of denudation; and also that in a wooded condition of the country, its streams, as we know from sad experience of the effects of clearings in America, are large in volume but equable in flow, and that the removal of the forest leads to great floods alternating with periods of desiccation, remarkably increasing and modifying the denuding power of the streams. Sir Charles Lyell gives some striking illustrations of this in his " Principles of Geology."

It is, perhaps, necessary here to refer to the conclusion recently developed at great length by Dr. James

Geikie, in his work, "The Ice Age," that the remains of Palæolithic men are not Post-glacial, but belong to a Pre-glacial or Inter-glacial period. This is, no doubt, a view forced upon him by his belief in a great continental "ice-sheet," which itself, as I have shown in former works, in all probability without good foundation.* He supports it principally on the geographical distribution of the animals supposed to have been contemporary with Palæolithic man, and which he tries to divide into two successive groups; and on the probability that the last period of continental elevation referred to in the table above was not of a character to change the insular climate of western Europe. With reference to the first of these reasons, Dawkins has shown, on the evidence of Cresswell Cave and other bone caves, that no such division of Post-glacial mammals can be made. The hyæna, the reindeer, and the hippopotamus occur together in the same deposits. Again, this Post-glacial fauna has been shown to be of the nature of a continental and prairie fauna, belonging to a state of Europe when it must have presented that condition of steppe-like plains and wooded hills and river courses which is, of all others, the most suited to a varied and abundant group of land animals. I may add that it is most unsafe to reason as to the climate required by extinct mammalia, especially in contravention of the evidence of contemporaneous existence afforded by the occurrence of their remains. Even the hippopotamus of the

* "Story of the Earth and Man." "Acadian Geology."

English caves and gravels may have been protected by a coating of fat like the walrus, or of hair like that of the seals. The elevated land of Post-glacial Europe, if it were partly clothed with forests, and partly grassy plains, would have precisely the climatal properties which we know in America and Asia favour the intermixture of the animals of different latitudes. Again, that so-called Palæolithic implements are not found over the boulder deposits of North Britain is merely a consequence of the fact that they are in the main limited to the chalk and flint districts, a circumstance which, as already hinted, throws grave doubts on their being even so ancient as usually supposed, and gives them a local rather than a chronological character. Further, in Eastern America we know that the higher condition of the land immediately preceding the Modern period was accompanied by a milder climate than that which now prevails, and that this occurred after the close of the Glacial period.* I must, therefore, reject this supposed later Glacial age intervening between Palæolithic and Modern man, and maintain that there is no proof of the existence of man earlier than the close of the proper Glacial age.

Some remarkable evidence has lately been found, bearing on the climate of Europe when occupied by the Post-glacial men, and showing that some measure of the rigours of the cold period still continued after their appearance. The presence of the reindeer, musk-

* "Notes on Post-Pliocene of Canada," by the Author, Montreal.

ox, glutton, and other northern animals is an indication of this, and we have reason to believe that the mammoth and the woolly rhinoceros were animals suited to extreme cold. On the other hand, the contemporaneous existence of the cave hyæna, the cave lion, and the hippopotamus tells a different story, and implies at least warm summers and facilities for migration over extensive plains. Possibly, however, these conditions were to some extent changeable, and at the height of the continental period the climate may have been warm in summer and somewhat cold in winter, while in preceding and subsequent periods of depression, it may have been cool and moist. One of the most convincing evidences of refrigeration in the later part of the Palæocosmic age, or older part of the Neocosmic, is that afforded by the deposit at Schussenried in Wurtemburg, described by Dr. Fraas, of Stuttgart. The place had been a camping-ground near a stream, and used apparently in the Reindeer age, possibly after the disappearance of the mammoth, and it had been overgrown with moss, in which Professor Schimper recognises the species now characteristic of Alpine and sub-arctic regions. It affords perhaps the best proof of a cold climate in Germany in the Reindeer age. This, let it be remembered, was the age of a population allied to the Laplanders, and probably after the disappearance of the stalwart Turanian race, characteristic of the continental mammoth period. In other words, this age of cold was the early Post-diluvial time.

It has been remarked that Palæocosmic man does not seem to have penetrated into Scandinavia, and I believe the same may be affirmed of the north of Scotland, Ireland, and other regions of northern Europe. Whether this has arisen from the continuance of glacial cold in these regions, or from other causes, we can only conjecture. The point has been discussed by Dr. Torell in a very interesting paper, in which he investigates the various discoveries of pre-historic remains in Sweden, with their probable ages.*

Torell arranges the later formations of Sweden in three great groups. The first includes the Glacial and Post-glacial formations, the second the Transition between the Glacial and the Modern periods, and the third the Recent deposits. The first contains the boulder clay, and the overlying clays and sands, with marine shells and a few plants of arctic types. The second consists of gravel terraces and superficial clay, and gravel of the plains. The third consists of elevated sea beaches, with modern shells, freshwater alluvia, and peat bogs. The latter contain remains of some quadrupeds now extinct in Sweden, as the aurochs, the bison, and the wild boar.

After a careful *resumé* of all the alleged discoveries of remains and works of man in these beds, he concludes that human remains are confined to the recent deposits, and that there is no evidence of anything older than the age of polished stone. In other words, in Sweden, as in America, man is contemporaneous

* "Compte-rendu du Congres Archæologique de Stockholm."

with the modern fauna, and objects of chipped and polished stone are contemporaneous.

Further, the physical changes which have occurred in Sweden within the Modern period are most instructive. For example, in enlarging the harbour of Ystad, in 1869, there was found at the depth of eleven feet below the sea level, a forest rooted *in situ*, and covered with a bed of peat, with freshwater shells, and this with about seven feet of marine sand. The peat contained weapons of stone and bronze, and a knife-handle referable to the 12th century, and the marine sand many objects, the oldest of which are referred to the middle ages. This evidence of great subsidence, growth of peat, and deposition of marine beds within modern times, shows how cautious we should be in referring superficial deposits to remote ages, or in supposing that changes of level necessarily require vast periods. This caution is more especially necessary with respect to the growth of peat, the period required for which, as tested by actual observation in Ireland, Scotland, and even in France, has been absurdly exaggerated in the case of the peats of Denmark and of the Somme valley.* It is to be observed, in connection with this, that the land of northern Sweden is now rising, and that there seems evidence in raised beaches that in the earlier part of the Recent period there was still greater depression than that evidenced by the peat and submerged forest of Ystad. Thus we have,

* See an able summary of the facts in Southall's "Epoch of the Mammoth."

within the Recent period, several oscillations of land in Sweden; and similar evidence exists in regard to many other parts of western Europe.

The facts above presented are suggestive rather than exhaustive; but they tend to show the necessity of suspending our judgment on the antiquity of man until larger inductions have been made, and until the facts known are better understood. Such caution is rendered the more necessary by the numerous instances, in the progress of this investigation, of errors current for a time, and then exploded. The archæological literature of the last ten years is strewn with the wrecks of supposed facts establishing the antiquity of man, but which more careful examination has shown to have been wrongly observed or misunderstood.*

If we attempt to reduce to terms of years such changes as those above discussed, which appear to have happened since the advent of man in Europe, there are two considerations often neglected, to which we must give their due weight. These are, (1) That

* It may be instructive to mention as instances, the calculations of time based on the Cone of the Tiniere, the peats of Abbeville and of Denmark, the excavation of valleys in northern France out of solid chalk, the growth of stalagmite in caverns, and the Sodertelje Hut in Sweden. These have been well exposed by Torell, Andrews, Southall, and others. Or we may refer to the evidences of Pre-glacial man supposed to be furnished by the Victoria Cave, the flint implements of Brandon, the bone cave of Dürnten, the Pliocene man of Denise, the cut bones of Tuscany, the Miocene chipped flints of Thenay and of the Dardanelles. All of these are now rejected, even by the most advanced advocates of the great antiquity of man.

in the north of Europe and Asia very important physical changes have occurred in what are properly historic times, and which may serve to give us some measure for the time necessary, at the same rate, for those which preceded them; and (2) That the rate of change in historic times is not a certain measure of that in pre-historic periods; but on the contrary, that there are indications of more rapid changes before the dawn of history, and in the early human period.

1. With reference to the great physical changes known to have occurred in historic times, I may refer to the fact that it is proved by the occurrence of marine shells and sea beaches at great elevations, that much of the land of the northern hemisphere was depressed under the sea to the amount of from 2,000 to 4,000 feet in the later Glacial period. † Evidence of this is accumulating from Great Britain, Scandinavia, eastern and western America. Now, the close of the Glacial age has been estimated on various data at from 7,000 * to 200,000 ‡ years ago. If we take even the longest of these periods, and suppose that during some considerable part of it the land has remained in a state of repose, or the sea at the same level, the rate of depression and elevation required for this enormous

* Andrew's calculations, based on the lake terraces of North America, give from 7,000 to 20,000 years. Winchell's, on the Falls of St. Anthony, in connection with the occurrence of our winter in aphelion 11,300 years ago, give 8,859 years.

† No. 2 of Table.

‡ Croll's calculations, based on precession of the equinoxes and eccentricity of the earth's orbit, and accepted by Lyell and others.

change becomes very great, since during some portions of the supposed period of 200,000 years the levels of sea and land must have been changing at the rate of four or five feet per century, even if the process was uniform, and not by successive abrupt movements, as the terraces on the margins of our continents would seem to indicate. But man did not, so far as known, appear till the continental period, which succeeded this great depression, and the changes which have occurred since his advent are comparatively small, and must have required a very small fraction of the time intervening between the glacial subsidence and the present time. This consideration alone, in my judgment, altogether negatives the claim for such high antiquities, as say 100,000 years, for man. Further, the state of preservation of animal remains, and the amount of atmospheric erosion observed on the raised terraces, at least of America, where alone I have studied them, forbid so great estimates as to time.

Again, there is reason to believe that in historical times, or since the foundation of the great historic empires of western Asia and northern Africa, say from 2,000 to 3,000 years before Christ, great areas in northern Asia, formerly sea, have become land, and large islands in the Atlantic have disappeared. The Hyrcanian ocean of the ancients has been dried up, and the continent of Atlantis has gone down. We have already seen that the Danish shell heaps belong to the later Stone age, and yet the shells found in them show that they antedate the present brackish water fauna of the Baltic, indicating a considerable rise of land, of which there are also indications in raised beaches in Scandivania, and in the canoes found in Scotland from seven to twenty feet above the present sea level. One of these canoes found near Glasgow, had a plug of cork, which must have come from the south of Europe; and with others implements of iron, as well as finely polished stone implements, have been found. On the other hand, the case already quoted from Professor Torell, and multitudes of submerged forests on the coasts of Europe, point to very considerable subsidence even within the Christian era. In volcanic regions, such as the south of Italy and the west coast of South America, such changes are much more rapid; but even in countries remote from volcanic centres, the oscillations of the earth's crust during the historic period have been so great that we do not require to allow very much longer time for the date of Palæocosmic man.

2. We are also liable to very grave error when we assume that the rate of change in particular cases has been no greater than we observe in modern times. Even the changes in the rate and character of erosion and deposit arising from the clearing of the forests, so familiar to all observers in America, and which so strongly impressed the mind of Sir Charles Lyell, seem often to be left out of the account. In Kent's Cavern the thin film of carbonate of lime which has formed over dates scratched on the rock more than two centuries ago, would lead to the belief that the thick

beds of stalagmite in that cave would require even half a million of years for their formation ; but observations in other caverns show that, under favourable circumstances, beds of this thickness might be formed in a thousand years. In point of fact, the solution of limestone by carbon dioxide, and its deposition again, is a process depending on the amount of organic matter going to decay and furnishing acidulated water, and on the exposure of this water to the air; and the activity of this process must, in any particular case, have varied very much in the lapse of time. The calculation of Boucher de Perthes as to the growth of the peat at Abbeville was supposed to give a period of 20,000 years for its accumulation, and yet it all belonged to the time since the newer or Neocosmic age. But his own observations show that it is a forest peat, the growth of which must necessarily have ceased since the original forest covering of the country was removed; and the observations of D'Archiac show that at present, in this same district, peat, where circumstances favour its growth, may accumulate at the rate of more than two feet in a century. This Abbeville peat was formed subsequently to the erosion of the Somme valley, and the deposition of its "palæolithic" gravels; and if the time required for the growth of the peat has been exaggerated, so has that for the older excavation and deposition. When one considers the little river Somme flowing quietly in its broad green valley, and asks how long time it would require to cut this valley out of the chalk, and to deposit the flint, gravel, and stones found in the terraces of its sides, not only may the time required be counted by tens or hundreds of thousands of years, but it may be said to be practically infinite; for no geologist, acquainted with the facts, and with the nature of river erosion, could affirm that the present river would ever produce such results. They require, in short, the operation of much more powerful forces, and whatever we assume these to have been, whether fluviatile, diluvial, or partly marine, they must have operated in a comparatively short time.

Such illustrations might be indefinitely extended. In short, the great difficulty of dealing with this subject consists in the immensity of the mass of imperfectly observed facts and crude reasonings that have accumulated with reference to it, and which become positively wearisome in their discussion. The above examples are sufficient to show their nature.

I conclude, then, that there is no adequate geological reason for attributing the so-called " Neolithic " men to any time older than that of the early Eastern empires, or say 2,000 or 3,000 years before Christ, and that the time required for the Palæolithic men need not be more than twenty or thirty centuries additional. What evidence the future may bring forth I do not know, but that available at present points to the appearance of man, with all his powers and properties, in the Post-glacial age of geology, and not more than from 6,000 to 8,000 years ago. This abrupt appearance of man in his full perfection, his association with animals the greater part of which still survive, and his introduction at the close of that great and as yet very mysterious revolution of the earth which we call the Glacial period, accords, as I have elsewhere endeavoured to show,* with the analogy of geological science, in the information which it gives as to the first appearance of other types of organic being in the several stages of development of our earth.

The reader may perhaps ask, If these conclusions are so plain, why has there appeared to be so general an admission of the great antiquity of man on the part of geologists and archæologists? The reasons of this are not difficult to discover. They are such as the following: the great intricacy and difficulty of the geological questions connected with the close of the Glacial age and the beginning of the Modern period; the difficulty of verifying alleged facts as to the occurrence of remains in superficial deposits, and of ascertaining the age of these deposits and their freedom from modern admixtures; the small number of geologists and archæologists qualified by knowledge and experience to deal with questions of this kind; the enthusiasm with which novel and startling discoveries, and especially those appearing to contradict old and received opinions, are welcomed at present; the exigencies of the new philosophy of evolution, one

---

* See the more full discussion of this subject in the " Story of the Earth," and the " Origin of the World," and in my Address as President of the Geological Section of the American Association, in 1876.

of the stumbling-blocks of which is the recent appearance of man, along with an exaggerated and unreasonable application of the doctrine of uniformitarianism in geology. Such reasons are, I think, quite sufficient to account for the swing of opinion in this direction. But there are already indications of a reaction.

It is a curious conclusion of this part of our inquiry that the history of man, as indicated by Lyell in the above table, presents, after all, such a striking parallelism with the sacred and traditional histories with which we have long been familiar. The second period of continental elevation is the equivalent of the early antediluvian times—a period, however, of which we have seen we really know little from archæology or geology, for they cannot, with absolute certainty' affirm that the oldest skeletons known are of this age, though this may be regarded as probable. If they are, their extreme rarity, and the paucity of works of art, with the exception of flint implements in the chalk districts, where this material abounds, give the impression not of a long, but of a very limited period of residence of antediluvian man in Europe. The period of continental oscillation is the correlative of the later antediluvian period, and the last of these oscillations may have been the traditional deluge. The last period is unquestionably that of the Post-diluvian world. A leading school of modern archæologists no doubt demands much more time than that of our ordinary chronology, but the succession is the same, Further, this succession, when critically examined.

gives no ground for the belief in the existence, even in the most ancient times, of any race of men more rude than the modern semi-civilized races, or less developed physically. The most ancient man whose bones are known to us may be referred to a race still extant, and perhaps the most widely distributed of all —a fact which tells strongly in favour both of the unity and moderate antiquity of the species, while it is directly opposed to all theories of evolution from brute ancestors.

CHAPTER IX.

PRIMITIVE IDEAS OF RELIGION: THE IDEA OF GOD.

MAX MÜLLER, in his lectures on the Science of Religion, rejects the ordinary division into natural and revealed religions, and adopts a threefold grouping, corresponding to the division of languages into Turanian, Aryan, and Semitic. Though not quite satisfactory, more especially in its treatment of revelation, this method is suggestive of some important thoughts and questions. While we regard, for example, our own religion as revealed, we must bear in mind that it necessarily includes also the elements of natural religion. Further, while it may be classed as Semitic, as coming to us through a Semitic people, yet, according to its own history, in its earlier stages it was much more general than this, and in its earliest stage universal. Still further, we must not forget that it was not all revealed at once—that Adam, for example, could have known very little of it, Noah a little more, Abraham a little more, and so on. Again, the natural religion to which St. Paul refers in the first chapter of the Epistle to the Romans, as sufficient to teach men the power and divinity of God, was never absolutely pure at any time subsequent to the fall of man, and must have always contained some mixture, and this usually more or less corrupted, of what those who believe in divine revelation would regard as revealed religion. These considerations, from the point of view of the Christian, greatly modify Müller's classification. They further lead us to suppose that the Semitic religions will be found to be those most impregnated with revealed truth as we hold it, for our God is the "Lord God of Shem." The Aryan religions will be those bearing most evidence of the exuberance of human fancy, for Japhet's destiny is "expansion," if not "delusion;" while the wild old Turanian races, which I have endeavoured to show in previous chapters are the most primitive of all, may be expected to have religions the least mixed with the later ideas of revelation, and most stamped with the impress of its earliest truths, as well as with the general features of natural religion.

We have seen that the aboriginal races of America are Turanian in features and in language and customs, and they existed unmixed with other peoples, and unvisited by missionaries of the "book-religions," up to a very recent period. We can learn with much certainty the tenets of their religious belief, as it existed in tribes and nations both in a state of barbarism and in various stages of civilization. We can scarcely propose to ourselves a more interesting question in the present state of religious controversy, than that which relates to the beliefs of these people. How much did they know of what we regard as truth, whether in the domain of natural or revealed religion?

and what relations have their religions to those of the ancient and pre-historic peoples of the Old World? What do primitive, untutored men like those whose stern, grave faces are presented in the two photographs of Chippewa chiefs reproduced here, believe as to the great questions relating to God and a future state? There is the more reason to ask these questions, since it has been too much the habit of modern writers to deny to such rude tribes the possession of any religious ideas, because they do not present the forms of religion best known to us. It would seem as if a people not possessing churches, or temples, or images, or pictures, or a caste of priests, must necessarily have no religion, just as for similar reasons the early Christians were stigmatised as atheists, and as Laud is said, on returning from a tour in Scotland, to have reported that he could perceive no indications of religion among the Presbyterian people of that country.*

Our first answer shall be from the narrative of the old Breton seaman, Cartier, who discovered the St. Lawrence three hundred years ago, and who can teach us all the better that he is no missionary, but merely a rough sailor, not recognising any similarity between the traditions of the Indians and those he himself believed. The creed of Stadacona, the ancient Quebec, according to him might be stated thus: "There

---

* For remarkable and curious illustrations of this prejudice, I may refer to the discussion of this subject in Lubbock's "Pre-historic Times."

THE PRIMITIVE IDEA OF GOD.

is one god, known by the name *Cudragny*.* He speaks often to men, and gives them warning of the changes of the weather; but when offended, he throws dust in their eyes, or makes them blind. When men die, their souls rise to the stars, and, descending with these to the west, are received into the happy plains where there are beautiful forests and delicious

Fig. 30.—CHIPPEWA CHIEFS, FROM PHOTOGRAPHS.
Showing the characteristic Turanian type of the American Aborigines.

fruits." This creed was that held in one modification or another by all the American tribes, and expressed the fundamental ideas of their religion. The Great Spirit might be the Great Manitou, or Oghee-ma of

* The word is allied to Mandan *Okee*, Sioux *Oghee*, Iroquois *Oke*, Esquimaux *Aghatt*, Algonquin *Oghee-ma*. It seems to mean the chief or highest one. It resembles the name of the ancient Hindoo god Agni, and is perhaps allied to the Og and Agag of the pre-historic peoples of Palestine.

the Algonquins; Okee, or Omaha of the Mandans; or approaching more nearly to the familiar Aryan Theos and Deus, he might be the Teo of the Mexicans; but in every case there was a Great Spirit, though there might be multitudes of inferior deities. So in all these religions there was a distinct recognition of immortality and a future life beyond the grave. Let us consider these two doctrines separately; and first, that of the existence of a supreme God interesting Himself in human affairs.

The American deity was not a Hindoo Brahma, isolating himself from all inferior beings. That is a later conception of a degenerate faith. He revealed Himself to men, and it was the general American belief that this took place in dreams, in "thoughts from visions of the night, when deep sleep falleth upon men," and such revelations were usually made to gifted and chosen men, prophets who had, like Balaam, "their eyes open, and heard the words of God, and saw the vision of the Almighty." The absurdly sounding name, "Medicine men," by which these prophets or Shamans are usually known, seems to be a corruption of the Algonquin word Meda or Medawin, by which their art was designated; a word which, like many others used by these tribes, has its allies in the Greek and other Indo-European tongues, and may be radically the same with our "medicine."

That these revelations should relate in great part to the weather, is precisely the same fact which we find in the Pelasgic mythology of Zeus, or the Scandinavian worship of Thor. In either case, the Great Spirit is not the god of the ether, merely, as some closet mythologists suppose, because of a fanciful deification of the elements, but because to a rude people the changes of the weather are the principal natural facts which concern and impress them, and which, being apparently capricious and irregular, they refer to the most direct kind of divine action. Hence it may be affirmed that among all primitive peoples the chief god is more or less a weather-god. In the Old Testament, Baal, the Phœnician sun-god, was eminently a deity of this kind, as was also the Great Amen-Ra, "prince of the dew," and "lord of beams," among the Egyptians;[*] and even the Elohim of the Hebrews does not disdain to be the Being whose voice is the thunder, who holds the lightning in his hands, who makes the clouds his chariot, and whom the winds and the waves obey. So in the old sacred book of the Quiches of Central America, one of the most remarkable monuments of ancient American religion, the Creator is the Heart of Heaven, the lightning-flash, the thunderbolt, and his name is Hurakan, the storm-god—a name introduced into our own language in the word "hurricane."

But like many other ancient nations, the Americans were not content with the simplicity of pure monotheism; they added many subordinate gods. First among these stands a deification of the sun, arising

[*] See the remarkable Hymn in his honour recently published in Bagster's "Records of the Past," vol. ii.

perhaps from a natural confounding of the glorious and world-enlivening orb of day with the Great Spirit his maker, but in many nations taking the form of a separate worship. Among the ancient Peruvians, and possibly also among the Toltecans, this identification of the sun-god with the Supreme Being seems to have been complete. The Mexicans, however, had a separate sun-god, Tezcatlipoca, and in this they agreed with the Iroquois and Algonquins, whose sun-god was a deified hero, the child of the great first mother. With sun-worship was naturally connected fire-worship, and it is interesting to observe that this, which seems to have been the principal cultus of the Alleghans, or extinct mound-builders of the west, and of the Natchez and other southern tribes, had extended from them to the Algonquin peoples of the north. A Chippewa tribe, for example, inhabiting Kewenaw Point, one of the former mining districts of the Alleghans, kept up, according to Schoolcraft, a perpetual sacred fire in a sort of hearth or open furnace. Its chief attendant was the " Great Sun," or " Chief Sun," and one of its priestesses was called the " Woman ever standing in presence of the God," or as it has been quaintly rendered, the " Everlasting standing woman," the Pythoness of this western fire-god. This worship was said to have been derived from the south, and it seems to explain the altar-hearths of the mound-builders. Among the Iroquois and Hurons the sun was in some sense an emblem of their Ares or Mars, *Areskoui* or Agreskoui, while the Mexicans had a separate war-god, regarded by some as the brother of him of the sun.

In most cases among the Americans the sun was a beneficent god, associated with light, fertility, and happiness, as was also the case among the Indo-European and Semitic races of the Old World; and he connects himself in some respects with the ideas of a mediator or redeemer. This last thought centres around the great fundamental tradition of the first mother, which figures in all the American mythologies. We may take the Iroquois version of it as given by the early Jesuits and by Schoolcraft. *Neo,** equivalent to Anu of the older eastern theologies, is the Great Spirit; *Atahocan* is the Master of Heaven; *Tarenyawogan,* or the Great Hare (of whom more hereafter), is the Keeper of Heaven. From this trinity originates Atahensic, the first woman, and the American equivalent of Alytta and Astarte of the East, Persephone and Artemis of the Greeks, and the mother-goddess of so many other ancient nations.† Married to one of the six first created men, who seem to represent the six creative days, and expelled from heaven, she produces twins,

* Supposed by some to be a corruption of the French Dieu, but more likely allied to Mexican Teo.

† In Smith's translation of the Assyrian account of the Deluge, as given on the clay tablets in the British Museum, Ishtar (Astarte) is introduced as appealing to the gods on behalf of men, as the children she has brought forth, and as weeping over their calamities (lines 110 to 120). This fact, which I noticed after the above was written, affords an absolute confirmation of the idea that the original Astarte is identical with the biblical Eve and the American Atahensic.

s

who are Darkness and Light, or "Good mind" and "Evil mind," and who introduce the knowledge of good and evil on the earth. She afterwards bears a daughter who has two sons, the elder of whom, Yoskeka, kills his brother, and afterwards becomes the parent of mankind. Finally, Atahensic is deified as the "Queen of Heaven," with the moon as her emblem; while Yoskeka also becomes a demi-god in the other world, and the sun is his totem or emblematic mark. In Hades, Atahensic, like the ancient Artemis, in one at least of her functions, and like the Scandinavian Hela, becomes a guardian, and also a judge and castigator of her children after death, while on Yoskeka devolves the more beneficent function of being their advocate and intercessor. This story, which is but a specimen of this part of American theology, as held in various forms by different tribes, bears no remote resemblance to our own familiar narrative of Eve and the Fall. But its significance is far greater than this. It shows the connection of the biblical Eve, the introducer of evil, and at the same time the mother of the Redeemer, who is the "seed of the woman," with all those primitive idolatries in which the first woman becomes the object of worship as the Queen of Heaven and mother goddess; and it shows how natural is that superstition which in like manner, in more modern times, transfers the adoration of the Saviour to his mother. Alike in the Atahensic of America, the two-horned Astarte of primeval Syria, and the virgin queen of modern Rome, we have precisely the same modification of a religious idea, that of the promised seed of the woman, which underlies all the biblical development of the doctrine of the Saviour, and in corrupt forms figures in a host of superstitions, both ancient and modern.

Perhaps even the old Phœnicians, in the worship of their Moloch, or Melkart, scarcely carried the idea of mediatorial atonement to so tragic a pitch of grandeur as did the Mexicans in their annual sacrifices to Tezcatlipoca. Their priests selected one of the most beautiful young men, at once a representative of the god and a sacrifice, and after feasting and honouring him as the impersonation of deity, slew him upon the high altar in the presence of adoring thousands, and held up his dripping heart as a sign that the sins of the people were atoned for.

The Messianic idea has, however, engrafted itself on the American religions in quite another way. All the Indian nations have traditions of a great benefactor, a teacher of arts, and introducer of humanity and civilization. Among the Peruvians he is Manco Capac; among the Mexicans, Quetzalcoatl; among the Crees, Gepuchican; among the Micmacs, Glooscap; and the Iroquois form of the tradition forms the basis of Longfellow's "Hiawatha." He is represented as a benevolent hero, or demi-god of the olden time, who has left the world or been spirited away, and is to return. We may compare him with Vishnu, Odin, and Balder, with Horus, with Hercules, and a hundred other heroes and demi-gods of the eastern continent, all of them outgrowths of the yearnings of the human mind for a great deliverer from all the evils which beset humanity, yearnings which belong to the higher spiritual instincts of our nature, and which for the Christian are satisfied in the person and work of Jesus the Christ.

I have mentioned above the Iroquois legend of the Great Hare, which forms another, if less intelligible, connection of the religions and superstitions of the East and of the West. This idea prevailed throughout North America, from Mexico to the shores of the Arctic Sea. As held by some Algonquin tribes it represented Manibozoo, the Great Hare, as moving on the waters, and making the earth out of a grain of sand from the bottom of the sea, and man out of the dead bodies of animals which had preceded him. The Great Hare is thus the creator, and also embraces some attributes of the Divine Spirit as introduced in the Scriptures. We can only conjecture the origin of this use of the hare as an emblem of God. It may have arisen from the harmless, simple, noiseless, and spectre-like habits of the creature, or from its expressive face and eyes, or from its habit of erecting itself on its feet, and its antics at certain seasons, or, as some think, from its whiteness in winter. But whatever its origin, it goes back into remote antiquity, and is of very wide distribution. One effect of it is the aversion to eat the flesh of the animal, which still lingers as a sort of superstition in some parts of Europe, and which I have noticed even in European settlers in America.

The Lapps, Greenlanders, and Hottentots, are said to refuse to eat hares, and so do the Samal Arabs, while even the Chinese are said to object to it.* The ancient Britons had the same superstition, and their conquerors, the Saxons, held the hare as sacred to the goddess Freya. The bones of the hare are not found in the Danish shell-heaps or the Swiss lake-habitations, whence it is inferred that the ancient peoples who have left these remains did not eat the hare. They do, however, occur in the *débris* in the cave of Mentone and in the Belgian caves; showing that the hare was not everywhere regarded with the same veneration among the earliest races of Europe, or perhaps that, as in America, where the Hare Indians and many other tribes feed much on this animal, while still regarding it with a certain traditional veneration, the regard for it as a religious emblem did not hinder its use as food. A recent writer, who mentions many of these facts, seems to think that they have some connection with the rejection of the hare as food by the Jews, which he wrongly states was owing to "a false impression about its chewing its cud," whereas this would have been a reason for regarding it as clean, the reason of rejecting it being that it had paws instead of hoofs. But the Jewish Scriptures have no trace of the superstitious regard for the animal, and the Algonquin and Iroquois traditions give us the most probable explanation of the religious veneration of the hare in regarding it as the emblem of the Divine Spirit.

* Lubbock, "Pre-historic Times."

One part of the Iroquois tradition above referred to relates to a deluge by which the descendants of Atahensic were all destroyed, and the earth was replenished with inhabitants by the conversion of beasts into men. The traditions of the Mexicans on this subject are well known, and they are but a type of those prevailing throughout all the American tribes, and pointing to a division of the human period into two portions by a great diluvial catastrophe. One Mexican tradition conects this, as did the Egyptians, with the disappearance of the great continent Atlantis, which in antediluvian times connected America with Europe, and whose name has perhaps as good a claim to be derived from the Mexican *Atl* (water), as from the somewhat conjectural root adopted by Greek linguists. Another Mexican tradition, preserved by Humboldt, relates that Tezpi, or Noah, embarked in a great acalli, or house, with his wife, children, and animals, and stores of grain. Tezcatlipoca, the second person of the Mexican Trinity, equivalent to Atahocan of the Iroquois, caused the deluge to abate. Tezpi sends out a vulture and other birds, and finally a hummingbird,* which returned to him with green leaves, and then Tezpi joyfully disembarks on the mountain of Colhuacan. This story bears very nearly the same resemblance to the Noachic account of the Deluge with that which we find in the Chaldean tablets translated by Mr. Smith, and with much the same amount

* This bird, like the dove among us, was also the emblem of the third person of the Mexican Trinity.

of local colouring, but with less of complication with a developed system of idolatry, and, therefore, with a more truly primitive aspect. We may well suppose that similar traditions with similar local variations, were repeated round the camp-fires of those hardy wanderers who first penetrated into Europe after the Post-glacial submergence, and served to explain the bones of the gigantic men and still more gigantic beasts that lay in the caves they inhabited.

In some sort of connection with the belief in a deluge was the belief of many American tribes that the souls of drowned persons could not attain to paradise until their bodies were recovered and buried with certain sacrificial rites, consisting of the burning of parts of the viscera before interment. This may also be connected with the belief in malignant spirits of the water—the kelpies of our own ancestors; and with the superstition in China and elsewhere, that it is unlucky to rescue a drowning person.

It may be said that the preservation of such a tradition as that of the Deluge is impossible, since it is held by some historical critics that an oral tradition cannot survive with any degree of accuracy even for a century. But the geologist knows that a footprint in the sand, which in some circumstances must perish in an hour, may in others survive for untold ages. So with traditions. Among a rude people, with few ideas, when fixed in a form of words, traditions may be handed down indefinitely. If once reduced to pictographs, like those of the Mexicans, or even recorded on quipus or wampum-belts, they become still more unchangeable. But even an oral tradition among such people as the Americans is more enduring than a temple or a pyramid.

The American in still another point conformed to the most primitive and also most modern religious tendencies of his eastern brethren. He believed in an infinity of inferior spirits, good and evil, haunting particular places, attached as guardian angels or genii to certain persons, families, and tribes, of various powers and properties, and of which any object, animate or inanimate, might be the emblem or material representative. Throughout the whole of the vast Algonquin family, these spirits were designated by the word "Manitou," which reminds us of the ancient Pelasgic or Etruscan "Manes" of the Romans, and the "Menim," fates or destinies, of the Chaldæans and primitive Arabians. Under other names they were worshipped by the western and northern tribes, and the belief in them seems to have been universal throughout America. Evil manitous were to be deprecated by offerings, and good manitous were special tutelary spirits to whom was committed the care of human interests. Every man or woman might possess such a spirit guardian, who was revealed in the course of a protracted fast, undertaken for the purpose at the time of entering into manhood or womanhood. The guardian genius usually revealed himself in the guise of some material object, and this became at once the emblem of the manitou, and the totem or armorial bearing of the person. It was pictured on his shield and other weapons; it was tattooed on his body; it became his designation; to it he made vows in circumstances of doubt and difficulty, and offered sacrifices of such things as he valued. (Fig. 37.) It is scarcely necessary to add that the idea of certain animals and plants being sacred to or emblematic of particular gods is not confined to America. It exists and has existed alike among the most rude and refined of the nations of the Old World.

Fig. 37.—Totems of Chiefs of the Penobscot Indians, appended to a treaty made with the English at Casco Bay, 1727. (*From the Archives of Nova Scotia.*)

This subordinate worship of the manitous necessarily formed a large part of the practical religion of the individual, and obscured the perception of the Supreme God. Its resemblance to the beliefs in seraphim, genii, and guardian spirits, saints and angels, must occur to every one, and need not be followed in detail. Nor need we doubt that the same faith existed among the primitive men whose bones are found in the caves of Europe. The fishes, reindeer, and mammoths carved on their bone implements were not merely works of arts, undertaken to amuse idle hours. As interpreted by American analogies, they were the sacred totems of primeval hunters and warriors, and some of the rows of dots and scratches, which have been called "tallies," may be the records of offerings made to these guardian spirits, or of successes achieved under their influence. Some of the strangely formed bone sceptres of these ancient caves may have had the further significance of being the *bâtons* or rattles of medicine men or prophets, who were supposed to be specially inspired by manitous, and hence to be themselves veritable "Manties," or men identified with the manitous, and uttering their commands. (Fig. 38.)

Like the American nations, the pre-historic peoples of Europe had also pictographs representing important events. In the first part of the "*Reliquiæ Aquitanicæ*" such a representation, on a piece of deer's antler, has been figured. It is from the Dordogne caves, and the learned editors avow themselves unable to attach any meaning to it. An American Indian would, however, readily decipher it, and his reading, if I am not much mistaken, would be this: It represents a man walking with a burden or weapon upon his shoulder. Behind him is the sea (indicated by marks representing the waves), and in it swims a large eel. Meeting the man on the other side are two horses (indicated by their heads). The intention is to show the annual migration of the owner of the object

THE PRIMITIVE IDEA OF GOD. 267

from the sea, where he subsisted on fish, to the inland regions, where he hunted wild horses. The number of bars representing the waves has perhaps the additional meaning of indicating how many times he had performed this migration; and on the opposite side of the piece of bone are two heads of the aurochs, which

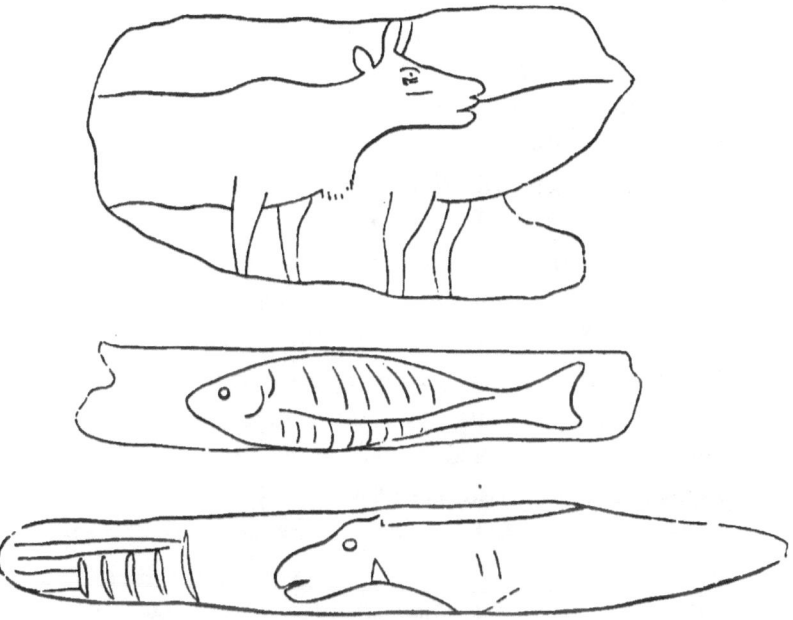

Fig. 33.—TOTEMS OF FAMILIES OF THE REINDEER AGE IN FRANCE.
(*From Christie and Lartet.*)

was perhaps his totem, or distinctive mark. Such a pictograph might, however, admit of a more precise interpretation. The aggressive attitude of the eel, with open mouth near the heel of the man, and the helpless and tame aspect of the horses, with the hasty movement of the man bending under his burden, may indicate an escape from an inundation rather than an ordinary migration. That even this may not be a strained interpretation may be seen from the Chippewa pictograph reduced from Schoolcraft (Fig. 40), which indicates the wishes of certain tribes with reference to certain territorial claims, and is also curious as an illustration of the use of totems. Fig. 39 is an outline of the French pictograph, which the editor of the *Reliquiæ* will excuse me for copying in consideration of the explanation above given.

In connection with the worship of manitous is the veneration of sacred places, of remarkable groves and trees, of strangely formed rocks, and of waterfalls, each of which is supposed to have its resident spirit, to whom offerings are made by the passing traveller. Rocks, more especially, have impressed the minds of primitive men in this way; and hence we have vast numbers of traditional sacred stones and sculptured stones, carved with the totems of their resident manitous, or with those of visitors desirous of propitiating them. Meteoric stones are known to have been held sacred by some tribes of Americans, probably because of their having been known to fall from heaven, just as similar facts are believed to have given origin to some of the most celebrated worships of Asiatic antiquity; as for example, to that of Diana at Ephesus. A more inexplicable superstition is the veneration paid to *green* stones, such as malachite, turquoise, and jade. Stones of this hue

Fig. 39.—Pictograph on a piece of Reindeer Horn from a Cave in the Dordogne.
(After Christie and Lartet.)

270   FOSSIL MEN.

seem to have been highly valued by all old races, both of the Old World and the New. The more civilized inhabitants of Central America and Mexico venerated blue or green stones, and mined for turquoise, as did the Egyptians, in their celebrated turquoise mines of the Sinai peninsula.

A remarkable example of a natural temple is that

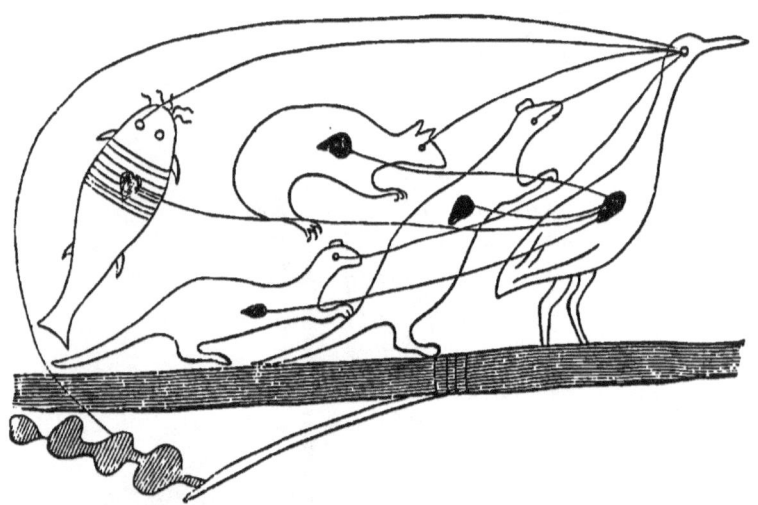

Fig. 40.—AMERICAN PICTOGRAPH FROM SCHOOLCRAFT, taken from a petition presented to the President of the United States, and showing that the chiefs represented by the totems of the crane, the marten, the bear, and the cat-fish, are of one mind and one heart with reference to the possession of certain lakes indicated in the rude map below them.

of the Roches Percées, on the plains of Western Manitoba, a province which derives its name from the manitou supposed to haunt a wave-beaten rock in one of its lakes.* These rocks are the fantastically

* See Frontispiece.

worn and eroded outcrop of certain sandstones of the Lignite Tertiary series, rising alone in the midst of a boundless prairie country, and striking the imagination of the traveller by a resemblance to ruined buildings. One of them forms a natural archway, resembling a fragment of an Egyptian temple, and is a veritable cathedral to all the wandering tribes of the West. Standing awe-stricken before this strange piece of nature's architecture, the Indian makes some simple offering, invokes the guardian spirit of the shrine, and perhaps engraves on the sandstone the mark of his own totem. The figures below (Fig. 41) show some of the marks thus made; and their resemblance in style to those on pre-historic implements of Europe must strike every one. Some of them are of course quite modern, but no one knows how far back in past ages these rocks have been venerated by the red man, who places on them his totem, or that of his tribe, with the same feeling with which an Englishman regards a monument in Westminster Abbey. The Indian, however, with an older and truer faith than that of many who despise or malign his simple worship, knows that the Most High "dwelleth not in temples made with hands," nor even in shrines of nature's workmanship, and regards these as merely the dwellings of the subordinate agents, who must obey the commands of the Great Spirit.

We can see in such a natural temple as the Roches Percées the original of the megalithic monuments which strike the imagination of the European antiquary,

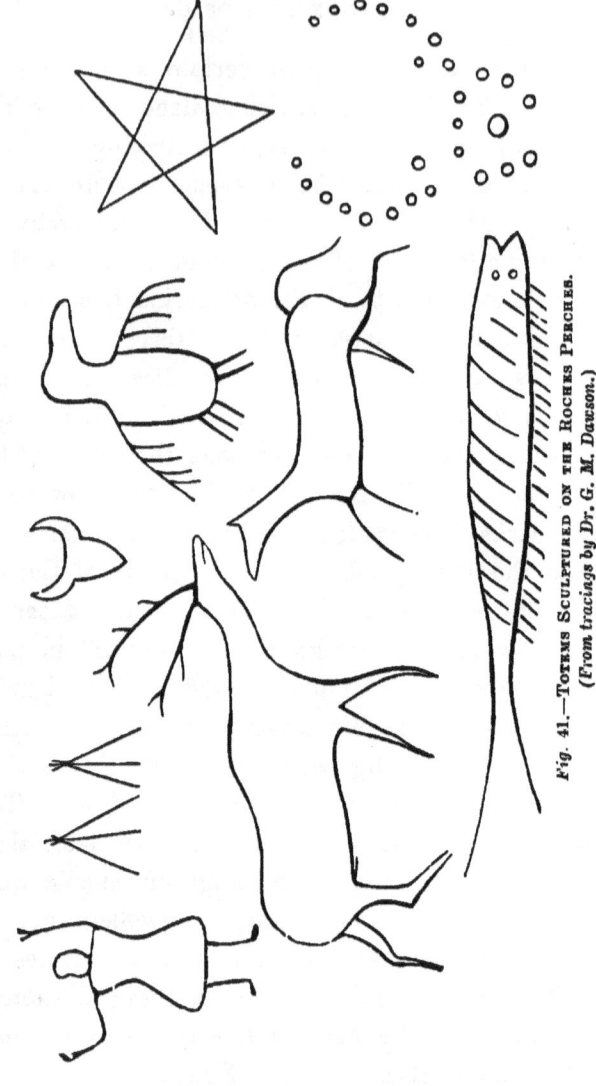

Fig. 41.—Totems Sculptured on the Roches Perchés.
(From tracings by Dr. G. M. Dawson.)

and also of the cave-like temples of ancient Egypt, of the massive teocallis of Mexico and Central America and even of our own huge cathedral piles. All are but the attempts of more civilized man to rival or surpass the grottoes and sculptured rocks which were revered by his remote ancestors as making more apparent to their untaught fancies the reality of the spiritual world with which fallen man seeks communion by so many quaint and strange devices, ever seeking to know God, yet ever confounding the creature with the Creator.

The fasts for manitous are connected with some of the most poetical tales of the American Indians—tales which rival in felicity of conception those of the ancient Greeks, however rude in expression. One of these, belonging to the Chippewas, and given in detail by Schoolcraft, may be summarised as follows:—A young man had reached the age proper for the manitou fast. His mother built him a lodge in a retired place, and he took up his abode therein and began his fast. At first his mind occupied itself with the shrubs and flowers around his shelter; and thinking of the goodness of the Great Spirit in giving so many varied gifts to man, he prayed that he might dream of something likely to be of use to his people. On the third day, while lying weak and faint in his bed, he saw a young stranger approach, dressed in green robes and with a green plume. He announced himself as a messenger from the Great Spirit, sent to grant his request, and invited the youth to a wrestling match. Weak though

T

he was, he endeavoured to obey, and after long trial his visitor said, "It is enough," and vanished. He returned a second and a third day, and the wrestling match was renewed, but the young man seemed to grow stronger with each contest, notwithstanding his abstinence. At length, on the seventh day of the fast, the youth, with a supernatural access of strength, overcame his visitor, threw him on the ground, and, obeying his directions, stripped him of his vest and plumes, and buried him in the earth. He visited the place again and again, carefully removing every weed, and at length he saw green blades spring up, and as the season advanced, strong stems shot forth, bearing ears of grain, and then in triumph the youth led his father to the spot, and showed him the ripened crop of maize. "It is monda-min!"—the spirit's grain —exclaimed the father; and thus the Indians first became acquainted with the culture of bread-corn. It is curious to note in this story the expectation of a heavenly revelation in the fast, the wrestling with the angel and prevailing, and the devout belief of the special provision of food for man—all features of a very primitive faith; while there is a touch of allegory in the green vesture and plume of the heavenly stranger stripped off, and his body buried, as emblematic of the seed-corn denuded of its green husk and feathery tassel and sown in the ground. Many other Indian tales, often very poetical and touching, are connected with the fasts for manitous. Still more protracted fasts were undergone by those who aspired to be medicine-men, in order that they might fully enter into communion with the manitous which were supposed to animate them; and there seems little doubt that these men, though often impostors, were sometimes possessed with a real religious frenzy.

A darker feature of the belief in manitous was the dread of those imagined to be evil-disposed, and which often filled the poor savage with extreme terror, and embittered his life with the apprehension of the ills that might be inflicted on him by those mysterious powers. In some cases, more especially, these superstitious terrors were excessive, and took possession of whole tribes, impelling to actions of folly and cruelty equal to those of our own ancestors in darker days, when they became afflicted with a witch-panic or with dread of the "evil eye."

I have already stated that the carvings on ivory and bone found in the caves of the Dordogne, in France, might be regarded as the totems of their possessors, the emblems of their guardian manitous. This has a bearing on the significance which we are to attach to the carving supposed to represent the mammoth, found in one of these caves, and which has so often been figured and described as an evidence that man existed before the disappearance of this animal. That some great warrior or chief of the Palæolithic age had the mammoth for his armorial bearing and for the emblem of his guardian genius is no doubt significant of a time when the creature was known, at least by tradition. Anything beyond that it does not certainly prove, any more than the figure of St. George and the dragon on an English coin would show that the saint and the dragon survived to the times of the Georges. Such a totem might, like the manatee carved on the pipes of the Ohio mound-builders, refer to an animal of a distant country, from which the owner or his ancestors had migrated, or with which they had intercourse. It might also be handed down as an heirloom for a vast number of generations, and might pass from tribe to tribe. Its actual last possessors might thus never have seen the mammoth, though they must have known it by tradition. Some of the Algonquin tribes had a tradition of the mammoth or mastodon as a great elk, with an arm projecting from its shoulder, and the Micmacs represent the bones of the mastodon as belonging to gigantic beavers which their great hero, Glooscap, destroyed. The mammoth was in any case the symbol of some pre-historic man or tribe of France: and in the cave of Bruniquel we find, along with beautiful fish-harpoons, figures carved on implements, and representing the horse, ibex, snake, reindeer, and salmon; so that if we knew the language of these people, we could decipher their names on their implements. An American Indian could in any case read them in his own tongue as pictographs, and might also conjecture the facts indicated by some of the significant marks and dots attached to them.

Lyell well remarks that these carvings teach us that the ancient tribes who hunted in the Dordogne, perhaps before the historical deluge, "did not belong to a less developed stage of humanity than some hunter tribes of the present day." He might have added that in their arts and superstitions, as well as in their physical characters, they approached very near to the somewhat noble type of semi-barbarous man still extant in America.

In summing up this subject, it may be well to refer to the probability that the race of men known by the general name Turanian is the oldest now extant. This race, occupying the northern parts of Asia, and identical in physical characters on the one hand with the American tribes, and on the other with the oldest races whose skulls are found in the European caves, seems also to have been that which preceded the Aryan races in India and in the south of Europe, and the Semitic races in western Asia. On the one hand, its religious ideas are identical with those still surviving in America and northern Asia, as well as to some extent in China, and with the oldest religions shadowed forth to us in the ancient records and traditions of Palestine, Aryan India, and Greece, and crystallised for us in the childlike narratives of the book of Genesis.* From these primitive ideas were developed on the one hand the Hebrew prophecy which culminates in the glorious truths of Christianity, and on the other all the wonderful myths of the Aryan polytheism.

* And also represented in the Chaldean legends of the Creation and Deluge, recently translated by the late Mr. George Smith.

If these general statements be conceded—and I think a vast mass of fact lying beyond the range of our present inquiry might be adduced to prove them, —then the following general truths may be accepted as to the primitive religious connections of the New World and the Old. (1) All the religions of America, and all the primitive faiths of the Old World, alike embrace the elements of a Supreme Creator, subordinate spirits of good and evil, a fallen human race, a first mother, who is the mother of a Saviour, and a division of human history into two periods by a diluvial catastrophe. (2) There is no trace of the origin of these ideas in any other source than historical fact and primitive monotheism. It is impossible to trace them back to mere worship of the elements and to fetichism. They are remnants of a higher and purer faith. (3) The American races must have diverged from the general mass of humanity at a period so early that the peculiar features of the Hebrew and Aryan religions had not yet developed themselves out of the primitive patriarchal faith, so that the origin of the American religions lies in the antediluvian and early post-diluvian time. (4) This accounts for the fact that some have seen in these American religions Egyptian, Indian, Hebrew, or Aryan influences, because the primitive ideas of all these exist in America, though undeveloped, or developed after a peculiar manner. (5) Both in language and religion such special affinities as exist connect the Algonquin tribes with the Aryan races, or rather, with the so-called Pelasgic elements which formed the front of the Aryan wave, and were perhaps as much Turanian as Aryan. In like manner, the same indications connect the Toltecans, Peruvians, and Alleghans with the south of Asia and Polynesia; and the Esquimaux, the Chippewyans, and the West Coast tribes with the Mongolian race of northern Asia. Still, all these elements must have been nearer to each other than they have been in historic times, when the early migrations to America took place. Lastly, all these elements of primitive faith point back to a golden age of simplicity and piety, corrupted and decaying under the influence of rudeness and barbarism on the one hand, or of a sensual and ungodly civilization on the other.

We thus learn how the aboriginal American, and probably, also, the primeval European, solved the great question of the origin of the earth and man, and of his own relation to the Supreme Being. With such dim light of nature as he had, he could at least conceive of higher spiritual beings and of a Creator, and could feel that God was nigh to him. He had, it is true, mixed up these primitive tenets with many corruptions and imaginings, but the substratum of his faith was identical with that of the patriarchal age, as revealed to us in Scripture, and whose truth is vouched for, not only by the connection with it of the subsequent superstructure of revelation, but by the natural and invincible persuasion of the existence of God, which is ineradicable from the human mind in all ages and places.

It is further instructive to observe that, except in the more civilized nations, he had not corrupted his faith with the apparatus of complex rituals and idols made with hands. These things in the New World, and no doubt also in the Old, were growths of immoral and hypocritical civilization. Again, the American religion was not materialistic or of the nature of fetichism. Even the rudest tribes were not, like some modern scientists, and perhaps some of the lower Papuan races, "Monists," who cannot conceive any primary existence except material forces—brute and inorganic—of which man is at once the product and the sport and victim. To arrive at this position requires either the utmost extreme of brutal degradation or of one-sided mental culture. Primitive man was evidently neither in one position nor the other. Neither was he properly pantheistic. He knew that man cannot be God, however much he might believe that there is a likeness between God and man; and though he might imagine a multitude of spirits connected with particular objects and places, yet they were all either ministering spirits of the Great Spirit, or manifestations of that Spirit himself in the things that his power had evolved from old chaos and night; and all essentially distinct from the objects which were their abodes, or their emblems, or the objects of their care. I by no means desire unduly to exalt prehistoric religions, but I wish distinctly to affirm that they, and what we call the heathenism or animism of untaught tribes, were nearer to God and truth than are either the ritualisms and idolatries or the materialistic scepticisms of more civilized times, when men, "professing themselves to be wise, become fools."

These primitive beliefs thus serve to confirm our faith in the inspired and historical records of humanity, in opposition to the crude theories which have been put forth in the misused name of science. In a practical point of view, the fact that all religions contain traces of primitive truth akin to that which was the original creed of the race, should encourage missionary effort even amongst the most degraded peoples, should warn us against despising either the simple theology of Genesis or the equally simple beliefs of untutored men, guided only by the light of nature; and should deter us from giving way to these æsthetic and merely outward corruptions of spiritual truth, which are equally absurd in their most antique and most modern forms, and are less excusable in the latter. "The past times of this ignorance God has overlooked, but now commands all men everywhere to repent."

CHAPTER X.

PRIMITIVE IDEAS OF RELIGION: THE INSTINCT OF IMMORTALITY.

As we prefaced the discussion of the Idea of God with an extract from Cartier, giving the creed of the ancient Stadaconians, we may in like manner introduce that of the doctrine of a future state with an extract from Carver, who visited the tribes of the great plains at the head of the Missouri in 1766 to 1768. He thus states the creed of one of the tribes of Dakotas or Sioux, a people then altogether unacquainted with any foreign religion. "They acknowledge one Supreme Being or giver of life, who presides over all things. The Chippewas call this being Manitou or Kitchi Manitai; the Nundowessies Wakon or Tongo-wakon,* that is, the Great Spirit; and they look upon him as the source of good, from whom no evil can proceed. They also believe in a bad spirit, to whom they ascribe great power, and suppose that through his means all the evils which befall mankind are inflicted. They hold also that there are good spirits of a lesser degree, who have their particular departments, in which they are constantly contributing to the happiness of mortals.

* Wakon or Augha is the same with the Canadian Oki or Agni; and the prefix Tongo may be compared with Mongolian Tong and Tang, and Chinese Tien, the name of the Sky-God.

To all of these they pay some kind of adoration. They doubt not but they shall exist in some future state; they however fancy that their employments there will be similar to those they are engaged in here, without the labour and difficulty attached to them in this period of their existence."

I give this extract more especially because it is the fashion at present with a certain school of archæologists to eliminate from the American religions the ideas of a Supreme Being, of good and evil, and even of immortality. Cartier and Carver, and a host of other unexceptionable evidences, could be quoted against this stupid sacrifice of facts to a prevalent but transient theory.

Among rude peoples the belief in immortality exhibits itself chiefly in their treatment of the bodies of the dead, and in the rites connected with burial, and it is information of this kind alone that we can have regarding pre-historic men; thus funeral rites must occupy a prominent place in this chapter. We must expect to find many of them crude and childish in the extreme; but we need not wonder at this when we think for a moment of the mixture of forms, heathen, mediæval, and scriptural, and the strange compound of grief, hope, and pageantry which attend burial among ourselves, with all our greater knowledge and more rational belief of immortality.

The Americans universally held the posthumous life and separate existence of the soul. When questioned as to the nature and properties of the disembodied spirit, they were, like ourselves, unable to give any definite answer, and compared it to a shade or ghost of the body, to a breath, air, or mist, or to the appearance of a bird—all, however, ancient and familiar representations among the nations of the Old World. They also most naturally believed that the tastes and desires of the dead were the same with those which had actuated them in life. Hence it was proper to bring offerings of food to the grave, and to bury with the corpse what the person had valued during life, or some model or miniature representation of it. In the case of eminent persons, costly gifts might be given by friends or dependents, or even by tribes and nations, for this purpose. They also believed that for a time after death the soul hovered over or remained with the body, before taking its final departure for the world of spirits, and it was supposed by some that the funeral feast held in honour of the dead was that which gave it its passport for the long journey.

The soul having thus departed was believed to make its way to the happy land, and the path thither was provided with accessories similar to those with which ancient mythologies have rendered us familiar. Some believed in the simple pathway of the stars, to which I have already referred.* Others believed in a long and dangerous journey, or in a river of death, whose Charon used a stone canoe, or which was crossed by a narrow and slippery bridge. There was a Cerberus, also, to be contended with, and the souls of the wicked might either perish altogether in the attempt

* P. 253.

to surmount these difficulties, or might be punished for their sins before entering the Elysian fields.

The happy land was usually in the far west, because thither the orbs of heaven went for their rest, and because the sunset sky daily opened up the glories of heaven's portal, to delight the eyes of men and to beckon them to immortality. Among the Americans, as among the Greeks, there were stories of adventurous men who had voluntarily descended into Hades to rescue the souls of their friends. Charlevoix found one of these stories, which he compares to that of Orpheus and Eurydice, and Schoolcraft has preserved two of them, which, as products of imagination, are not unworthy of a place beside classical stories of this type, themselves probably older than the times of Greek civilization.

The belief in future happiness beyond the grave was not a shadowy imagination, but a firm and practical conviction. The early Jesuit missionaries record with wonder the stoicism and stern joy with which the savage met death, and his certain assurance of a blessed hereafter. If the dying man was the head of a family, he chanted in advance his funeral song or oration, giving parting advice to his children and sorrowing friends, as in that wonderful death-song of Jacob preserved to us in Genesis. It may be well to remark here that the gifts of oratory and song were not rare among the Americans, nor are they rare among other rude tribes. Though without a written language, they had already entered on the path of literary composition, and such orations and songs as have been preserved to us are sometimes by no means despicable efforts. The dying speech having been finished, presents were given to the sick man by members of his family, and the relatives took their last farewell, wishing him a happy journey, and consoling him with the hope of the joys at its termination, and with the assurance that his children would sustain the reputation of his name. Among one northern tribe, according to Charlevoix, it was believed that when old persons survived until their dotage, they would have to begin their new life in the other world as mere infants. To avoid this, so strong was the conviction of eternal life, old persons verging on decrepitude were in the habit of beseeching their relatives to strangle them, that they might enter the future life in the full possession of their powers. *

The faith of the survivors in the immortality of their deceased friends was exhibited in the care of the body, and in the simple rites and offerings by which they hoped to promote the welfare of the disembodied spirit. First among these may be mentioned the securing of companions and assistants to the departed shade. The terrible expedient of immolating prisoners, slaves, and wives, on the tomb, so prevalent in the Old World, was not unknown in the New. Among the northern tribes, their only domestic animal, the dog, was obliged to accompany his master into the

* The same belief and practice are recorded by Hunt as existing among the Fijians.

land of death, just as among the ancient Scythians and some modern Americans, the warrior's horse was slain to bear him on his long journey. The dogs, killed immediately after death, usually formed a part of the funeral feast, but this did not conflict with the idea that the spirits of these sagacious animals might guide the shade to its final abode. Cranz, a Greenland missionary, relates that it is a practice with the people of that forlorn region to place the head of a dog in the tomb of a child, "in order that the soul of the dog, which can always find its way home, may show the helpless infant the way to the country of souls." Some of the arctic navigators who have opened Esquimaux graves confirm the statement of the missionary. Nilsson quotes this touching instance of care for the soul of the deceased child in illustration of the fact that skulls of dogs occur in ancient burial-mounds of the Stone age in Sweden, which in many other respects resemble the burial-places of the Greenlanders. A similar association of remains of the dog with those of man has been found in a pre-historic Irish tumulus,* and in Peru the skeleton of the same faithful friend of man is sometimes found in the family sepulchre.

It has been remarked with reference to some European interments, that flint implements and weapons appear to have been buried with the dead, even after the close of the Stone age. This may be explained by the superstitious reverence which came to

* Knock Maraidhe, Dublin.

be entertained for the ancient weapons. It was fit that the Modern should appear in presence of his ancestors with their ancient and time-honoured appliances. But American analogy affords another explanation. The medicine-man provided himself with all ancient and curious things, as old weapons, curiously formed stones, or fossil shells. These paraphernalia of his trade might be placed with him in his grave, and thus afford a strange association of objects. Even the ordinary Indian might have a medicine bag, in which were old arrows or flint flakes, carried as talismans, which would also be buried with him, even in cases where no other objects might be so interred. To take a modern instance. When the late Prince Imperial of France was slain by the Zulus, his body was stripped, but a reliquary worn suspended to his neck was left, because to have taken this would have been a sacrilege according to the primitive belief of the African. Had the body been buried where it fell, this "medicine bag" and its contents would have been the only objects to indicate its date or nation.

To return to the funeral ceremonies. Among the Canadian tribes, the corpse, immediately after death, was placed in a sitting posture at the door of the hut, its face painted, dressed in the best robe of the deceased, and with his weapons beside it. Thus seated in state, it was visited by friends. It was then taken to the place of burial, and laid in a grave carefully lined with the richest furs, as if the last resting-

THE INSTINCT OF IMMORTALITY.

place were to be a bed of peaceful sleep. The grave was covered with a rough roof of split wood or bark; a post was set up on which were carved the emblems of the dead, and some rude marks to indicate his actions. (Fig. 42.) And on this, or on the grave,

Fig. 42.—ADJEDATIG, OR GRAVE-POST OF WABOJEEGSE, THE "WHITE FISHER," a Chippewa chief, who died in 1793 (*from Schoolcraft*). The reindeer at the top is the totem of his family; it is inverted to indicate death. The horizontal marks denote the number of his war parties and other military achievements. The three perpendicular lines indicate three wounds received in battle. The head of a moose commemorates a combat with one of these animals. The other emblems are supposed to indicate his influence as a ruler, and the animal below is perhaps his dog, represented as dying with his master.

were placed offerings to the spirit, as weapons or useful utensils; while for the time when the spirit was supposed to haunt the grave, daily offerings of food were supplied. In the case of infants, mothers have been seen to shed the milk from their breasts on their little graves; and I have been informed that among some tribes there is more mourning for the death of a child than for an adult, on the ground of its greater helplessness in the lone land of spirits. The woodcut (Fig. 43) of Chippewa mourners is from a photograph, and shows the roofed grave with objects suspended on it as offerings, and an opening to introduce supplies of food, and the grave-post whereon to hang other offerings or emblems. After the funeral, presents were given to the relatives of the dead by their friends or by the tribe collectively, and a funeral feast was held by the family. This was accompanied by games, ending, says Charlevoix, who records these rites, with songs and cries of victory.

In some cases the offerings to the dead took the form, not of valuable articles, but of mere models of these, like the tissue-paper garments burned by the Chinese as sacrifices to their ancestors. This may be regarded as the creeping in of hypocrisy or ritualism, properly so called, into a practice once high and noble. Different from this, however, was the practice of defacing and rendering useless, either by mechanical injury or by fire, the objects offered to the dead, an act which implies the final renunciation of them on the part of the living, and may have also been understood as a species of death ushering them into the other world for the benefit of the dead. All this has its analogues in the Eastern continent, even in historic times.

Fig. 43.—Chippewa Graves and Mourners.

(*From a Photograph taken by photographers on the B. N. A. Boundary Commission, 1873.*)

In front of the nearest grave is seen the grave post, with leaves and a vessel for offerings tied to it. In the end of the wooden structure covering the grave is a hole for inserting offerings of food, and at top it is ornamented with leaves. At the side is hung the worked knife-case of the deceased, and above is a head-dress of feathers. The Indians represented belong to a decaying tribe, now poor and degraded by intercourse with the whites, but still retaining to some extent its ancient customs and beliefs, among which are Feasts for the Dead.

Last of all came the great octennial or decennial feast of the dead, most important of all the national ceremonies of the St. Lawrence tribes. Arrangements were made as to the time and place, and a master of the ceremonies was appointed, and friends were invited from neighbouring villages. When all was ready, they proceeded in procession to the cemetery, disinterred and cleansed the bones, amidst the lamentations of the women, wrapped them in new furs, and then, with many ceremonies, feasts, dances, and games, conveyed them to the great national pit or ossuary, where they were finally interred with the richest funeral gifts, and covered with the heaped-up soil.

> "Here bring the last gifts, and with them
> The last lament be said,
> Let all that pleased and yet may please
> Be buried with the dead."

The arrangements of burial differed among different tribes. In ancient Micmac graves, in Prince Edward Island, the bones have been found wrapped in birch bark, and with a little parcel of arrow or spear-heads interred with them. Some of the western tribes leave the corpse and its property in its lodge, which thus becomes its tomb. Some raise the bodies of the dead aloft on stages, a custom which prevails as far off as Papua, where the people have also long, communistic houses, inhabited by many families, like the Iroquois and Hurons. Some tribes buried their dead in caverns; and the old Alleghans, and other agricultural tribes of the west and south, erected great mounds over the dead, some of which, as the Grave-Creek Mound, in Virginia, seventy feet in height and a thousand feet in circumference—are among the greatest burial tumuli in the world. The elaborate subterranean sepulchral chambers of the old Peruvians are well known, and are, like the graves of the Greenlanders and the "gallery graves" of the ancient Scandinavians, miniature houses furnished with the utensils or weapons of the dead.

Such differences in manner of burial might depend merely on difference of circumstances, and various modes might prevail among the same race. It is probable that the extinct Bœotics, or Red Indians of Newfoundland, were not an Algonquin people, but an eastern extension of the great Chippewyan or Tinné race, intermediate between the Algonquins and the Esquimaux, and entering America from the northwest. These people were destroyed partly by European settlers, and partly by their hereditary enemies, the Micmacs of Nova Scotia. In 1827 an expedition was fitted out, under the auspices of the Newfoundland Government, by the explorer, McCormick, with the view of ascertaining if any remnant of them existed. He penetrated to the Red Indian Lake, their former head-quarters, but there found nothing but the ruins of their huts and their graves. The interments had been of various kinds; some were in carefully-built huts of bark, others on stages or poles, others under heaps of stones. The body of an unfortunate young woman, taken prisoner by the whites, among whom she died, and after death was left to be recovered by her tribe, was recognised by the remains of European clothing which these poor savages had scrupulously buried with her. If we ask the reason of this variety, the climate affords a ready answer. In Lower Canada at this day, the bodies of those who die in winter are preserved in vaults until spring, when they can be properly buried; so among the Red Indians, any one dying in winter could not be interred in the frozen ground or buried under stones, but must be placed in a bark cabin or on a stage. In like manner it is quite conceivable that under different circumstances the same tribe might bury their dead, or dispose of them by cremation, as the Kutchin of north and west America, a branch of the same stock with the Bœotics, now do.

But however different in details, all these modes of burial rested on the belief in immortality, and on the idea that the care of the body and the provision of suitable offerings had a connection with the soul's welfare in a future life, and perhaps the meanest and basest thing in modern literature is the attempt made by some writers on this subject to explain away these beliefs as held by pre-historic men. A further illustration of these beliefs, and also probably of some dim notion of a resurrection of the body, is afforded by the desire of the American Indian to be in death "gathered to his fathers." A touching instance of this feeling is afforded by the story of the aged Micmac Sachem, or Sagamo, Mambertou, a man of high character and influence among his people, and evidently of great personal qualities. He became an early convert of the missionaries, and when attacked with his last illness was carried to Port Royal for medical assistance; but finding this of no avail, and his end approaching, he asked the Governor, Beincourt, to promise that his body should be taken to his native village and buried with those of his ancestors. The promise was given, but no sooner was it known to the Jesuit missionaries, than they were filled with horror; their noble convert could not be buried with infidels, his bones must lie in consecrated ground. Beincourt suggested that they might consecrate his grave in the Micmac burial-place, but this was out of the question, unless all the old infidels in the cemetery could first be disinterred and removed. The quarrel threatened to be serious, and the angry monks withdrew, and declared that if Mambertou persisted in his unreasonable wish, they would have nothing to do with his death or burial, and would withhold the rites of the Church. No modern Ultramontanes could display more faithful ritualism or more genuine antagonism to all that is holy and spiritual in religion and in man; and the Jesuit narrative records with satisfaction that their firmness triumphed; for the dying chief, unable to struggle against their fanaticism, quietly gave way, and his bones lie in the old French cemetery of Port Royal.

America, we have seen, is rich in examples of the belief in a future state. We may now turn for a little to pre-historic Europe, and note the parallelism. We may here at once affirm that the oldest "Neolithic" mounds and cave interments of Europe bespeak beliefs similar in every respect to those of America. I have already referred to this in the case of the "gallery graves" of Scandinavia, and it is equally apparent in the sepulchral tumuli. But how was it with those oldest tribes of men supposed to have been contemporary with the now extinct Post-glacial mammals? Unfortunately, most of the remains of this period are not of a character to give much information as to rites of sepulture or religious beliefs. There are, however, some which partially make up for this defect, and I shall refer here to a few instances.

Among the caves on the banks of the River Lesse, described by Dupont in his book on the Pre-historic Ages, one of the most curious, the Trou de Frontal, in Belgium, is a sepulchre of the so-called Reindeer Age, which intervenes between the earliest Palæolithic or "Mammoth" Age, and that of Polished Stone. It is rather an overhanging ledge or shelter than a cave, except at its inner side, where there is a chamber about two yards in length by one in breadth. This inner chamber had been used as a sepulchre, in which were found bones referable to sixteen persons of different ages. The mouth of the cave had been closed with a slab of dolomite, and on the terrace in front, and under the overhanging ledge, was a hearth of stones which had been used for funeral feasts, and around which were the bones of many animals, all recent, but some now locally extinct, as, for example, the reindeer. With regard to the age of this sepulchre, it is later than the earliest human age of Europe, when we know from other evidence that the country was inhabited by a race of gigantic stature and physically similar to the best developed of the American races. But it is older than the historic age, and belongs to a time when the earlier race had been replaced by another of smaller stature, but still Mongolian or Turanian in features, and corresponding to the Lapps in Europe and the Esquimaux in America. These, again, at some unknown period, were replaced by the historic Celtic and Germanic races. Let us now consider the manner in which these people buried their dead.

The mixed and disjointed condition of the bones shows that either the burials took place at long intervals of time, or that the place was a sort of ossuary, into which bones taken up from a first burial were put, in the manner we have already described. With the dead were buried their ornaments and implements. Among these were pierced pieces of fluor spar and perforated shells, used no doubt as beads or wampum, and chipped flint weapons. A plain earthen jar, not unlike some of those found in ancient American burial-places, but less ornamented, was found in fragments, and had probably held provisions for the dead. The survivors had attempted to perpetuate the memory or achievements of their deceased friends; for two slabs of sandstone were found, one with unknown markings, the other with the figure of an animal, probably the totem of the family or tribe to whom the vault belonged. Feasts for the dead must have been a recognised institution, as evidenced by the hearth built for them, and by the quantity of charcoal, ashes, and bones upon and around it. Dupont enumerates more than forty species of quadrupeds, birds, reptiles, and fishes, which had been used in these repasts, and which show that these people were as omnivorous in their tastes for animal food, and as skilful in gratifying them, as are the American Indians. This cave, which in many respects resembles that of Aurignac, so well described by Lartet and Lyell, and other tombs of this age, tells in a manner too plain to admit of contradiction, of the same hopes with reference to the dead which we have seen in the funeral rites of pre-historic America.

But there was in Europe a still earlier race. Were they cognisant of this sublime hope? We have, it is true, few indications of their beliefs; but what we have show that, while physically a superior race to that which succeeded them, they were equally, in their own judgment, heirs of a future life.* I have already referred to the carvings in the cave of Bruniquel, in France, probably belonging to this most ancient human age, as evidence of their belief in God. Of the sepulchral caves of this period I may take that of Mentone, already noticed, as evidence of their identity with the Americans in the belief in immortality.

* It should be noted however, that the Bible gives reason to believe that the chief sin of antediluvian times was a disregard of God and a future life.

The first human skeleton found in this cave has been beautifully illustrated in the photographs published by Dr. Rivière. It was discovered under about twenty feet of material, which is characterized as chiefly ashes and cinders of fires, mixed with the bones of recent and extinct mammalia, flint flakes, and shells. The locality, as described by Dr. Rivière, is not likely, unless great changes of level have occurred, to have been inhabited by a settled tribe, but is rather a maritime pass between France and Italy, where large bodies of men may have resided for a time in the course of migrations, or of hunting and military expeditions. The skeleton is that of a man of great stature, who must have been a hunter or warrior, of physical type decidedly Turanian, and akin to that of the aborigines of North America; while his limb-bones have the development of muscular processes characteristic of men who walk much through rough forests, and his arm-bones are those of a hunter rather than of a man familiar with steady manual labour. This body lay extended in an easy position, as if, says its discoverer, he had died in his sleep. There is no evidence of violent death, though he may have died from the effects of a flesh or internal wound, not leaving traces on the skeleton. He had evidently been buried by his friends in a cave previously used as a habitation, and afterwards occupied for a long time in the same way.

As interpreted by American usages, the interment may be explained thus. A war-party returning from an unsuccessful expedition into France or Italy, halted

at the caves of Mentone; and here a wounded man,
whom they had been carrying with them, expired, and
was hastily buried in the cave, perhaps in the hope
that they might be able to return at some future time
and convey the bones to the tomb of his fathers. They
laid a few stones around the body of the dead, as a
substitute for the cromlech, or funeral cyst, and buried
him with an ornamented helmet of shell on his head,
shell armlets and anklets, and his robes of fur wrapped
around him. His arms had probably been left on the
field of battle, and there were no spoils to bury with
him. The only thing they possessed, or which the
neighbourhood afforded, to promote his welfare in the
land of spirits, was a little iron oxide, carried with them
to be ground into war paint. With this they, no doubt,
painted his face; but they appear to have sprinkled it
over him, and to have placed a little additional supply
in a hollow in front of his head, that he might appear
in his proper character in the spirit land. All this was
precisely what American Indians would do in a similar
case; and perhaps his companions, before they sorrow-
fully departed, sang his death-song, and kindled over
his grave the fire of a funeral feast, as well to honour
his memory as to prevent pursuing foes from disturbing
his remains. The next occupants of the cave probably
knew nothing of the burial, and the friends of the dead
did not return to reclaim his remains; so he lay undisturbed till disinterred by Dr. Rivière, and removed
to the Parisian Museum.

If, as there is every reason to believe, this is an

interment of the oldest Palæolithic or "Mammoth" Age, the antediluvian age of history, we learn from it that the people of that age were of very high physical organization, and very closely resembled the American type; and their manner of interment shows that they shared with the Americans and with their successors of the Reindeer Age a belief in a hereafter, along with its accompanying regard for the proper interment of the dead.

Before leaving this part of the subject, it may be well to refer to the very small number of human remains of the Palæolithic Age found in Europe. Not only have few burial-places been found, but those discovered contain very few skeletons compared with those found in American cemeteries and ossuaries. This cannot be accounted for by supposing that the dead were left unburied, since it is clear that in the case of both the men of the Mammoth and Reindeer Ages burial was practised, and this in the case of women and children as well as men. It is, however, quite possible that, like the Americans and Papuans, they may have ordinarily placed their dead on wooden stages or in shallow graves covered with wood and bark, and that the cave interments may be exceptional. If not, then it is evident either that these primæval tribes, were sparsely scattered over the country and very small, or that the period of their occupancy was very limited.

It is also worthy of remark that the different kinds of burial, as in the earth or on stages, in the sitting posture or extended, in caves, in ossuaries, or under tumuli, and also cremation, have their representatives on both sides of the Atlantic. What may be called the house-tomb, representing the habitation of the deceased person when in life, is world-wide in its extension. It is seen in the lodge of the western Indian or the winter-house of the Esquimaux closed up and converted into a sepulchre, in the gallery graves, dolmens and chambered barrows of Europe, and in the rock-cut tombs of Etruria, Egypt, and the East, and the chamber-tombs of Peru. In all cases it points to the idea of a house of the dead corresponding to that of the living, and has no obscure connection with the belief in a resurrection of the body. The tumulus, in every style, from the little grave-mound of a country churchyard, or of an ordinary Indian burial-place, to the ossuaries of the Hurons, the huge mounds of the Ohio, the barrows of Europe and Asia, and the pyramids of Egypt, which are merely great stone tumuli, is common to the most varied tribes, and in its grander forms is a regal tomb, equally in America and the Old World. The descriptions of such burials in Homer, probably refer to customs of extreme antiquity even in his days, and they are obviously identical with those of the more civilized tribes of America. The body laid on the pyre and buried with precious offerings and with animal sacrifices, and the whole covered with a lofty mound of heaped-up earth, not forgetting the war-dance around the pyre and the funeral feast, are all equally applicable to the Alleghans and other tribes of America, to whom the Homeric song of the burial of Hector or Patroclus would be as intelligible as the death-song of one of their own warriors.

What shall we say, then, of this instinct of immortality, handed down through all the generations of pre-historic and savage men, and prompting to costly funeral rites? Is it a mere fancy, a baseless superstition? Is it not rather a god-given feature of a spiritual nature yearning after a lost earthly immortality, and clinging to the hope of a better being in a future life? And is it not, after all, inseparable from the belief in a God, whose children we are, and who can transfer us from this lower sphere to better mansions in His own heavenly home? Is the "Monist" or Materialist who looks with indifference on death as the close of certain physical changes and nothing more, or who shrinks from it as a hopeless annihilation, on any higher mental or moral platform than the savage who departs chanting his death-song and looking forward to meeting with the shades of his fathers in the happy hunting-grounds? Is he not rather on a level with those more degraded savage tribes, if there are such, who have lost the pre-historic faith without receiving anything better, and who regard the future either as a mere blank or as an unknown and terrible mystery? How much happier than either are those on whose last days shines the brighter hope of the light and immortality revealed by the Gospel!

In the present state of religious opinion among ourselves, and in view of the strange and absurd logomachies which have raged as to the doctrine of a future life in the Old Testament, it may be necessary to refer to the actual connection between the doctrines of the Holy Scriptures and the instinct of immortality referred to in the preceding pages. In Genesis man appears at first as endowed with an immortality both physical and spiritual. This tradition of primitive immortality, and the instinctive longing for an immortal life implied in it, the Christian should hold as not a possession of the Hebrews only, but of the whole human race; and it should be, as it is, next to the belief in God, the second great doctrine of universal religion. The promise of a Redeemer to restore the immortality lost by the fall, is the next doctrine of the revealed religion, and, as we have seen, this also is embodied in all the creeds of the nations, though in strangely distorted forms. The translation of Enoch in antediluvian times is another primitive testimony of the Old Testament, which, if we regard it as an historical fact, must have served to deepen the belief in the future life both of body and soul. It is to be observed that all these primitive testimonies go to establish not only the immortality of the soul, but also of the body; that is, the doctrine of the resurrection. It is clear, therefore, that these doctrines lie at the base of the religion of the Old Testament, and that without them it would be nothing. If they are not often dwelt upon in the Hebrew Scriptures, this is because they were not doubted or disbelieved even by the heathen, and because there was more need to insist on the immediate beliefs and duties of life.

At the same time, in the ancient Hebrew Church, and still more among the heathen, much obscurity hung over the immediate future of the human soul. Death was ever a patent fact, and what the state of the disembodied soul in "Sheol," and how or when it would be reunited to a body, were not known to man. Job might believe, notwithstanding the decay of his body, that with his own eyes he would see God, but this would be in the latter days. Martha might know that her brother would rise again at the last day. This was the common-sense faith of readers of the Old Testament before the Christian era; but it remained for Jesus to raise the veil from the intermediate state, and to bring "life and immortality to light." This He does by His own teaching that the believer in Him can "never die;" that is, that to him death is not really death, but the entrance at once into a higher and broader life in and with Christ, who is Himself the "resurrection and the life;" by His declaration to the thief on the cross, "To-day shalt thou be with Me in Paradise;" and by His own personal resurrection as the "first fruits of them that sleep." Thus to the Christian, not only are the future life and the resurrection more sure and plain than they could be to the Jew, but all the terrors of the intermediate state are taken away—the soul unclothed by death is at once "clothed upon," to be absent from the body is to be "present with the Lord," to leave the earthly tabernacle is to enter a "mansion in the Father's house" prepared by the risen Saviour. True it is that these doctrines are yet only partially received by many calling themselves Christians; but surely happy are they who believe, and whose lives are heightened and ennobled by such belief. Yet it is well for them to remember that, to some small extent, these beliefs have been shared by the pious souls of all ages and peoples, and that the existence of the belief in God and immortality, even among the lowest races, is an element of hope, as presenting some opening and implying some capacity for higher truths.

CHAPTER XI.

UNITY AND CONTINUITY.

If any definite impression has been left on the mind of the reader of the preceding chapters, it must have been akin to that which fixed itself upon the wisest of the Hebrews when he exclaimed, "The thing that hath been is that which shall be, and that which is done is that which shall be done, and there is nothing new under the sun." This is in some respects an unsatisfactory result, falling far short in its sensational effect of the discovery of a new and extinct species of man, or even of a very essential difference in manners and habits of thought between the men of hoar antiquity and those of to-day. Yet this conclusion, tame and prosaic though it may appear, opens most important questions both as to the past and future of our race, some of which we may profitably discuss.

What is the ultimate meaning of that marvellous resemblance which obtains between pre-historic and modern men? Does it point to a common origin and historical affiliation of all races? Is it the result of some process of necessary evolution through which every race must pass, as the individual man passes through successive stages from infancy to maturity?

Is it a consequence of a fixed instinct, like that of the bee and beaver? Is it merely the effect of the action of similar powers and wants on similar resources; or, to put it in the other way, of similar surroundings on tendencies and powers in the main similar?

Views of one or other of these kinds have floated before the minds of writers on the subject, either singly or in combination of two or more of them. Nor are they inconsistent with one another. Primitive instincts and tendencies implanted in man at the first may have tended to develop themselves along certain lines among all peoples, and the influence of surrounding circumstances and means may have been in the main similar, though with subordinate differences of detail. These have been the material or terrestrial causes of the unity with diversity which characterises our species, and to these we have only to add such spiritual influences from without as may have acted directly on man's soul either for good or evil, and such new thoughts and purposes as may have been struck out from the interaction of human minds, or by the appearance of men of rare and exceptional powers.

Looking thus upon the current of human affairs, two great truths are apparent. First, unity of result from the influence of all these complicated causes upon human nature implies to the naturalist unity of origin and genetic affiliation, just as surely as if the perfect genealogical tree of the human race from its origin were in our hands. Second, the earliest arts, inventions, and beliefs of the race are those which must determine its course in all time. In ever-widening circles they may decay in power, or may be crossed and affected by other ripples on the surface, but they must proceed to its circumference in time and space. With unity of origin and continuity of descent, it is certain that modern men must be the product of the original nature of man, with the effects of all the causes acting on it from the first, and that the earliest of these influences must be the most potent and the most widespread.

Any true science of man must therefore go back to his origin, and trace out his primitive conditions and their results, and our best means for doing this are the remains of primitive men, and those less modified races which still exist. It may depend on our previous tendencies and the methods we pursue, whether we find ourselves, with many modern inquirers, brought back to the presence of a simian ancestor of our race, destitute of nearly all that now characterizes it, or to a perfect primeval man endowed by his Maker with all those qualities which essentially distinguish humanity. I propose in this concluding chapter to show by American facts that the latter is the true conclusion of archæology, as it is of sacred history, and in doing this I shall refer to some additional points not previously mentioned, so as to give greater interest to the discussion, and to notice shortly some important facts relating to primitive man, which space has not permitted us to consider in detail.

It is a common popular statement, that the languages of the American continent are innumerable and mutually unintelligible. In a very superficial sense this is true; but more profound investigation shows that the languages of America are essentially one. Their grammatical structure, while very complex, is on the same general principles throughout. But grammar is after all only the clothing of language. Its essence consists in its root words, which bear a definite relation to the mental habits and vocal organs of the speaker, and very often equally definite relations to the things spoken of. Now, multitudes of root words are identical in the American languages over vast areas, some of them with precisely the same senses, and others with various shades of analogical meaning. If we leave out of the account purely imitative words, as those derived from the voices of animals and from natural sounds, which necessarily resemble each other everywhere, it will be found that the most persistent words are those like "God," "house," "man," which express objects or ideas of constant recurrence in the speech of everyday life, and which, in consequence, become most perfectly stereotyped in the usage of rude peoples. Further, a very slight acquaintance with these languages is sufficient to show that they are connected with the older languages of the Eastern continent by a great variety of the more permanent root words, and with some even in grammatical structure. So persistent is this connection in time, that pages might be filled

with modern English, French, or German words which
are allied to those of the Algonquin tribes, as well as
to the oldest tongues of Europe and the East. The
time is probably approaching when it will be admitted
that all languages are radically the same, and that
they all have their roots in those archaic forms of
speech to which we apply the term Turanian. Whence
this unity of language ? Can it have sprung from the
independent growth of thought and language in many
centres, or from the slow development of speech
through countless generations of semi-brutal and
semi-articulate men ? Does it not rather point to
the formation of language at no very distant date
chronologically, and among rational and thoughtful
beings, and also to a time when the earth was of
"one tongue and of one speech" ?

We have had frequent occasion to mention the
identity of implements and weapons in the Old World
and the New in pre-historic and modern times. This
may arise from the fact that in all countries the same
substances are in the main offered as the raw material
of human industry. Stone, clay, wood, bone, and
native metals have similar properties everywhere.
The sharp edges of flint chips, the toughness of greenstone, the ductility of native gold and native copper,
commend themselves alike to the aboriginal artisan
in all countries. Rising a step beyond this, the
different specific gravities of different substances,
the leverage gained by handles, the use of elasticity
in urging projectiles, and other properties of bodies,

might readily attract the attention of men everywhere. Still further, the use and preparation of pigments and dyes, of various kinds of medicinal herbs, of narcotics and stimulants, of pyrite and flint and drills as means of securing fire, are less obvious, but still not difficult to be reached. The natural cave or leafy bower may suggest a house or hut, and the means of constructing it. The rudest savage may cross a river on a floating log. Thought and invention lead him to hollow the log into a canoe, or to construct a lighter and more portable vessel of bark or hide, and in doing this he has already mastered all the elements of the ship. Clay may be moulded by a child into any form it pleases; accident, observed and reasoned on, may teach that it can be baked, and the art of the potter arises. That such things have been done among all races and in all times bespeaks not merely similar resources, but the action on these of the same human thought; and also that this must have been active at a time so early that similar arts have branched into all races of men, yet so modern that the time is historically recent when many aboriginal arts were universally practised in their most primitive forms.

Indeed, when we consider the identity of the arts of implement-making, fire-kindling, basket-making, spinning and weaving, pottery, carving, and many others; with special peculiarities,—as in the boomerang, the ornamentation of vessels, the special patterns of harpoons,—we can scarcely avoid the conclusion that not only are all men of one origin, but that in early antediluvian times there must have been a special mental activity in the way of invention and discovery, not surpassed in subsequent ages, and perhaps not equalled until our modern days. With all this accumulated knowledge, man must have made his *début* in the early seats of post-diluvian population.

The tally as a means of recording numbers is found on pre-historic human sites in Europe, though, as already suggested, some supposed tallies may in reality have been used in playing games. It is universal among rude tribes, and occurs, to some extent, among civilized nations. Man must have begun his existence as an enumerator, and counting is a difficult matter, especially where large numbers are concerned.* Further, so soon as we begin to add and subtract, we have launched ourselves on the boundless sea of mathematics. So the tally, with its outgrowth of the quipa, the wampum string, and the abacus or reckoning frame, came into use to economize thought and memory, and to preserve records of numbers. But thought and memory must have already existed before even the rudest tally could be of use. Catlin records, in his notes on the American Indians, a curious illustration of the failure of this primitive method, in the case of two Indians from the western prairies, who, being about to travel in the United States, undertook to reckon up the lodges of the white man as they

* Custom makes us unfamiliar with the primary difficulty of abstract numeration, which we perceive, however, in children and in some low savage tribes, in whom disuse has impaired this faculty or prevented it from being developed.

would have done those of the encampment of a neighbouring tribe. They provided themselves with long wands, and as they dropped down the Missouri, made a notch for every house. The rods were soon filled, and then they provided others; but still the numbers grew, and at length, when the steamer reached the city of St. Louis, they threw their tallies into the river, and gave up the hopeless attempt. The tally and its analogues mark man as a reckoning animal with mathematical possibilities, and while they take us very near to the beginning of all things in this direction, they introduce us to a being so like ourselves, that when we are required to reckon up any large number, we are fain to have recourse to his primitive expedient. Pre-historic and antediluvian genealogies must have been kept on tallies akin in principle to the knotted cords of the Peruvians; and it is not impossible that some of these may yet be recovered for comparison with the numbers in Genesis which have excited so much scepticism and controversy. We are told that the Peruvians thus kept the reckoning of the events of their lives, and their personal quipas were buried with them; and this even in the case of young children, the events of whose lives might be represented by a very few knots. Careful search should be made in all repositories of the remains of prehistoric men for records of this kind; and judging from American analogies, it may be found that some of the unintelligible marks on old stone monuments are intended to denote dates and numbers.

One of the most remarkable of the links which bind together all nations of men as of one blood, is the method in which they reckon consanguinity and descent. The truth is, that some of the rudest peoples have more systematic methods of this kind than those known to ourselves, and that these primitive products of human thought and experience have been handed down through the channels of descent from the most remote times. Morgan,* in his elaborate work on the "Systems of Consanguinity and Affinity of the Human Family," has shown that two distinct systems now exist—the Descriptive, in which a few terms expressing primary relationships are combined so as to express the more divergent and distant connections till they disappear in nameless divergences; and the Classificatory, in which the divergent relationships are brought back to the main line by classifying them with the relationships most resembling them, as when my brothers' sons, are called my sons instead of being, as in the other mode, my nephews.

Between these two methods men have from a very early age been divided. The Indo-European or Aryan nations, the Semitic nations, and that portion of the Turanian stock known as the Uralian, use the descriptive mode. The whole of the peoples of Eastern Asia, Polynesia, and America, use the classificatory mode; and as this is the mode of the most stationary and unprogressive peoples, it is probable that it is the primitive method, from which the more advanced

* "Smithsonian Contributions," vol. xvii.

nations diverged into the descriptive system. In illustration of this, I may state that while the reckoning of consanguinity among the Greeks, Romans, and Celts is the same with our own, that of the Tamil races of India, the Chinese, and the Mongolians of North Asia, is identical with that of the American races.

Nothing can more distinctly mark a unity of origin and descent than such facts as these; but their significance is far more profound than at first appears. Morgan holds, as do also Lubbock and McLennan in treating of this subject, that the classificatory mode points back to a time when there was no institution of marriage or family relationship. In this, however, they go beyond the limits of fair deduction. The reckoning of consanguinity in any form presupposes the family relation, without which man would be in this matter on a level with the lower animals, and it can give no information as to any previous state in which no family relation existed. Further, the helpless condition and slow growth of the human infant, physiologically imply that man is eminently a pairing animal; and thus even animal analogies preclude the supposition that there ever was a time when marriage did not exist. Where promiscuous intercourse, polygamy, or polyandry occur, we have evidence of vicious social inventions unsuited to the healthy continuance of the race.

It is clear, however, that the classificatory system points back to a time when there were no prohibited degrees of relationship, and this accords with its high antiquity; for the origin of men from a single pair implies in the earlier generations of mankind the intermarriage of the nearest relatives. The Book of Genesis, it is true, passes this over in silence, but we can detect evidence in the marriages of Abraham and the patriarchs, that even in their days the union of near blood relations was considered proper; and even the Mosaic prohibitions were only written for the great brotherhood of Israel, into which all Israelites were supposed to marry. It is further undoubtedly implied in the Old Testament history, that the classificatory system of consanguinity was that of antediluvian times, and perhaps continued in full force till the divergence which is indicated in the story of the dispersion from Babel.

As a special illustration of the primitive laws of consanguinity in force among the Americans, we may take those of the Iroquois as detailed by Morgan, and this will introduce us to a new and curious parallelism with the Old Testament. Among these people each nation was divided into eight tribes, designated respectively by the totems of the Wolf, Bear, Beaver, Turtle, Deer, Snipe, Heron, and Hawk. No member of any of these tribes could marry within his or her tribe. The husband or wife must in every case be from a tribe of different name. Further, the tribal descent was in the female line, the husband joining the tribe of his wife, and the children being reckoned as of her tribe. All the women of a tribe or family were thus nearly related, while the men might be derived from different tribes. It was consequently easy for large numbers of families to live together in "long houses," or in communistic edifices, and to have all things in common, for the women, on whom the domestic arrangements devolved, were all relations, and had been brought up together from infancy. The union of the women in this way also gave them great power and influence. These arrangements were widely spread, probably almost universal, in primitive America, and constitute the key to the social institutions of the people as well as to their reckoning of consanguinity. It will be found in detail in Morgan's book already referred to; and Lahontan enters into a curious defence of it in an imaginary dialogue with a Huron chief, who contrasts most unfavourably the selfishness and avarice which arose from the European arrangements, with the morality of his own people. Had the Huron chief been instructed in the Old Testament, he might have strengthened his argument by a reference to the saying there attributed to the first man: "Therefore shall a man leave his father and mother, and shall cleave unto his wife," which implies that the husband goes with the wife rather than the wife with the husband. If I am not mistaken, this also appears in the negotiation of Eleazar for a wife for Isaac, and in the claim of Laban that Jacob should remain in his tribe as having married his daughters. It is probable that this primitive relation of the sexes was before our Lord's mind when He quoted this passage in opposition to the Jewish practice of divorce, with the comment, "From the beginning it was not so." This is not the only instance in which we have seen archaic customs recorded in the Book of Genesis cropping up in our investigations of pre-historic men, and vindicating the statement that from the beginning ma was the same thinking and organizing being that he still is. Perhaps some social reformers of our own day might be more successful if, instead of looking back to dreary ages of barbarism, out of which we are supposed to have emerged, they could refer to a "beginning" in which, if simpler, men were wiser than they are now. If they will not go back as far as Adam and paradise, it might even be profitable to study the classificatory relationships of the old Turanians and the tribal communism of the American Indians, as the only possible kinds of community of goods in the present imperfect condition of human nature, and as having been successful even in the great communistic tribes of the Pueblo Indians and ancient Toltecans and Mexicans, to which I referred in a previous chapter.

In his recently published "Etruscan Researches," Isaac Taylor has arrived by other routes at many of the conclusions sketched in this chapter. He regards with much reason the ancient Etruscans as a Turanian people, either aborigines of Italy or migrants into it in pre-historic times, or partly of both origins. He shows that among them descent was in the female line, as among the Americans and Old World Turanians, and that it is probable that "exogamy," or the marriage of women with husbands of other tribes prevailed among them. Following other writers above referred to, however, he falls into the error of tracing these customs to a supposed primitive period of promiscuous intercourse of the sexes. He further shows that the Etruscans, as tomb-builders, as believers in the immortality of the soul, and in manitous or spirits, and in having medicine-men, or shamans, rather than priests, were essentially Turanian and American. Much that he says of the tombs of the Etruscans is perfectly applicable to those of the Peruvians and of the Alleghans, and the relations which he traces between the funeral rites and sepulchres of these more civilized nations and the ruder Ugrian tribes of Europe and Asia are precisely parallel to the similar relations of the more cultivated and ruder nations in America. The words in which he sums up his conclusions on these points deserve quotation here, as most significant with reference to our present purpose. "The vast and numerous monuments which constitute the tombs of this (the Turanian) race can always be recognised; they exhibit a most remarkable and most significant unity of design and purpose. These tombs are all developments of one hereditary type; they are all the expressions of one hereditary belief, and they all serve the purposes of one great hereditary cultus. The type on which they are modelled is the house. The belief which they express is the fundamental truth which has been the great contribution of the Turanian race to the religious thought of the world—the belief in the deathlessness of souls. The cultus which they serve is the worship of the spirits of ancestors, which is the Turanian religion. The creed of the Turanians was Animism. They believed that everything animate or inanimate had its soul or spirit; that the spirits of the dead could still make use of the spirits of the weapons, ornaments, and utensils they had used in life, and could be served by the spirits of their slaves, their horses, and their dogs, and needed for their support the spirits of those articles of food on which they had been used to feed." Hence, he goes on to say, we find in their tombs the warrior with his weapons, the woman with her domestic utensils, the child with the faithful dog to guide it to the better land, and the tomb in all respects the counterpart of the house, only more durable and costly. Nor can we fail to see in the Animism of the Turanians and Americans the remnants of a rooted belief in a spiritual intelligence above man. In the Hebrew Scriptures the Spirit of God moving upon the face of the waters is the initial step in evolving order out of chaos, light out of darkness, life out of the inanimate. Hence the Hebrew not only recognised the Divine Spirit as a light of his own soul and the origin of the inspiration of prophets, but as shining in the sun, glowing in the flowers, singing in the birds, rustling in the wind. To him all nature, the whole cosmos, was the product of the one Spirit. So it should be to us also

Y

in the Christian dispensation; and in so holding, though we rise above the primeval Animism, we justify it as at least a low and childlike way of recognising the one God, just as the funeral gifts buried with the dead constitute a simple testimony to the belief in the immortality of the soul.

We have passed from the tribal communism and the descent in the female line to the doctrine of immortality, but not unintentionally. Just as we find these things united in that old primitive race, whose fragments exist everywhere over the world, so do we find them in our oldest written history. The God-given woman, the man leaving father and mother and cleaving to his wife, the lost immortality by the woman's means, and its destined recovery by her seed, are no less familiar doctrines to every Sunday-school child among us than they are ingredients in the creeds of all primitive peoples, from the days of the pre-historic cave-dwellers until now. Are they not landmarks of some importance in connection with all inquiries as to the origin and unity of our species?

Pre-historic and other ancient men, both in the Old and New World, must have had poetical tendencies, leading them to attribute their own views and feelings to natural objects. We read this even in their carved implements and ornaments; and the same mythical and poetical representation of nature which we see in the most ancient poetry is still extant among the ruder races. Multitudes of poetical tales and legends have been written down from the lips of old Indian men and women. As a specimen, I may mention an unpublished myth collected by Mr. Rand among the Micmacs. It is a story of the adventures of the "Rushing Wind and Rolling Wave," personified as young men who set out on their travels, and who pass through many adventures, all more or less related to their proper characters. They combine to overthrow the cabins of a village that they may enjoy the confusion of the inmates. They go on a hunting expedition, and drive before them multitudes of birds and fish, and they throw down trees to kill the deer and other wild animals of the forest. Finally, after roving around the world and working much mischief and some good on land and sea, they are married to two lovely girls, named respectively the Calm and the Sea-foam, and by these their rude energies are subdued, so that always the storm and the calm alternate with each other, and waves rage only for a time, and then subside in stillness and creamy foam. Such plays of fancy are obviously the rudiments of true poetic myths, and would require only the knowledge of letters to be developed into poetry like that which comes down to us from ancient India and Greece.

As a specimen of a lighter style, I may give from Schoolcraft the Song of the Frog in Spring, when it awakes from its winter torpor and complains in its shrill and monotonous evening songs of the long oppression of the frost and snow. Every one who has listened to the batrachian chorus which in a spring evening in America issues from every swamp and pond, can appreciate the natural fact to which it relates. The verbal parallelism in this little piece is as characteristic of American song as of that of the early East.

Song of the Okogis.

See how the white spirit presses us,
Presses us,—presses us, heavy and long,
Presses us down to the frost-bitten earth.
Alas! ye are heavy, ye spirits so white;
Alas! ye are cold—ye are cold—ye are cold.
Ah! cease, shining spirits that fall from the skies,
Ah! cease so to crush us and keep us in dread;
Ah! when will you vanish and spring-time return?

The names of the constellations come down to us from the most remote antiquity, modified by Greek myths, but not of Greek origin; and they testify both to that tendency to transfer our own thoughts to the universe around us to which I have already referred, and to the application of the totemic system of emblems to the heavenly bodies. It is, therefore, not wonderful that the Americans should, like the men of the East in the days of Job, have names and symbols for those most important in their relations to man, but it is a more striking and significant fact that these apparently arbitrary names should be the same with those of the Old World. It is still more curious that they should in some cases serve to supplement and illustrate the application of these names. The Great Bear, from its prominence in the northern sky and its connection with the pole-star—" the star that does not move "—of the Americans, is as likely as any other to have had its name handed down from age to age. Accordingly, it is named the Bear among the Algonquin tribes. The Greek fable explains the name by the story of Callisto, one of the attendants of Artemis, who is the equivalent of Atahensic, the first mother. Through the jealousy of Juno, Callisto is changed into a she-bear, and Zeus, fearful that the hunters would destroy her, transferred her to the heavens as the magnificent constellation still named the Great Bear. Whatever the origin of the story, it has a very archaic aspect. The Greek Bear, however, comes down to us without the hunters, and consequently, in our maps of the stars, it is furnished with a preternaturally long tail, which has apparently led to other names being given to it. The Micmacs, however, who call it the bear (*Mouin*), name the stars of the tail the three hunters, and these have as their totemic names, *Pules* (the pigeon), *Chigogeck* (the titmouse), and *Chipchawitch* (the robin); all of which, by the way, are onomatopœtic, and recall similar names in more familiar tongues. A small star near one of the hunters is the Kettle which he carries, and Berenice's Hair is the Bear's Den. We can scarcely doubt that this myth and its astronomical application belong to a time when the root-stocks of the Hellenic or Pelasgic populations were still one with those of the Algonquins, that the importance of the Great Bear as a mark in the sky has caused its name to be perpetuated, and that among the Americans the tradition survives in a more complete and less corrupt form than among ourselves.

It seems a general fact that primitive men have traditions of giants and dwarfs of the olden time. Our own ancestors believed in Iotuns, huge and terrible, and in elves and fairies; and we still have in our sacred writings the Nephilim of antediluvian times, and in our literature the Titans of classical mythology. So the old Micmacs of Nova Scotia and their relatives of the Algonquin race had Kukwes, or *gigantes*—men in form but immense in stature, gifted with magical power, cannibals, and associated in their minds with the power of the frost and ice—veritable Iotuns or Titans, and with stories connected with them in every way comparable with those in our own folk-lore. They had also little people, or fairies, with the same attributes with those of our nursery tales; and Kitpoos, or Gepuchican, was their Puck, or Gobelin, of whom the most strange and romantic stories are told. He is a giant-killer, and represents the victory of intellect and cunning over brute force without intelligence, as embodied in the giants. I have before me many genuine Indian tales relating to these beings, but it would be tedious to reproduce them here. The main questions are as to the origin of such stories and the reason of their general diffusion. The only satisfactory explanation is, that they are based in some way on historical facts. Nilsson has conclusively shown that the giants and skrelings of the northern sagas represent respectively the Scandinavian and Finnish races, as contesting in early times the possession of Scandinavia, though the names may refer to still older facts than these. It is no longer possible to smile at the antediluvian giants of Genesis, since we now know from actual remains that the earliest race disinterred from caves in the Old World was of gigantic physical power, and that this was succeeded by a feebler race, who must, locally at least, have been contemporary with the other. Here we have undoubtedly the primitive historical truth that includes all these traditions, which, though coloured by the fancies of different races of men, are essentially the same all over the world.

The traditions of our race point back to golden days of simplicity and innocence. They tell of retrogression rather than of improvement, and attribute the advance in the arts and the elevation of the race to great heroes of the times of old. Is there a basis of archæological and historical truth for this?

The first answer to the question is an obvious one. Man must have originated in a mild climate, and must primarily have been a gatherer of the fruits of the earth. Even though the oldest remains of men ever found should be those of rude hunters living in cold climates, it will still remain an irrefragable physiological deduction from the structure of the human frame, that this could not have been the earliest condition of man. This accords with the American facts, which show that, leaving out the irruptions of rude races from Northern Asia, the primitive peoples existed in the fertile plains of the south, and lived on the produce of the soil. Let it be observed, also, that this is in the main the condition of the Australasian and Polynesian peoples, and of the primitive men of Southeastern Asia, the most isolated and least modified of men next to the Americans. It follows that the first industry must have been agriculture, or more probably horticulture; for, as in America and Polynesia, the tillage of the soil by man probably began ages before he had any domestic animals to aid him. Without realizing this, and picturing to ourselves the condition of the primitive populations, tilling the ground with rude implements and human toil alone, and with little agricultural skill, we cannot fully sympathize with that wail of the patriarch Lamech, which comes to us over the ages, when he named his son Noah—rest—saying: "This same shall comfort us concerning our work and toil of our hands, because of the ground which the Lord hath cursed." Even in his time the earth was yielding her riches in too niggard a manner for the increasing multitudes of men, and the violence born of selfishness was making life still more hard and dangerous. He could look back to an Edenic age, when the land was not cursed; he could look forward to a reformer and improver to come, and his lamentation and his hope recorded in these archaic stories of Genesis have their parallel in the difficulties and hopes of every generation of men.

The invention of fire and the use of clothing, both of the most remote antiquity in the history of our race, enabled men to subsist in the less genial climates; and tradition concurs with sacred history in affirming that lawlessness and violence, arising perhaps in the first instance from struggles for fertile portions of land, broke up the original unity of mankind and produced migrations and the separation of rude and more polished races, which have ever since continued. On the one hand, these movements and contests have been fertile sources of degradation and retrogression. On the other, they have stimulated the energies of men, and have tended to bring to the surface the more vigorous races.

Here arises an inquiry of the highest importance. How has it happened that the majority of men have continued for ages in a stationary condition? How, on the other hand, has the higher culture, and especially that which we call Aryan and Semitic, grown out of the archaic dead level of the old Turanian stock, whether agricultural or merely in the hunter and fisher condition? On the one hand, we have a picture of stagnation and fixity; on the other, of marvellous advance.

It cannot be denied that pre-historic men were, in bodily vigour, in volume of brain, in skill of manipulation, on a level with their modern successors; and even in their ruder tribes they must have had their senses and perceptive powers sharpened to a high degree of perfection by the constant struggle for food, or against enemies and wild animals; while their implements and ornaments show patient industry and much taste and skill. Thus gifted, we would naturally suppose that primitive man would speedily rise to a higher state. Yet the opposite of this is so notoriously the case, that it has been a matter of keen controversy whether the inferior races can raise themselves to any higher condition, or tend to do so in even a very slight degree. The Bashkirs of the Ural are said to be at this day in precisely the condition in which their ancestors were found by Herodotus, 2,300 years ago. The negro and Arab tribes are as nearly as possible in the same state in which they were in the times of the Pharaohs. There is no reason to believe that the Australians, Polynesians, or Americans, if undiscovered by Europeans, would have been in a more civilized condition a thousand years hence than they were when first made known to the rest of the world. Why is this?

One reason is, that it is so much more easy to imitate than to invent. Only the more rare and exceptional minds can strike out new paths. Another is, that the rude man has few wants, and these few can be supplied by the means he already has. A third is, that after he has developed to their full extent a certain number of industries, he can get no further without some large and difficult step, as, for example, the reduction and working of metals, or the introduction of materials from distant parts of the world. Again, such large steps may be made by accident, as we say, or, in other words, the active mind may meet only at rare intervals with those combinations of causes which lead to invention or discovery. Native gold and copper found in river gravels were, no doubt, the first metals known. Gold is the earliest mentioned in Genesis. Meteoric iron, a literally heaven-descended gift, first made man acquainted with that metal; but the step from the native iron to the richer ores resembling it somewhat in aspect, was so long and difficult, that it is likely a vast lapse of time intervened before it was made. Some old metallurgist working in a region like Cornwall, where the ores of copper and tin occur together, mixed them and produced bronze, just as the Chinese are said to have originated nickel silver by smelting mixed ores containing copper, zinc, and nickel. It follows, from these considerations, that after the invention of a few arts, indefinite periods of stagnation might ensue, and the same arts and customs might be stereotyped for many generations. It follows also that these arts and customs might be propagated among numerous nations and tribes without material modification; everywhere, as we have seen, bearing evidence at once of the unity of man and of his comparatively short residence on the earth.

If we ask how an impetus is to be given to humanity, so that change and movement shall occur, history gives us two answers only, and these closely allied to each other. One of these we obtain in a very definite form in sacred history, which we are sometimes apt to forget represents primitive man, while innocent and happy, as destitute of even the rudiments of material civilization. Its story is, that certain gifted men, in a very primitive age, made the great discoveries on which material progress has ever since been based.

Tubal-cain, the first metallurgist, Jubal, the first musician, and Jabal, who first exchanged the cavern or the wooden hut for the skin tent of the nomad, and tamed the larger beasts of burden, these were heroes of old, men to be deified by succeeding ages. Under various names, and with various attributes, these and other great inventors are to be found in all the mythologies of the Old World, and to this America adds its testimony. Every American nation has its great demi-god or hero, to whom it ascribes the origin of the arts of life. Manco Capac of Peru, and Qetzalcoatl of Mexico, are familiar to all readers of American history, and Hiawatha, of the Iroquois, is but the same personage known under different names among all the American tribes. Among the Micmacs of Nova Scotia he is Glooscap, a benevolent giant and wonder-worker, who dwelt apart, but was always near and accessible to those who sought his aid. He taught them the arts they knew, had marvellous influence over all living things, used the wild animals as messengers, and rode over the sea on whales. Great rocks and hills represent his kettles and his wigwams, and the bones which geologists call those of the mastodon, belong to the gigantic beaver which he hunted. He has been driven from the earth in disgust by the wholesale destruction of wild animals, and the marring of the face of nature by the settlements of the whites, but one day he will return to his people and redeem them from their sins and evils, and restore them to welfare and happiness.

The second answer is that which we receive from the later ages. It relates the advent of more civilized strangers, who taught the rude nations what they themselves knew. Perhaps this is implied in the story of the Peruvian Manco Capac, child of the sun. The savage aborigines of Greece were visited by Phœnician traders, and soon themselves learned to voyage to the East and bring home its stores of knowledge. Our own Celtic aborigines were indebted first to the Phœnician traders visiting the tin islands, next to the intercourse with Gaul, and then to the Romans, for their early lessons in civilization. The missionary of new things may come as an invading soldier, or in the guise of a trader, of a shipwrecked mariner, or of a self-denying and laborious teacher; but he must come in order that humanity may awake from the stagnation of semi-barbarism. These two answers are mutually related. The primary stimulus must arise from a God-given genius, or a heavenly baptism of the life-giving Spirit, and when this is given it may propagate itself from nation to nation by human agency; but thus far the stagnant water of humanity has far exceeded its living and fertilizing streams.

More especially we see these principles in the divergence of the two great Aryan or Japetic and Semitic branches from the old Turanian stock. The motto of the Japetic race has been enlargement and dispersion, with the eager quest of things new and strange. The Semitic motto has been to retain the old landmarks and cultivate the old ground up to its highest point of productiveness. The first impulse in these directions must have been given by great minds in pre-historic times—probably by minds which, if contemporary, were violently antagonistic to each other, and may have rent asunder the old primitive patriarchal communism by their struggles. Out of this Babel God has worked His own plans, giving to the Semitic culture the higher revelations of His spiritual nature, and to the Japetic culture the higher control of physical forces and the greater power of expansion and of propagandism; while among the Turanians, the old primitive instincts and habits of pre-historic men have crystallized themselves into fossils, or have been weathered away and disintegrated into barbarism. " God shall enlarge Japhet, and he shall dwell in the tents of Shem ; and Canaan " (the representative here of unprogressive humanity) " shall be his servant."

We are now prepared to give, by the help of our American analogies, a common-sense answer to the much-agitated question of the primitive barbarism of man and the origin of civilization. Sacred history and the materialistic archæology of the day concur in the belief that man at first was destitute of the arts. But from this point they diverge. The former teaches that man without arts was pure and holy, and in unison with his Maker, and that, falling from this condition, one part of mankind simply sunk into barbarism, the other grasped at arts and civilization, introduced by great inventors, as a substitute for or in connection with a higher spiritual life. These several portions have been acting and re-acting on each other ever since, and also have been acted on by the remnants of primitive religion and by new influences emanating from God. The latter, knowing no God and no spiritual nature in man, supposes him at first a mere animal in whom the life of intellect and of higher tastes and feelings has been struck out by physical causes acting on his organism. There can, I think, be no hesitation in affirming that our old Biblical doctrine is the more complete and scientific of the two, and also that which is most in accord with the evidence of history and archæology; while even the "Animism" of pre-historic peoples may claim kinship with some of the higher doctrines of spiritual religion, and so also may the "Shamanism" of the ancient Turanians and Americans, and of which we find traces even in Palæocosmic men.

Among the American tribes, except perhaps some of the more civilized and advanced communities, no distinct system of priesthood had been developed. In this they resembled the men of those patriarchal times in which the kingly and priestly functions were conjoined, and were exercised by persons of great age or of high and recognised gifts. The "ancients" were the authorities in all religious and ceremonial matters. The professed medicine-men, or jugglers, or prophets, rested their claims on a totally different basis from that of priestly caste or appointment. By long fasts and urgent invocations, they had acquired such intercouse with a beneficent genius or demon, that through his means they could give information as to what was passing at a distance or would happen in the future, discover the sources and cure of diseases, advise in all difficulties, interpret dreams, and secure the Divine favour for all enterprises. They were in the habit of steaming themselves in a vapour bath and working themselves up into a frenzy before delivering their predictions, which were sometimes given in song. So correct, occasionally, were their anticipations, that the French missionaries believed that they were actually inspired by the Evil One. They had, however, no political status or authority, and practically their chief function was that of physicians and diviners. The better to aid in these functions, they were not only collectors of herbs and simples, but of any object of a strange, abnormal, or curious character that came into the possession of the tribe, so that the cabin of the "medicine-man" might be a sort of museum of things rare and curious, or believed to have some mystic powers. It is very probable that the Silurian fossils and grotesquely shaped or sculptured stones found on aboriginal Canadian sites have been part of the apparatus or collections of these jugglers; and there is reason to suspect that a similar explanation may be given of some anomalous objects found in pre-historic repositories in Europe, as well as of some of the fossils found in such places. To this origin should probably be referred some at least of the carved bones and antlers called by the French antiquaries, "Bâtons of command." Such objects might have been the horns which conjurors wore on the head or attached to their rods or staffs, or which formed part of the rattles or drums which were used in ceremonies. All these functions constitute what has been termed "shamanism" among the Mongol tribes; and it has been recently shown by Taylor that the same system prevailed in Etruria, and was the origin of the Roman augury. It was in full force among the Canaanites and other ancient peoples mentioned in the Pentateuch; and Balaam, as presented to us there, is evidently only a superior sort of medicine-man.

Here, again, we have an ancient and universal instinct of humanity; and, however corrupted, we may recognise under it a great and Divine truth—that of the possibility of revelation of the will of God to man—an instinct capable of the noblest elevation and also of being the subject of the vilest corruptions and impostures. It marks out man as a being from the first not content to be the sport of mere inanimate forces, and so rising to the conception of a divinity. It shows him also as feeling in danger, sickness, bereavement, and approaching death, the need of aid from above, the presence of a God who could succour him, the yearning that God would abide with him and bless him. Let me add, that as an original and God-given gift, this universal religious instinct, and its survival among even the most depraved peoples, explains the universal adaptation of the Christian religion to the wants of man. Paul perceived that the Athenians were "very religious" because they had an altar to the unknown God; and so in every human heart there is an altar to God as known or unknown, as a father and a friend, or as an equitable ruler. So the missionary can find everywhere some response to the proclamation of Christ, the substitute of sinful man, the Revealer of the will of God, and to the doctrine of the Divine Spirit, the Comforter, dwelling in and renovating the human soul. Let us not despise this precious testimony to God written by Himself in the heart of man, and let us endeavour to cultivate it to its highest point of Christian spirituality, and to rescue it from the scathing hand of superstition and the frosty breath of materialism.

My object, as stated in the first chapter of this work, has been to bring the testimony of facts relating to the existing or recently extinct tribes of America, to aid in correction and counteraction of the crude views prevalent among European archæologists as to the origin and antiquity of the pre-historic men of the caves, gravels, and peats of the Eastern continent. The treatment of the subject has necessarily been meagre and imperfect; but it will have served its purpose if it has been suggestive of lines of thought in harmony with higher views as to the origin and destinies of men than those which spring from monistic and materialistic hypotheses of the spontaneous evolution of consciousness, reason, and morality from merely animal instincts. Perhaps they may also serve to widen our sympathies with the men of all times and of all grades of practice and belief, and to show more clearly the underlying unity which subsists in all the higher hopes and aspirations of humanity.

These considerations must constitute my justification for entering into the subjects discussed in this and the two preceding chapters. To examine the relics of fossil men, without regard to the evidence which they afford of the higher aims and sentiments of human nature, would surely be as unscientific and unprofitable as it would be to study the structures of fossil shells and corals without considering their probable conditions of existence and habits of life.

APPENDIX.

THE subjects treated of in this work are so much discussed and so rapidly changing in their scientific aspects, that while the sheets were passing through the press many new points have presented themselves. A few only of special interest, more particularly with reference to American facts, will be here noticed.

ADDRESS OF DR. TYLOR.

Some of the latest aspects of the subject are presented in Dr. Tylor's able address before the Department of Anthropology of the British Association (August, 1879). He is struck, in looking back, with the fact that many of the most important causes of change in language, physical features and other properties of man, must have done their chief work "in times before history began." But history, as he understands it, extends back only to the rise of the old Oriental monarchies, say 2000 to 2500 B.C. He takes no note of antediluvian history, though this is vouched for not only by the record of Genesis, but now by the lately disinterred records of other Eastern nations, as well as by almost universal tradition. This antediluvian age, covering at least twenty centuries, must on every account have been more fertile of change than any following period of the same duration, and judging from the state of the arts at the dawn of post-diluvian history, must have been more fertile of invention and discovery than the whole time that has since elapsed. The neglect of these facts, as well as inattention to the geological evidence of abrupt changes of the earth's surface, before and since the introduction of man, greatly influences much of the reasoning of anthropologists. Tylor also directs attention to the fact, that the swarthy Turanian races are the founders of civilization;

that while in most countries an age of stone preceded an age of metal, this is by no means universal; and that doctrines as to nature-myths supposed to have given origin to religious beliefs, have been pushed to a ridiculous extreme.

MEASUREMENTS OF SKULLS.

From an interesting paper read before the French Association for the Advancement of Science, in 1878, I take the following average measurements of skulls, given in cubic centimetres:—

Historic.		Pre-historic.	
French (city of Paris)	1·558	L'Homme Mort	1·606
German	1·521	Solutré	1·500
Croats	1·499	Cro-magnon	1·550
Russians	1·471	Grenelle	1·530
Tchuchtchs	1·468		

This high development of the brain in palæocosmic men justifies the remark of Tylor, that they may have fallen off from a "higher ancestral state."

PRE-GLACIAL AND POST-GLACIAL MEN.

In a paper read before the Victoria Institute, Professor Hughes disposes of the alleged cases of Pre-glacial men in Europe; though, on grounds similar to those held by Sir C. Lyell, he is still disposed to assign a high antiquity to even Post-glacial man. He seems not to have been aware that the supposed "wattle" found in the interglacial brown coal of Dürnten, in Switzerland, has been shown by Steenstrup to be probably the work of beavers; nor does he notice the odd theory of Gaudry, that the supposed Miocene flint implements found in France may have been made by the extinct apes of the genus *Dryopithecus*. In the proceedings of the same society Mr. Southall has ably summed up the arguments bearing against the great antiquity of even Post-glacial men. The whole question of the glacial age in connection with man, is involved in grave difficulties at present, owing to the extreme doctrines as to continental glaciation now prevalent, and against which the writer, as well as other geologists, have long contended. A short paper, by Feilden, in the Proceedings of the Royal Dublin Society, reduces the solution of these questions, and also the theory of interglacial periods, into a nutshell, by directing attention to the comparatively temperate climate of Grinnel Land in N. latitude 81° 40′ to 83° 6′ with the glaciation of Greenland "in the same parallel of latitude, and on the opposite shore of a channel only twenty miles across." In a paper in the *Quarterly Journal of the Geological Society*, November, 1879, Professor Boyd Dawkins details some interesting new explorations in Creswell caves. Two deposits by water seem to have taken place in the caves explored before the appearance of man, and two others subsequently. First, a bed of white calcareous sand without fossils. Second, beds of red clay and ferruginous sand containing bones of extinct Pleistocene mammalia, but no remains of man. Third, a bed of red sand with bones of the mammoth, woolly rhinoceros, horse and reindeer, and rude quartzite implements, with a hatchet of ironstone and "pot-boilers." Fourth, breccia and upper cave-earth, with human bones and better formed implements of flint and carved bone objects. The animal remains were a mixture of recent and extinct species; but the bed had been much disturbed. The two beds, numbers 3 and 4, must have been formed under different circumstances, and probably at some distance of time apart. Both are Post-glacial, but there seems every reason to believe that the one represents the Palæocosmic, and the other the earlier Neocosmic age. There is no reason to suppose that the implements in either represent the best work of their time; but if the pot-boilers of the oldest deposit are genuine they must represent savages of somewhat advanced type, and with vessels for cooking,

Skertchley, in a recent paper, calculates the age of the alluvial deposits of the "Wash," and the bordering peats, and, measuring by the deposits of the Roman period, assigns to peats holding "Neolithic" implements an age of 7000 years. But there is no real distinction between Neolithic and Palæolithic, and there is no reason to believe that the deposit of either silt or peat has been as rapid since Roman times as before. On the contrary, it is in every way likely that it was much more rapid previously.

JADE IMPLEMENTS.

There has been some discussion respecting the alleged jade found in Swiss lake habitations. It seems that there is a probability that it is not the Oriental jade, but the Saussurite which is found in Switzerland itself. In fact, the so-called jades are not all of one composition, and are found in various countries. A recent writer informs us that while jade implements occur in America, the rock itself is not known; but Dr. G. M. Dawson informs me that it occurs in British Columbia, and therefore not unlikely in various parts of the metamorphic districts of the Pacific border. Perhaps the most interesting fact respecting it is that it has been utilised in so many parts of the world, from New Zealand to Tartary and that like other green stones, it has been an object of superstitious veneration.

MAKING OF FLINT ARROWS.

Mr. Redding, of San Francisco, has contributed to the *American Naturalist* an interesting paper on the manner of making flint implements in Alaska. It seems that obsidian is used, that a flake is struck off with a stone hammer, and chips are then *pressed* off the edges with a pointed bone, till it is worked into shape. The notch is made by similar pressure with a more finely pointed bone. An arrow-head of perfect workmanship can be made in forty minutes. It is evident that this method has been nearly universal, as almost all well-made implements of so-called chipped flint bear evidence of being worked by pressure on the edges. Chipping, properly so-called, would suffice only for ruder implements, or for the first blocking out. The art of making flint implements by pressure must have originated at a very early period, and in the cradle of the human race.

PALÆOLITHIC IMPLEMENTS IN AMERICA.

In the Reports of the Peabody Museum of American Archæology, Abbott has published two papers on the implements found in the gravels of New Jersey. These may be older than any other human remains known in Eastern America, but they are obviously Post-glacial, and not dissimilar in their mode of occurrence, from those of the European river gravels discussed in the body of this work. They require additional examination, from a geological point of view, before their precise relation to the modern period can be determined. In the same Reports, Schumacher describes the manufacture of stone pots and mortars by the ancient Indians of California, and shows that they used in this manufacture tools of purely Palæolithic type, though the pots were beautifully formed out of material detached with great labour from the solid rock. Mr. Putnam gives an interesting account of a similar manufacture in New England. One manufactory of soapstone pots seems to have existed at Christiania, Lancaster Co., Pennsylvania, while numerous fragments of pots and rude stone implements have been found. Another ancient quarry has been found near Providence, R.I. At this place a bed or vein of steatite had been so extensively quarried that in re-opening it over three hundred cartloads of *débris* of the manufactory, mixed with rude stone implements and fragments of pots, had to be removed. The chisels were of hard stone rudely chipped, from 5 to 8½ inches in length, rounded roughly at one end, and pointed at the other. The method used in working out the round or oval masses of steatite to be cut into pots, was precisely that employed in California on the opposite side of the continent. Another ancient quarry of this kind has recently been discovered in Virginia. Had any of these quarries been situated on the bank of a river subject to floods, and especially those ice-floods which in early spring sometimes devastate the valleys of our American rivers, gravel beds full of palæolithic implements must have resulted.

"PLIOCENE" MAN IN CALIFORNIA.—THE CALAVERAS SKULL.

The mention of stone pots and mortars leads to a consideration of the circumstances under which these have been found at great depths in the auriferous gravels of California. Since the remarks on these in the text were written, I have seen a memoir by Professor Whitney, in which he re-states the evidence which he believes exists for the occurrence of man in California in Pliocene times. After carefully weighing it, I must say that it appears to me altogether inconclusive, for the following among other reasons :—

1. None of the specimens, either of bones or implements, appear to have been seen *in situ* by any competent scientific observer, and most of them are open to the gravest doubts as to the undisturbed character of the material. Even the Calaveras skull was found in a shaft now full of water, and the facts respecting it were collected some time after its discovery.

2. The age of the deposits is not certainly known; but from the remains of plants and animals found in them they would seem to date from the period of the Pliocene Tertiary, when the fauna and flora of the American land were quite different from the present, before the glacial period, and before the main valleys of the Pacific slope were cut out. It is very unlikely that man can be the sole survivor of the fauna of this distant period.

3. This improbability is increased by the fact that the skull discovered, while American in form, is of large size and of better development than those of the modern rude tribes of California, and that the implements found are similar to those of the semi-civilized agriculturists and miners formerly inhabiting some parts of the West. Further, it is well known that many shafts and mines have been excavated in these gravels both before and after the European conquest.

4. The manner in which Whitney accounts for the occurrence of the Calaveras skull is so fanciful and improbable, that it throws doubt on the whole of his conclusions. To show this, I shall quote, at some length, his own words, premising that this skull is believed to have been taken from a shaft, at Bald Mountain, sunk through beds of gravel and lava, amounting in thickness to 130 feet:—

"The skull was unquestionably dug up *somewhere*, and had unquestionably been subjected to *quite a series of peculiar con-*

ditions.* In the first place it had been broken, and broken in such a manner as to indicate great violence, as the fractures go through the thickest and heaviest parts of the skull; again, the evidence of violent and protracted motion, as seen in the manner in which the various bones were wedged into the hollow and internal parts of the skull, as for instance, the bones of the foot under the malar bone. The appearance of the skull was something such as would be expected to result from its having been swept, with many other bones, from the place where it was originally deposited, down the shallow but violent current of a stream, where it would be exposed to violent blows from the boulders lying in its bed. During this passage, it was smashed, and fragments of the bones occurring with it were thrust into all the cavities where they could lodge.† It then came to rest somewhere, in a position where water charged with lime salts had access to it, and on a bed of auriferous gravel. While it lay there, the mass in which it rested was cemented to it by the calcareous matter deposited round the skull, and thus the base of hard mineral tufas and pebbles which was attached to it when placed in the writer's hands was formed. At this time, too, the snail crept in under the malar bone, and there died.‡ Subsequently to this the whole was enveloped in a deposit of gravel, which did not afterwards become thoroughly consolidated, and which therefore was easily removed by the gentlemen who first cleaned up the specimen in question, they only removing the looser gravel which surrounded it."

To any one acquainted with the usual modes of occurrence of fossil bones, the conditions above stated may well seem "peculiar." That the skull and other bones of the skeleton, and even a bead used for ornament, or perhaps put into the mouth as an obolus to pay the Stygian ferryman, in whom some American Indians as well as the Greeks believed, should keep together while rolled down the bed of the torrent, and be

---

* The italics are ours.
† From another statement, it would seem that a shell bead was also attached to the roof of the mouth, and pieces of charcoal introduced into the skull during its rough transit down the stream!!
‡ A modern snail, *Helix Mormonum*, still living in the country.

deposited in one place along with pieces of charcoal and a snail shell, seems quite incredible.* If the supposition had been that the whole body, with its dress and ornaments, was drifted down, or that it was a fossil from some older deposit already sealed up in a hard nodule, the theory would be more coherent, though still not quite in accordance with the facts. As it is, supposing the shell to have been found as alleged, the whole appearances are those of an interment, or of loss of life in some old shaft or tunnel, and this is rendered the more likely by the fact insisted on by Whitney, that the surrounding beds belong to a time when the "animal and vegetable creations differed entirely from what they are now": that is, always excepting the modern Indian and modern snail.

5. The so-called "fossilised" condition of the skull proves nothing. That it contains, as shown by analysis, 62 per cent. of calcium carbonate, implies merely that the pores and cancellated structure of the bone have been infiltrated with that substance after decay of the animal matter, and this under favourable conditions would not require a long time.

The above reasons are, I think, quite sufficient to warrant any geologist in declining to accept the human remains of the California gravels as other than those of American Indians of the modern period.

Men of the Gravels and Caverns.

It will be observed that I do not regard the distinction recently insisted on by Dawkins between the men of the river gravels and those of the caverns as valid in a general sense. Tribes dwelling on river banks or coasts during summer, would naturally resort to caverns in winter, if such shelters were accessible. Cave-dwellers would resort to river banks and shores to chip flints, which they might more carefully work up at home. Rude invaders might occupy river valleys

* It would seem that the name of the locality, Calaveras, means a place of skulls, and that loose skulls and bones are found in the Calaveras River. It would be interesting to know the age and source of these, and their connection, if any, with the Calaveras skull.

and more cultivated people might be driven to the hills. Both kinds of deposits belong to one great period, and this the oldest human age known to us; and there are some reasons to believe that portions of the cave deposits date as far back as Lyell's Second Continental period, while some of the gravel beds must have been deposited in the following times of subsidence. Thus the difference in the contents of these deposits must often be merely local rather than due to lapse of time, and their contemporaneity or order of succession must be worked out for each separate region independently.

CLASSIFICATION OF THE PLEISTOCENE AND MODERN.

In the appendix to the last edition of the "Story of the Earth," I have given the following classification of these Periods, which I believe to be more accurate than that on p. 233 supra:—

I. PLEISTOCENE, including—

(a) *Early Pleistocene*, or First Continental period. Land very extensive, moderate climate.

(b) *Later Pleistocene*, or glacial, including Dawkins' "Mid Pleistocene." In this there was a great prevalence of cold and glacial conditions, and a great submergence of the northern land.

II. MODERN, or Period of Man and Modern Mammals, including—

(a) *Post-glacial*, or Second Continental period, in which the land was again very extensive, and Paleocosmic man was contemporary with some great mammals, as the mammoth, now extinct, and the area of land in the Northern Hemisphere was greater than at present. This represents the Late Pleistocene of Dawkins. It was terminated by a great and very general subsidence accompanied by the disappearance of Paleocosmic man and some large mammalia, and which may be identical with the historical deluge.

(b) *Recent*, when the continents attained their present levels, existing races of men colonized Europe, and living species of mammals. This includes both Prehistoric and Historic periods.

THE MEN OF THE "NEOLITHIC" AND BRONZE AGES.

In his work "Early Man in Britain," Dawkins has admirably illustrated the marked distinction between the old paleocosmic men of the gravels and caves and the smaller race, with somewhat differently formed skulls, which succeeded them, after the great subsidence which terminated the Second Continental period and inaugurated the Modern epoch. The latter race he identifies with the Basques and ancient Iberians, a non-Aryan or Turanian people who once possessed nearly the whole of Europe, and included the rude Ugrians and Laps of the north, the civilized Etruscans of the south, and the Iberians of the west, with allied tribes occupying the British Islands. This race, scattered and overthrown before the dawn of authentic history in Europe by the Celts and other intrusive peoples, was unquestionably that which succeeded the now extinct paleocosmic race and constituted the men of the so-called "Neolithic period," which thus connects itself with the modern history of Europe, from which it is not separated by any physical catastrophe like that which divides the older men of the mammoth age and the widely spread continents of the post-glacial period from our modern days. This identification of the Neolithic men with the Iberians, which the writer has also insisted on, Dawkins deserves credit for fully elucidating, and he might have carried it farther to the identification of these same Iberians with the Berbers, the Guanches of the Canary Islands, and the Caribbean and other tribes of eastern and central America. On these hitherto dark subjects light is now rapidly breaking, and we may hope that much of the present obscurity will soon be cleared away.

Another curious point illustrated by Dawkins, with the aid of the recent re-discovery of the tin-mines of Tuscany, is the connection of the Etruscans with the introduction of the bronze age into central Europe. This, when viewed in relation to the probable ethnic affinities of the Etruscans with the "Neolithic" and Iberian races, remarkably welds together the stone and bronze ages in Europe, and explains their intermixture and "overlap" in the earlier lake habitations of Switzerland and elsewhere.

The Deluge in its Relation to Geology.

A very important speculation arising from the facts recently developed as to prehistoric men is the possible equivalency with the historical deluge of the great subsidence which closed the residence of paleocosmic men in Europe, as well as that of several of the large mammalia. Lenormant and others have shown that the wide and ancient acceptance of the tradition of the deluge among all the great branches of the human family necessitates the belief that, independently of the biblical history, this great event must be accepted as an historical fact which very deeply impressed itself upon the minds of all the early nations. Now, if the deluge is to be accepted as historical, and if a similar break interrupts the geological history of man, separating extinct races from those which still survive, why may we not correlate the two. The misuse of the deluge in the early history of geology, in employing it to account for changes that took place long before the advent of man, certainly should not cause us to neglect its legitimate uses, when these arise in the progress of investigation. It is evident that if this correlation be accepted as probable, it must modify many views now held as to the antiquity of man. In that case, the modern gravels spread over plateaus and in river valleys, far above the reach of the present floods, may be accounted for, not by the ordinary action of the existing streams, but by the abnormal action of currents of water diluvial in their character. Further, since the historical deluge cannot have been of very long duration, the physical changes separating the deposits containing the remains of paleocosmic men from those of later date would in like manner be accounted for, not by slow processes of subsidence, elevation, and erosion, but by causes of more abrupt and cataclysmic character.

INDEX.

Ages of stone, etc., 5.
Agricultural Implements, 124.
Agriculture, Primitive, 154.
Algonquin Race, 50.
Alleghan Race, 50.
American Races, Distribution of, 48.
American Races, Origin of, 48.
Animals, Extinct, contemporary with man, 220.
Animism, 321.
Antediluvian Agriculture, 129.
Antiquity of Man in America, 205.
Antiquity of Man in Europe, 212.
Arithmetic, Primitive, 314.
Arrow-heads, 122.
Arts, Origin of, 307.
Astronomy, Primitive, 324.
Atahensic, 258.
Axes, Stone, etc., 117, 131.

Barbarism, Primitive, 324.
Beads, 139.
Belgrand, M., 128.
Beluga of St. Lawrence, 25.
Bone Implements, 134.
Brain, Characters of, 181.

Broca, Prof., 193.
Bronze Age, 6.
Building Materials, 81.
Burial, Rites of, 286.

Calaveras Skull, 206, 184, and Appendix, 344.
Canada, Prehistoric, 25.
Cannibalism, 100.
Cartier, his Voyages, 18.
Carver, 115, 282.
Catlin, 57.
Cavern Deposits, 222.
Ceramic Art, 86.
Chippewyan Race, 49.
Chisels, 131.
Christie and Lartet's "Reliquiæ," 3.
Chungke, Game of, 113.
Cities of the Stone Age, 70.
Commerce, Primitive, 163.
Communism, Tribal, 318.
Communistic Homes, 83.
Consanguinity, 315.
Copper, Native, 61.
Cresswell Caves, 218.
Cro-Magnon, Men of, 188.

Dawkins, Prof., 161, 218.

Dawson, Dr. G. M., 176.
Dead, Burial of the, 283.
Deluge, Tradition of, 263.
Distribution of Races in America, 48.
Dried Meat, Preparation of, 172.
Drilling Stone, 147.
Dupont, 160, 216, 296.

Edenic Age, 327.
Eries or Neutrals, 62.
Esquimaux, 48.
Etruscans, 315.
Extinct Mammals Contemporary with Man, 220.

Fasts for Manitous, 273.
Female Divinities, 258.
Fences for Hunting, 170.
Fish-Clubs, 119.
Fish-Spears, 136.

Gambling Sticks, 144.
Gaspé Indians, 22.
Geographical Knowledge, 160.
Giants and Dwarfs, 326.
Glacial Age, Date of, 242.
Glooscap, 259.
God, Idea of, 250.
Gouges, 132.
Great Spirit, 253, 282.
Grimes Graves, 173.

Hammers, 112, 171.
Hare, The Great, 260.
Hiawatha, 259.
Hochelaga, Agriculture of, 154.
„ Cartier's Visit, 28.

Hochelaga, Ethnic relations of, 46.
„ Fate of, 30.
„ Houses of, 83.
„ Remains of, 70.
Hoes, 124.
Home, Mr. Milne, 231.
Huxley, Prof., 178, 193.

Immortality, Instinct of, 282.
„ in Old Testament, 309.
Implements of Bone, 134.
„ of Stone, etc., 110.

Jones on Southern Indians, 113.

Lake-Dwellers, 103.
Language, Unity of, 310.
Lost Arts, 146.
Lyell, "Antiquity of Man," 3, 233.

Magical Weapons, 174.
Mammoth as a totem, 275.
Manibozoo, 260.
Manitous, 264.
Mentone, Man of, 298.
Messiah, Idea of, 259.
Micmacs, 20.
„ Arts of, 168.
Moquis or Village Indians, 57.
Morlot on Swiss Lakes, 3.
Mother of Men, 257.

Native Copper, 60.
Needles, 136.

INDEX. 353

Neocosmic Men, 218.

Origin of Arts, 307.

Palæocosmic Men, 108, 193, 218.
"Palæolithic" Age, 11.
   „   Implements, Nature of, 214.
Peat, Growth of, 245.
Pemmican, Making of, 172.
Pfahlbauten, 103.
Physical Changes, 228.
Physical Characters of Primitive Men, 177.
Pictographs, 268.
Picture Writing, 268.
Pipes, Tobacco, 92.
Poetry, 322.
Pogamaugan, 116.
Pottery, 86.
Progress, Causes of, 329.
Prunières, M., 109.

Quarries of Flint, 126, 173.
Quipus, 144.

Races, Successive, in America and Europe, 186.
Rau, Prof. 147.
Red Indians, Arts of, 169.
   „   of Newfoundland, 19.
Relationships, 315.
Religions of American Tribes, 252.
Religions, Classification of, 250.
Religions, Origin of, 278.

Rivière, Dr., 299.
Roches Percées, 270.
Schoolcraft, 256, 268.
Sculpture, Primitive, 153.
Skulls, Forms of, 178.
   „   as Vessels, 145.
Slung Stones, 115.
166.
Soloutre, Village of, 107.
Southall, 240.
Spades of Stone, 124.
Spears, 136.
Squier and Davis, 149.
Stadacona, 26.
Stalagmite, Deposits of, 222.
Stations of Prehistoric People, 166.
Stone Age, 6.
   „   Implements of, 110.
   „· Weapons of, 111.
245. ʼ
Sugar making, 132.
Swallow, Prof., 55.
Sweden, Recent deposits of, 239.

Table of Physical Changes, 233.
Tallies, 144.
Tinné Race, 49.
Tobacco Pipes, 92.
Toltecan Race, 50.
Torell on Scandinavia, 239.
Totems, 268.
Trou de Frontal, 88.
Turanian or Tartar Race, 203.
Tylor, Dr., 175, 6.

Unity of Man, 307.

A A

Village Indians, 57.

Wampum, 139

Weapons of Stone Age, 111.

Whitley on Stone Implements, 216.

Wilson, "Prehistoric Man," 3, 8, 45, 64.

WORKS BY THE SAME AUTHOR.

I.
MODERN SCIENCE IN BIBLE LANDS.
With Illustrations. Crown 8vo, 7s. 6d. [Preparing.

CONTENTS.—The-Fire-Belt of Southern Europe.—Men who lived before History.—Antediluvian Arts and Culture.—Palestine as an Early Home of Man.—The Valley of the Nile.—The Present and the Future, etc.

This work is intended as a supplement to the Author's previous volumes, entitled, "The Story of the Earth," "The Origin of the World," and "Fossil Men," and more especially to bring out the new information obtained in his recent travels in the East, and his matured conclusions respecting certain debated points not treated of, or only slightly noticed, in the works named above.

II.
THE STORY OF THE EARTH AND MAN.
With Twenty Illustrations.
Ninth Edition. Crown 8vo, cloth, 7s. 6d.

"This is a book of rare excellence. Dr. Dawson has been for twenty years a geologist of high repute, and has gained a world-wide fame in connection with the discovery of the celebrated Eozoon Canadense, the earliest known fossil. We turn to his book with high interest and keen anticipation. And we are not disappointed; for we find an account of the geological history and the past life of the earth—full yet concise, accurate yet pictorial, and almost poetic. And we most heartily commend to our readers a book so full of interest, so radiant with truth."—*British Quarterly Review.*

III.
THE ORIGIN OF THE WORLD, according to Revelation and Science.
Fourth Edition. Crown 8vo, cloth, 7s. 6d.

"Any one who will study Dr. Dawson's three recent volumes, will not only gain much trustworthy information on matters of romantic interest, but will make the acquaintance of a writer who is as vigorous as he is modest, and as modest as he is vigorous; who knows how to throw the air of genius around even the minuter facts and details of philosophical inquiry; and who combines a true scientific independence of thought with a reverent faith in the Scriptures and the Gospel."—*London Quarterly Review.*

IV.
FOSSIL MEN, AND THEIR MODERN REPRESENTATIVES.
An attempt to illustrate the Characters and Condition of Pre-Historic Men in Europe by those of the American Races.
With Forty-four Illustrations.
Third Thousand. Crown 8vo, cloth, 7s. 6d.

"It will be especially acceptable to those who refuse to accept the high estimate of man's antiquity which modern science has brought forth, for they will find here their case stated with much ability, and illustrated by a wealth of material drawn from sources not sufficiently known in this country."—*Athenæum.*

LONDON: HODDER AND STOUGHTON, 27, PATERNOSTER ROW.

A STUDY OF ORIGINS; or, the Problems of Knowledge, of Being, and of Duty.

By E. DE PRESSENSÉ, D.D., Author of "Jesus Christ: His Times, Life, and Work," "The Early Years of Christianity," etc. Translated by ANNIE HARWOOD HOLMDEN.
Crown 8vo, cloth, 9s.

STUDIES IN THE LIFE OF CHRIST.

By Prof. A. M. FAIRBAIRN, D.D.
Fourth Edition. 8vo, *cloth, price* 9s.

"It scarcely needs be said that these studies are full of spiritual penetration, profound philosophy of moral life, and literary beauty. Devout in feeling, and evangelical in theological view, they are yet characterized by great freedom and independence of thought. We do not know where to look, save perhaps in Pressensé's 'Jesus Christ,' for a like combination of reverent belief and broad independent thinking."—*British Quarterly Review.*

A PRACTICAL COMMENTARY ON THE GOSPEL ACCORDING TO ST. MARK.

By JAMES MORISON, D.D.
Fifth Edition. In one Volume, 8vo, *cloth,* 12s. 562 pp.

"We are happy to call attention to this painstaking and exhaustive work. No student can well do without it. It is a marvellous display of learning and labour."—Rev. C. H. SPURGEON, *in "Sword and Trowel."*

"This great work is a long way beyond and above our criticism. The unanimous verdict of the best judges, of men differing most widely in their theological opinions, has declared it to be one of the ablest expositions of Holy Scripture produced in any age or nation."—Rev. J. AGAR BEET.

HISTORY OF RELIGION IN ENGLAND.

From the opening of the Long Parliament to the end of the Eighteenth Century.

By JOHN STOUGHTON, D.D.

Third and Carefully Revised Cheap Edition. In Six Volumes. Crown 8vo, price £2 5s. Handsomely bound in cloth.

I.—THE CHURCH OF THE CIVIL WARS.
II.—THE CHURCH OF THE COMMONWEALTH.
III.—THE CHURCH OF THE RESTORATION.
IV.—THE CHURCH OF THE RESTORATION.
V.—THE CHURCH OF THE REVOLUTION.
VI.—THE CHURCH IN THE GEORGIAN ERA.

HISTORY OF THE RISE OF THE HUGUENOTS.

By HENRY M. BAIRD, Professor in the University of New York.
In two Volumes. Crown 8vo, cloth, 15s. *With Maps.*

"Professor Baird has produced a work which for carefulness of investigation and completeness and accuracy of statement, is far in advance of all predecessors. We thank Professor Baird for a book of great historical and moral value, of untiring patience, scrupulous fairness, noble sympathies, and the deepest religious interest."—*British Quarterly Review.*

LONDON: HODDER AND STOUGHTON, 27, PATERNOSTER ROW.

www.ingramcontent.com/pod-product-compliance
Lightning Source LLC
Chambersburg PA
CBHW030744250426
43672CB00028B/392